D1198910

Rivers and the British landscape

Rivers and the British landscape

Sue Owen,
Colin Pooley,
Andrew Folkard,
Chris Park,
Gordon Clark,
Nigel Watson

Carnegie Publishing

First published in 2005 by
Carnegie Publishing Ltd
Carnegie House
Chatsworth Road, Lancaster LA1 4SL
www.carnegiepublishing.com

Text copyright © the contributors, 2005

ISBN 10: 1-85936-120-X
ISBN 13: 978-1-85936-120-7

British Library Cataloguing-in-Publication data
A catalogue record for this book is available from the British Library

Designed, typeset and originated by Carnegie Publishing
Printed and bound in the UK by CPI, Bath Press

Contents

Preface

This book arose from a happy coincidence of interests and enthusiasms. A number of researchers in the Department of Geography at Lancaster University have long-standing interests in both the physical and human aspects of rivers, and in changes to British landscape, environment, economy and society. In 2001 Tony Wilkinson contacted us and explained his ideas for a book on British rivers that would reflect his interest in and enthusiasm for this topic. Rather like a river, from this small beginning a substantial project grew! Although there are many books on particular aspects of rivers, especially their physical characteristics, and some volumes on specific major rivers, to our knowledge nothing has been published that provides an integrated account of the physical characteristics and human uses and associations of British rivers. We proposed such a volume and Tony Wilkinson agreed to fund the research needed to write the book. Sue Owen was appointed as research associate for the project and the book was researched and written during 2002 and 2003. A further fortunate coincidence led us to Carnegie Publishing Ltd, also based in Lancaster, where Alistair Hodge expressed enthusiasm for the manuscript we had produced and agreed to publish a volume that included the substantial illustrations that we had always envisaged.

The finished book is aimed at a number of audiences. Although it is written by academics and meets high standards of scholarship and research, it is written in an accessible style. Detailed and scientific explanations are avoided, though the interested reader is given references where these ideas can be followed up. The book aims to convey our collective knowledge of and enthusiasm for rivers in a way that will interest, entertain and stimulate further study both in the library and along the riverbank. We thus expect the book to be of interest to a wide range of general readers with an interest in landscape, environment, local history and popular science. It may also be useful as an introductory text for courses in Geography and related subjects in schools, colleges and universities. The book's holistic approach, combining physical and human studies of rivers with extensive illustrations and an appendix of factual information on a range of British rivers, ensures that every reader will find much of interest.

Many debts are incurred in the production of any volume. First, and most importantly, we must acknowledge the vision and generosity of Tony Wilkinson without whom this project would not have been initiated. Second, there are many colleagues at Lancaster who, though not formally associated with the project, contributed to it in various ways. In particular we thank Harriet Orr for comments on sections of text, Gemma Davies for assistance with GIS, Chris Beacock and Simon Chew for cartography, and numerous other colleagues with whom we have discussed ideas about the project. Detailed credits for pictures and other sources of information are given elsewhere, and we thank all those who have given permission to reproduce material. Finally, our thanks go to Alistair Hodge and his team at Carnegie Publishing for carefully seeing the book through its production process.

In many ways this has been an unusual and exciting project for a group of academic geographers. It has challenged us to move beyond our specialist areas of expertise, to think about the links between physical and human processes in a creative way, and to write for a non-academic audience. Although each chapter has its principal named author, the book has been a genuine collaboration. We have enjoyed the experience, and the sharing of knowledge about rivers that the project has required has led us to view the rivers of Britain in new ways. If, in reading the volume, others can be enthused to visit rivers and to see them with fresh eyes then the book will have served its purpose.

Sue Owen
Colin Pooley
Andy Folkard
Chris Park
Gordon Clark
Nigel Watson
Lancaster 2004

Foreword

The architecture of geology holds for us mere humans some of the greatest stimuli in our lives. Rivers and waterfalls, along with mountains, have the greatest impact. For those of us who are impressed with these things, and we are legion, it is a lifetime love affair. There is an irresistible urge to stop at any spot where there is moving water. Rivers, like people, are unique and hold in them depths of mystery about which we always wonder. Like human beings, they also have a life force which in their case, however, is much longer lived. If we knew all that there was to know about them, life would be less interesting. We are their pupils and they are the teachers. This book is intended to help to guide those interested through the earlier stages of what the writers hope will become a lifetime engagement.

Tony Wilkinson

Acknowledgements

The authors would like to thank all those who gave permission to reproduce copyright material. Detailed acknowledgements are given adjacent to the relevant illustrations. Permission to quote from copyright works was granted as follows:

A Son of War by Melvyn Bragg, reproduced by permission of Hodder & Stoughton Limited; *Twopence to Cross the Mersey* by Helen Forrester, published by the Bodley Head, reprinted by permission of the Random House Group Ltd; *A Lakeland Mountain Diary* by A. Harry Griffin; *The House at Pooh Corner* © A.A. Milne, copyright under the Berne Convention, published by Methuen, an imprint of Egmont Children's Books Limited, London and used with permission; *Tom's Midnight Garden*, by Philippa Pearce (OUP, 1958), reproduced by permission of Oxford University Press; *The River Humber*, courtesy of the estate of James MacGibbon; *Invasion on the Farm in Song at the Year's Turning. Poems 1942–1954*, London: Rupert Hart-Davis; *Welsh Landscape in Song at the Year's Turning. Poems 1942–1954*, London: Rupert Hart-Davis.

All reasonable efforts were made to contact copyright owners of all the works used within the text. In those cases where no contact was made if the copyright owner would like to contact us then a full acknowledgement will appear in any future editions of the book.

Thanks also to the many staff at Lancaster University, Department of Geography, who contributed to the production of the book, especially Chris Beacock, Simon Chew, Gemma Davies and Harriot Orr.

CHAPTER I # Introduction to British rivers

Chris Park

Introduction

Rivers play a fundamental role in the economic, social and cultural life of most societies. They have provided power for industry; they may provide water for industrial use or human consumption; they can be a means of communication and transport of goods; and they are sites of leisure and pleasure. Most large towns are situated on a river; most people are attracted to water; and rivers feature prominently in literature and art. Rivers can also pose threats, particularly from flooding or pollution. They thus have to be managed and regulated, especially when there is urban and/or industrial development close to a river. Rivers are also a central feature of the natural landscape, providing a mechanism that shapes landforms as well as a range of habitats for flora and fauna. There are few aspects of contemporary life that do not interact in some way with rivers. Whereas there are many books which deal with specific aspects of rivers, this book is unusual in that it draws together all of these topics to provide an integrated account of rivers within the context of the British landscape.

In this volume we deal exclusively with British rivers. By Britain we mean Great Britain, which consists of England, Scotland and Wales. We have deliberately adopted a broad-brush approach, in seeking to describe and account for rivers in the British landscape. The scope is huge, and to avoid the risk of simply producing a tourist guide to British rivers and make our task manageable we have focused on specific themes in separate chapters. It will become clear that while landscape features such as lakes, canals and estuaries are often important elements of the 'river story', our primary focus in this book is on the rivers themselves. There are few entirely natural rivers left in Britain, so inevitably much of what we describe relates to modified or managed rivers. We have not attempted to mention or describe each of the major rivers in Britain, but have adopted a thematic approach – with chapters dedicated to particular river themes – illustrated with examples drawn from around

Britain. We explore British rivers from multi-disciplinary perspectives, because
each contributor views rivers through a different lens and our own
professional interests in rivers are different but complement each other.

This chapter provides a broad overview of rivers and their importance, and
in it we define key terms (such as 'river' and 'drainage basin'), set British rivers
in context (by scale and importance), outline why rivers are important
elements in the British landscape, and describe the features of a typical British
river from source to sea. In chapter 2 we look at why we have rivers in Britain,
and in doing so we outline how the water cycle operates at various scales,
describe how rivers form and how river networks function, and consider the
range of geological processes which created landscapes that British rivers have
exploited over the past 10,000 years. Chapter 3 outlines how rivers work in
terms of flows (of water and sediment) and forms (physical features of rivers
at a range of scales). These themes are taken further in chapter 4, which
considers sediment movement and its relevance to channel form and change,
outlines the impacts of water chemistry on river ecology, and describes the
types of plants and animals that are characteristic of many British rivers. Next,
in chapter 5, we explore the role and history of rivers as an economic
resource, looking at the importance of rivers for water and energy, the use of
rivers for recreation, fishing and commerce, the management of rivers
(including canals), and the development of land beside rivers. In chapter 6 we
move on to look at rivers as a cultural resource. We explore how rivers and
culture interact, with particular reference to ways in which rivers create a
sense of place or identity, how rivers inspire creativity and how this is
expressed through different media. Chapter 7 tackles the important theme of
river management, examining the ways in which humans have adapted and
changed rivers, both to provide water resources and to minimise flooding.
The final chapter focuses attention on a single river, the Severn, and integrates
the key themes of the book through an illustrated journey down the river
from source to sea. Finally, the bibliography and appendix provide further
reading and some statistical data on British rivers for those who want to take
further some of the themes introduced in the book.

What is a river?

Our first task is to define the term 'river', to make sure that we are all talking
about the same thing! According to the *Collins Dictionary of the English
Language* a river is 'a large natural stream of fresh water flowing along a
definite course, usually into the sea, being fed by tributary streams'. The
etymology of the word *river* is interesting. It was first used in the English
language in the thirteenth century, and it was adapted from an old French
word *riviere*, from the Latin *riparius* meaning 'of a bank'.

The convention, when referring to the sides or banks of a river, is to name them looking in the downstream direction; so, with your back to the source, the river's right bank is on your right. Thus, for example, the Houses of Parliament are situated on the left (north) bank of the River Thames in London, as the Thames flows from west to east. Upstream means looking towards the source of the river; downstream is looking in the direction that the river is flowing in.

The dictionary definition of 'river' highlights five important properties of rivers – they are natural features of the landscape; they carry and are shaped by fresh water; they are defined by the river channel (the 'definite course'); they transport water (and the sediment it carries) from land to sea; and they are made up of networks of streams that are integrated together rather like the veins on a leaf. We will explore these properties, or themes, in the chapters that follow. Suffice it to say, here, that rivers serve as drains or gutters, or act like the arteries in a body. Another metaphor that is sometimes used for rivers is the conveyor belt, because they move things (water and sediment) along in one particular direction – downstream or downslope.

The drainage basin

While rivers are the most obvious sign of water movement across the land-scape in Britain, to understand fully how rivers work we need to treat them in their proper setting, which is as part of drainage basins. A drainage basin (also called a river basin or a catchment) is the area of land which is drained by a particular river and its tributaries. Drainage basins take the name of the main river which flows through them. Thus, for example, the River Tweed drains a large area of south-east Scotland; that land is the Tweed drainage basin, named after the main river running through it. The principal drainage basins in England are the Severn, Thames, Humber, Tees, Tyne, Avon, Exe and Mersey. In Scotland the main basins are the Tay, Spey, Clyde and Tweed. The Wye and Severn flow from Wales into England, but the Usk and Dee are also important Welsh drainage basins. Figure 1.1 shows the ten largest catchments in Britain. The boundary of a drainage basin is defined by the drainage divide (also known as an interfluve or watershed), which is the line of high ground that separates adjacent basins. This can be defined both in the field and on maps, and it determines which way water will flow when it reaches the ground, and thus which river system it will become part of. The area within the divide is referred to as the drainage (or catchment) area.

The drainage divides for individual river systems define the direction in which rivers flow. A major divide can be identified, running down the backbone of the Pennines in Northern England (Figure 1.1), which separates the main east-flowing rivers such as the Ouse and the Trent, which flow into the North Sea, from the west-flowing rivers such as the Lune, the Ribble and the Mersey, which flow westwards into the Irish Sea. Nearly all parts of the Earth's surface belong to a river system, so that drainage basins fit together spatially rather like the pieces of a jigsaw. Drainage basins are convenient units for sustainable development, land-use planning and natural resource allocation (particularly water resource management) because they represent definable and meaningful units on the ground. They are also important units because of the inter-play and inter-relatedness of all of the processes that take place within them (as we shall see in chapter 2).

Table 1.1 The world's ten longest rivers

River	Continent	Length (km)
Nile	Africa	6,648
Amazon	South America	6,275
Mississippi–Missouri–Red Rock	North America	6,210
Ob–Irtysh	Asia	5,569
Yangze	Asia	5,519
Hwang Ho	Asia	4,670
Congo (Zaire)	Africa	4,666
Amur	Asia	4,508
Lena	Asia	4,269
Mackenzie	North America	4,240

Source: Park (2001)

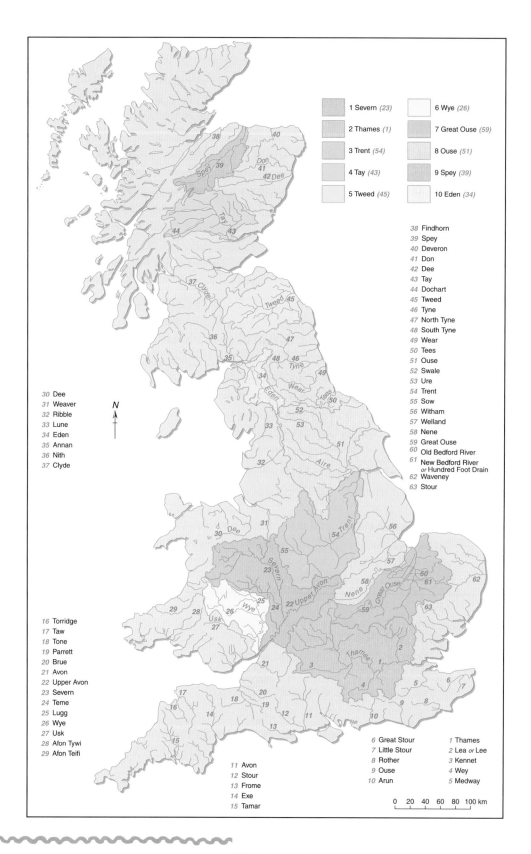

1 Severn (23)	6 Wye (26)
2 Thames (1)	7 Great Ouse (59)
3 Trent (54)	8 Ouse (51)
4 Tay (43)	9 Spey (39)
5 Tweed (45)	10 Eden (34)

38 Findhorn
39 Spey
40 Deveron
41 Don
42 Dee
43 Tay
44 Dochart
45 Tweed
46 Tyne
47 North Tyne
48 South Tyne
49 Wear
50 Tees
51 Ouse
52 Swale
53 Ure
54 Trent
55 Sow
56 Witham
57 Welland
58 Nene
59 Great Ouse
60 Old Bedford River
61 New Bedford River
   or Hundred Foot Drain
62 Waveney
63 Stour

30 Dee
31 Weaver
32 Ribble
33 Lune
34 Eden
35 Annan
36 Nith
37 Clyde

16 Torridge
17 Taw
18 Tone
19 Parrett
20 Brue
21 Avon
22 Upper Avon
23 Severn
24 Teme
25 Lugg
26 Wye
27 Usk
28 Afon Tywi
29 Afon Teifi

11 Avon
12 Stour
13 Frome
14 Exe
15 Tamar

6 Great Stour	1 Thames
7 Little Stour	2 Lea or Lee
8 Rother	3 Kennet
9 Ouse	4 Wey
10 Arun	5 Medway

0 20 40 60 80 100 km

The scale of British rivers

There is no denying the fact that, by world standards, British rivers are very small (see Appendices 1–4). Ward (1981, p. 9) describes them as 'miniscule' compared with some of the world's major rivers. Even Britain's two longest rivers – the Severn (354 km) and the Thames (336 km) – are dwarfed by big rivers elsewhere (Table 1.1) that drain large continental landmasses, and often flow through a variety of climate zones.

left Figure 1.1. Map of largest catchments and longest rivers in Great Britain.

DEPARTMENT OF GEOGRAPHY, LANCASTER UNIVERSITY

In global terms, Britain is a small island – just under 1,000 km from top to bottom, no wider than 500 km, and with a total area of only 243,000 km² (the Amazon Basin, at nearly 7 million km², is 30 times the size of Britain!). No place in Britain is further than 120 km from the sea. Even though some areas receive more than 1000 mm of rainfall each year, and many areas are underlain by impermeable rocks – both of which factors give rise to a large number of rivers and streams – we have no very large rivers in Britain. The Thames – described by Joseph Addison (1672–1719) as 'the noblest river in Europe' – drains an area of just under 10,000 km², which is large by British standards but tiny on the world scale. The Amazon basin, for example, is seven hundred times bigger than the Thames basin. In Europe the Danube drains 816,000 km² (more than 80 times that of the Thames), and the Thames could fit into the Rhine sixteen times over. Another way of measuring the size of a river is by discharge, which is the volume of water it carries (expressed as the number of cubic metres of water per second; m³ s⁻¹). The average discharge of the Amazon, over a year, is around 180,000 m³ s⁻¹. By comparison, the Danube has an average discharge of around 7,000 m³ s⁻¹, the Rhine is about 2,000 m³ s⁻¹ and the Thames is a mere 70 m³ s⁻¹ (Ward 1981).

If we have no really large rivers in Britain, at least we can take pride in having lots of them. Figure 1.1 shows the 61 largest rivers in Great Britain, defined either in terms of length or size of drainage area. For water management purposes the country has been divided into hydrometric areas (hydrometry is the measurement of water movement); there are 105 of these across the United Kingdom (Ward 1981). But these cover large river systems only, and within each of these there are countless tributary rivers. Exactly how many rivers there are in total is impossible to say, because there is no standard way of defining the point at which a small stream becomes a river. Counting all of the rivers in the field would take for ever, so hydrologists have tended to use Ordnance Survey maps as a basis. Map scale is important, because large-scale maps are more accurate and show more rivers than small-scale maps. Smith and Lyle (1979), using maps at a scale of 1:625000, counted 1,445 river systems within Britain, but within each of these there are many individual rivers and streams. Inland areas tend to have the longer rivers, and

The Lynmouth
flood, 1952
THE DAILY MIRROR

the shorter rivers tend to be concentrated around the coast, particularly in Scotland, Wales and southern England.

British rivers in context

Size is not everything. Many British rivers are well known for their role in history. The Thames and the Severn (see chapter 8) are good examples. Other British rivers are well known because of the trouble they have caused. The East and West Lyn in North Devon, which flooded badly in 1952 killing 34 people and either destroying or damaging beyond repair some 93 houses and other buildings in the village of Lynmouth, is a case in point. While Britain does not have a Mississippi or a Yangtze to call its own, rivers have played a hugely important part in shaping the land, and affecting what happens on it and how people use it.

Britain's rivers have long attracted attention. In 731 an English monk, the Venerable Bede, wrote an *Ecclesiastical History of the English People* in which he described Britain as 'rich in grain and trees, and is well adapted for feeding cattle and beasts of burden. It also produces vines in some places, and has plenty of land and water fowl of divers sorts; it is remarkable also for rivers abounding in fish, and plentiful springs.' Gregory (1997) noted that 'the prominence of rivers and streams in the British landscape has been echoed by landscape painters such as Constable and Turner, and it has been emphasised in prose and in poetry, for example by Ted Hughes (1983) in his book *River*. Rivers in the British landscape have often been associated with leisure, and Isaak Walton's book *The Compleat Angler*, first published in 1653, has run to no fewer than 300 reprints.

Naturally, there is nothing absolutely unique about British rivers; they are simply rivers that happen to be in Britain. They are shaped by the same factors, have the same features, and present many of the same problems and opportunities as rivers anywhere in the world.

Why are rivers important?

It should become clear, in the chapters that follow, why rivers are important, both in general, and particularly in Britain. As well as having practical utility, rivers are quite simply key features in the British landscape, and they

Two thousand years of interaction between humans and rivers is shown here at Bath: the eighteenth-century Pulteney Bridge is located close to the original Roman river crossing, while the river has been weired at this point in order to power a watermill at least since late-medieval times.
PHOTOGRAPH, CARNEGIE

contribute in various ways to the special character of particular places. The long and distinguished heritage of rivers in Britain is preserved in many place names, such as Stratford-on-Avon, Newcastle-upon-Tyne, and Tynemouth. Many British towns get their names from the rivers that flow through them – Lancaster is derived from Lune Castle (castle on the River Lune), for example.

As a small country, surrounded by sea, we have long relied on our rivers to provide fresh water for all manner of different purposes. This dependence on river water has also driven the growth of water resource management schemes in Britain, including the great Victorian period of dam building, which has so visibly altered much of the British landscape. Periodic river flooding has traditionally been a free source of fresh silt and nutrients on floodplains, which have helped make much of Britain – particularly in the lowlands – such fertile farming land. Of course, flooding brings bad news as well as good, and many parts of the British landscape bear the scars of past flooding. Much effort and many resources have been invested over many centuries in trying to tame and control the rivers which flood most seriously. Water flowing down rivers also provides a means of redistributing material downstream across a landscape, including soluble pollutants, washout of fertilisers from farmers' fields, and fine material from industrial spoil heaps and dumps.

Rivers provide other resources, too, including gravel and other material for building, and land (on flat floodplains) on which to build. Rivers have traditionally provided means of transport, and river valleys have long been exploited as reasonably accessible corridors and transport routes. Little surprise, therefore, that most of Britain's major towns and cities are built on or beside rivers. Rivers also provide defensible sites for settlements, particularly inside a large meander bend, such as the River Wear which sweeps around the core of Durham and made it a relatively safe site on which to build a cathedral in a turbulent part of the country shortly after the Norman Conquest.

Over a longer timescale, rivers are major agents of landscape change in Britain. While ice and frost action during the Pleistocene Ice Age created much of the landscape we see today across most of Britain, particularly in the north and west, rivers played an important role before that in creating and shaping the major valley systems that glaciers flowed down. In post-glacial times rivers have altered the landscape left by ice and frost, and created what we see today. Landscape is sometimes described as a palimpsest, meaning a manuscript or ancient document which still contains traces of earlier writing, much of which has been over-written by more recent text without completely obscuring what lies beneath. In this sense, some of the old text and much of the new text on the landscape of Britain was written by rivers!

Durham Cathedral and the river Wear.
BILL OXBURY

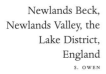

Newlands Beck, Newlands Valley, the Lake District, England
S. OWEN

From source to sea – the anatomy of a river

The character of any river changes considerably along its course, as it flows through different country and itself changes *en route*. One way to make sense of these variations is to describe a typical river from source (where it starts) to sea (where it ends). To keep things simple, we can divide that river into three sections – upper, middle, and lower. Bear in mind, though, that no one river is absolutely 'typical' in every respect. Each river is unique, in the sense that it has evolved in its own location, driven by a climate which has changed through time, exploiting the opportunities presented to it by the underlying geology (over which it has no control), and the surrounding landscape (much of which, in Britain, is a legacy of ice and frost processes during the Pleistocene Ice Age), and – more recently – influenced both directly and indirectly by the imprint of human activities. That said, each river operates under exactly the same physical laws and processes as every other river anywhere in the world, so it is no surprise that we find common features and patterns between rivers, even in very different environments and climates.

Upper section

The upper section of a river includes the area where the river 'rises' or has its source, and the stretch downstream from there in which the river flows through upland, surrounded by hills or mountains. Such a river is often called a headwater stream.

It is often quite difficult to define exactly where a river rises, because – depending on climate and flow conditions – the point at which flowing water appears in a channel can be some distance downstream from the first appearance of a channel. Under wet conditions, flow starts closer to the head of the channel; under dry conditions, it starts further downstream (because groundwater is lower, and soils are drier). This means that the network of channels in a headwater area is dynamic, changing through time. The channel and flow conditions are given names that reflect the extent to which flow is continuous. *Perennial* flow (or a perennial channel) never ceases, even under the driest of conditions. *Intermittent* flow is discontinuous (through time and along the channel): it flows during or immediately after a storm has produced a major input of water into the area, and can continue flowing some time afterwards while water makes its way through the drainage basin water cycle (which is described in chapter 2). Flow ceases when the water supply dries up, and it resumes only when more water is supplied, usually as a result of a rainstorm. *Ephemeral* flow tends to be short-lived, and it only occurs during or immediately after rain. So, you would normally expect to find a zonation along a headwater stream, starting with ephemeral flow at the outer limits, followed by intermittent flow further downstream, and then perennial flow

some distance further again downstream. Whether or not it contains flowing water when you view it, most rivers are very narrow at their source. You can often stand with one foot on either side of the stream, where it rises, whereas further downstream it requires a bridge to cross a much wider section of the same river.

As we move downstream the headwater streams join together to form a river, which continues to grow larger as more and more streams join it and flow into it. The streams that join the main river are referred to as tributaries, and they meet at a confluence.

Many upland rivers have bedrock exposed on their bed, and often in their banks as well, which is why they are described as bedrock channels. Some channels are cut entirely through local bedrock, but these tend to be relatively rare and are almost always confined to the upper section. Bedrock in and beside streams is sometimes pitted by potholes. These are circular depressions which look as though they have been literally drilled in the surface of the rock, and they often contain quite well-rounded gravel. The gravel gives clues to the origin, because potholes are formed when particles of sediment gets trapped in a small depression in the top of the rock; the particles are swirled around within the hole by flowing water. The hole continues to grow bigger through time, and more gravel can fall in under flood conditions. The hole keeps growing as the process keeps going.

above The confluence of the rivers Kent and Sprint, near Kendal, Cumbria. Bankside vegetation is evident, in some places covering the large boulders installed for bank protection.
S. OWEN

left The confluence of the river Lune and Bowderdale Beck
S. OWEN

An important property of the upper section of most rivers is that the small river flows across a land surface which it did not itself create, often within a steep valley left behind from the Ice Age. A river will always flow along the lowest part of a landscape, because it is driven by gravity, so in the upper section the river exploits the steepest line along the ground. For this reason, headwater streams are often quite straight, but they can also suddenly change

Bedrock channel, River Greta, North Yorkshire. This river has carved a course through Carboniferous limestone, so – unlike an alluvial river which has bed and banks of movable sediment – the channel here is constrained by bedrock, which means that the channel cannot readily adjust to changes in river discharge or sediment load. The river has a relatively high solution or dissolved load, because the limestone rock is soluble.

In this type of river channel, the main erosion processes are solution weathering of the solid rock, and abrasion (physical or mechanical weathering) as solid particles rub against the rock and grind its surface, somewhat like coarse sandpaper against a block of wood.

C. PARK

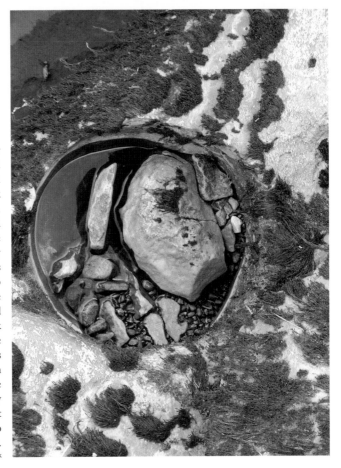

Pothole in the limestone bed of the River Greta, North Yorkshire. Potholes are formed where particles of sediment get deposited in slight undulations in the surface of the rock either in or adjacent to a bedrock channel, and water flow causes the particles to swirl around in that depression, through time grinding a distinct hole which is usually circular. Once the process starts, it drives itself, because the particles are unable to escape from the depression so the erosive force of tumbling them round and round makes the depression grow. There is a check on this process, however, because as the particles rub against the rock they themselves are worn down, so they get smaller through time and gradually lose their ability to erode the pothole further. Potholes are commonly found in clusters, although it is not uncommon for a few major ones to dominate a stretch of river.

C. PARK

direction as they exploit the underlying topography. Another consequence of this close contact between the channel and surrounding ground is that sediment can often fall straight into headwater rivers (for example, from scree slopes adjacent to the river, or by the mass movement of soil on adjacent hillslopes). Sediment loads in such rivers are rarely supply-limited.

The slope of the river bed is usually relatively high in this upper section, which has the tendency to make the water run fast. But small headwater channels usually contain relatively large blocks of sediment, and this – combined with the rough (in a hydraulic sense) character of the bedrock – produces friction that slows water velocity down. So steep headwater rivers are often deceptive – water crashing over rocks and through rocky ravines, seemingly flowing fast, but in reality flow is constrained by the 'rough' channel conditions. Many upland rivers which flow across boulders and coarse gravel have a tendency to braid (that is to flow through several channels linked by mid-channel bars) rather than follow one single course. We explain how this process operates in chapter 4, but we can note here that the only British river which is braided over much of its course is the River Spey in the Scottish Highlands.

Water crashing over rocks in a headwater stream, upper Borrowdale, Cumbria
S. OWEN

Another feature of many upper sections is the waterfall. These are usually created by a band of hard rock underneath the course of a stream, which offers extra resistance and takes much longer than the surrounding rocks for the river to wear down. One of the most famous waterfalls in Northern Europe is the Falls of Clyde, near Lanark in Scotland. The English Lake District also has many waterfalls, including Scale Force (172 feet) near Crummock Water, described by Wordsworth as 'a fine chasm, with a lofty, though but slender, fall of water'. Hardraw Force (100 feet) in the Yorkshire Dales is the highest unbroken waterfall in Britain. By world standards these are small, but where waterfalls do occur they create interesting scenery and add valuable variety to the riverscape (Appendix 7).

Rivers have access to a great deal of sediment in their upper sections, because in Britain they are usually reworking parts of a landscape that has been created mainly by ice and frost action during the Ice Age. This means that they often carry quite high sediment loads, particularly of rock, deposits and other solid material – the so-called 'particulate load'. Particles are worn down by rubbing and crashing against each other in the river, and by being smoothed by the running water. The particles thus become smaller, smoother and often

Thornton Force, part of the Ingleton Waterfalls in North Yorkshire. The series of waterfalls and dramatic scenery here is dominated by the Yoredale Series which comprise layers of relatively hard limestones and softer mudstones, sandstones and siltstones. In post-glacial times the rivers have cut down through the different layers of rock, finding it easier to cut through the mudstones, sandstones and siltstones. The more resistant limestones often provide the steps for waterfalls. Here the River Twiss falls 14m over a resistant layer of limestone, and you can see how much easier it has been for the water to erode down and back the underlying softer rocks, creating attractive scenery and an unusual play area for children of all ages.

C. PARK

Cobbles and gravel on the riverbed of the upper river Derwent, Cumbria.

S. OWEN

rounder as they move progressively downstream. This is true particularly of the bedload particles, which make up the bed of the river and are moved along the bed under high flow conditions, when water depth and flow velocity both increase. Headwater streams also carry solution load (materials dissolved in the flowing water), the precise quantity and composition of which reflects variations in rock type (soluble rocks such as limestone producing high solution loads) and land use (fields which have fertilisers

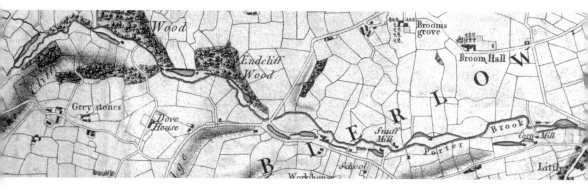

added to them produce run-off with a high dissolved content). Compared with middle and lower sections, solution loads in the upper sections of most rivers are quite small. Industrial sources of water pollution are relatively rare in upper sections of most rivers, too.

Most rivers, in their upper section, act like conveyor belts in transporting sediment further downstream. Relatively little of the material is deposited in the upper section, so the river has only a limited ability to shape for itself a channel that is in equilibrium with the water and sediment it must carry. Erosion processes tend to be dominant in such rivers, and the upper section is often described as an erosional environment. Since the Industrial Revolution, the upper reaches of a number of upland rivers in Britain have been managed and modified in order to produce sustainable flows of water to drive turbines (and thus power machines). Before that, many of Britain's water mills were located on upper sections of rivers, where the steeper slopes guaranteed a greater head of water (that is, a regular flow usually controlled by a small local storage dam).

Middle section

In the middle section of a typical river, downstream from close contact with the adjacent hills, the river flows across a floodplain. It is now usually described as an alluvial channel, which no longer flows directly on bedrock. Alluvium is sediment deposited by the river, so the character of this river is now shaped largely by interactions between the flowing water, the sediment it carries, and the channel it has made for itself. The river is generally much wider and deeper than in its upper section, so crossing it usually requires a bridge.

River slope is now much more shallow than in the upper section, but – perhaps contrary to what you might logically expect – flow velocity is usually higher. The reason for this is that flow is more efficient in the bigger channel, where proportionally more of the water can flow downstream without being held back by friction contact with the channel bed and banks. Increased flow

A detail from William Fairbank's map of Yorkshire, 1795, showing a section of the Porter brook which flows from high in the Pennines eastwards into the Don near Sheffield. Along much of its length the Porter was diverted into a series of millponds to drive cutlers' wheels and a range of other industrial processes. By the end of the eighteenth century the Porter had an average of five water-powered sites per mile of river.

efficiency more than compensates for reduced slope, so the river runs faster.

Now that the river runs through alluvium rather than on solid rock or in a confined valley, it has a much greater ability to shape a course that suits its needs. In other words, it can adjust itself to the water and sediment it has to carry, and to the landscape it crosses. Solution loads are usually higher than further upstream, partly because of the inputs from successive tributaries but also because of washout from fields. The river usually carries more

A middle reach of the river Duddon, Cumbria.
S. OWEN

A lower reach of the river Duddon, Cumbria, showing a wide channel with smooth surface water conditions.
S. OWEN

particulate load than in the upper section (because of tributaries), but it is made up of finer material that can be deposited or picked up and put in motion again, depending on flow conditions.

The river now runs in a channel composed mainly or exclusively of alluvial (river-based) materials – particulate sediment of differing sizes, which has been deposited by the river under flood conditions in the past, and which can build up to form a relatively flat floodplain adjacent to the river channel. Under low flow conditions streamflow runs within the channel. But heavy rain can cause an increase in discharge which, in turn, makes the streamflow deeper and faster within the channel. If flow reaches the bankfull stage (i.e. the top of the banks), and continues to rise, water spills out from the channel and flows over the adjacent floodplain. As it flows over the floodplain, the flow velocity is reduced (by friction with the floodplain) and particulates of sediment are deposited on the surface of the floodplain. Through time a balance is reached between the water and sediment load a river carries, so that the channel is adjusted to carry both in an efficient way. Over-bank flooding occurs with a fairly predictable regularity (on average every 2.3 years in most natural rivers, regardless of climate or geology), and the surface of the floodplain remains relatively stable (that is, it ceases to be built up or worn away).

Under these reasonably stable conditions, the natural river is able to make for itself a channel which works with optimum efficiency (in carrying water and sediment). If conditions change, the channel can adjust to re-establish or maintain that efficiency. It can adjust in three dimensions simultaneously, by changing its cross-section and altering its path (that is, changing its plan and thus its slope). This balance within the river is what William Wordsworth had in mind when he wrote, in *The River Duddon* (1820), 'Still glides the Stream, and shall forever glide; the Form remains, the Function never dies.'

Cross-section changes are fairly common, both along a river and through time, either as a progressive change, or perhaps as a response to a major flood or period of low flow. A channel can adjust vertically, by changing the level of its bed. If a river erodes its bed, thereby making itself deeper, it is changing its cross-section to accommodate changed flows of water and/or sediment. It might adjust the other way, by depositing sediment on its bed and thus decreasing its depth. A channel can also adjust laterally (sideways), by under-cutting one or both of its banks in order to make itself wider, or by depositing sediment on one or both sides to make itself narrower (to cope with a smaller discharge). A channel becomes bigger (wider and/or deeper) to adjust to a larger discharge; it becomes smaller (narrower and/or shallower) to adjust to a decrease in discharge.

Many of the rivers downstream from major reservoirs in Britain have adjusted their channel cross-sections in response to reduced flows (because

Burrator Reservoir Dam, Dartmoor. This Victorian masonry dam, on the south-west section of Dartmoor in Devon, was built in 1898 to provide a reliable water supply to the city of Plymouth some twenty miles away. It also serves as a flood control dam, reducing the risk of major flooding downstream along the River Meavy. Like most dam structures built across rivers, Burrator has changed the natural pattern of flows of water and sediment along the river. The particulate sediment which was previously washed downstream is now deposited within the reservoir, so that through time the storage capacity is being reduced by siltation. High flows downstream have been reduced by the impounding effect of the reservoir, and as a result the river channel downstream is likely to have adjusted to the new flow regime by shrinking (particularly via reducing its channel width and depth). The Dartmoor National Park has developed a Burrator Reservoir Circuit for cyclists and walkers, which is 3.5 miles long and offers terrific views of the reservoir and sections through exotic woodland and plantation. The reservoir is stocked with rainbow trout and offers good fishing under licence.

C. PARK

water is now stored behind the dam rather than allowed to flow downstream uninterrupted). Other rivers, or other parts of the same rivers, have adjusted to the increased flows brought about by large-scale urban development, which replaces natural soil and vegetation with impermeable surfaces, and supplements natural streams with dense networks of artificial drainage systems.

Probably the most characteristic feature of the middle section of a natural river is the meander, the gently curving path followed by the river as it flows across the floodplain. This is the river feature that Samuel Taylor Coleridge describes in *Kubla Khan* – 'five miles meandering with a mazy motion, through wood and dale the sacred river ran.'

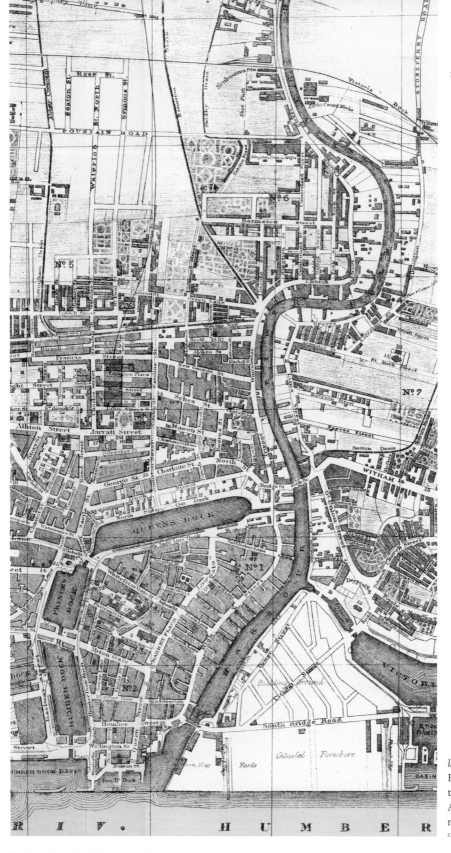

right A sinuous meandering course is the most natural path for a river to follow, except where it is constrained in some way from doing so. Typical meanders have a relatively uniform shape, smoothly sinuous, with a wavelength of around ten times the channel width. From the air meanders often look like a regular sine-wave. Here, the River Wharfe flows through an alluvial channel, so it has been able to adjust its course to a fairly typical pattern, in equilibrium with the flows of water and sediment through this reach.

C. PARK

left The River Barbour flows into the Humber at Hull. A map of the mid-nineteenth century.

CARNEGIE COLLECTION

below Newcastle East Quayside.

SEAN GALLAGHER

Straight channels are relatively rare, except where there is an obvious constraint (such as an outcrop of resistant bedrock, or perhaps where a river runs along a fault-line). Rivers meander naturally, and natural rivers usually have clearly defined and quite regular sequences of meanders along their middle and lower sections. Studies of many rivers of different sizes and in different environments (geology and climate) have shown some remarkably stable geometric patterns: for example, most rivers are rarely straight for longer than ten times the channel width; the downstream length of meanders

Floodplain deposit within the bank of the River Wharfe, North Yorkshire. This is a close-up view of one of the meander bends shown on page 23, showing a typical stratigraphic sequence (set of layers of deposits) within the channel bank, and which also occurs throughout the alluvial floodplain of the river. Very fine material represents over-bank deposits, mainly sand, silt and clay sized particles, which have been deposited by the river under flood conditions on the adjacent floodplain. Larger particles, typically well rounded and often well sorted and of similar size by being transported along the river bed, have usually been deposited within the channel, either during a flood (as a result of scour-and-fill on the bed of the channel, or by being deposited by the slower-moving water on the inside bend of meanders, as point bars) or simply by being rolled along the bed as normal bedload movement. The location of the coarse gravel layer within this river bank indicates that the floodplain here has been formed by repeated migrations of the river laterally across the floodplain; a former point bar is here preserved in the bank, and has been uncovered by more recent channel migration.

C. PARK

is generally between two and four times the cross-valley width; and the sinuosity (the ratio of distance along channel to distance down valley) is often around 1.5.

In taking a longer route to pass the same distance downstream than a straight channel, meanders alter the efficiency with which water and sediment are moved along the conveyor belt, and this is an important way in which a river creates and maintains equilibrium. Put simply, a river can increase or decrease that route, by increasing or decreasing the number and size of meanders within a given stretch of river. The adjustment is achieved by cross-sectional change within an existing meander bend, which moves progressively in one direction; the river deposits sediment on one bank while at the same time eroding and undercutting the opposite bank. This leads to a progressive shift in the size and location of the meander. This process, by which meanders move across an alluvial valley floor (lateral migration), can also be traced in the sub-surface deposits of a typical river floodplain, where the coarse point-bars and much finer over-bank deposits are often well preserved in the sequence of sediments beneath the ground surface.

Some meander bends can be stable for long periods of time. But old maps and repeated photography, coupled with field evidence of floodplain stratigraphy (sediment sequences) and topography (surface expression), often show that meanders move across and down floodplains through time. Lateral (side-to-side) migration of meanders tends to redistribute floodplain sediments, and repeated cycles of lateral planation over a long period of time can produce very flat, featureless floodplains. You can sometimes also find evidence of meander migration preserved on the floodplain surface in the form of an oxbow lake or cut-off. These banana-shaped depressions, often filled with stagnant water, are formed by the erosion of a tight meander bend which leaves the former meander separated from the main channel (Figure 1.2).

The formation and migration of meanders is partly a response to slope, in the sense that the river uses adjustments of its course as a way of preserving efficiency in its adjustment of form (channel size, plan and slope) to function (transport of water and sediment). For example, bed slope can be increased (which increases flow velocity and ability to transport sediment) by reducing the size of meanders, and forcing the river to flow more directly down-valley rather than taking the sinuous route via meander bends. Conversely, slope can be reduced by increasing the number and size of meanders within a particular reach of river.

Lower section

If the hallmark of the middle section of a natural river system is the attempt to preserve balance (equilibrium) between the form of the channel, and the task that channel has to perform (carry water and sediment), this is also true

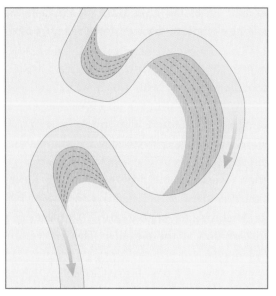
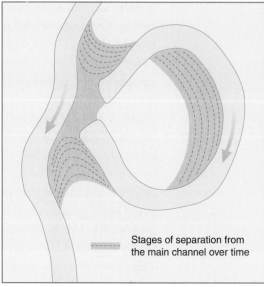

Stages of separation from the main channel over time

Figure 1.2.
The development of an oxbow lake.
(PARK, 2001)

of the lower section. Now the river is even wider and deeper than in its middle section; it has larger meanders and a lower bed slope; it flows faster; and it carries a relatively high sediment load (particulate and dissolved, the particulate material usually now much smaller and more uniform in size but higher in concentration than further upstream).

The river also now flows across a wide relatively flat floodplain on its way to the sea. By this point along the river the hills which in the upper section were adjacent to and dominated it are separated from the river by the floodplain, so that what happens in and to the river is controlled largely by what reaches the river from upstream. Compared with the upper reaches, this lower section of a river is usually dominated by deposition, particularly on the floodplain during over-bank floods. A typical British floodplain scene is evoked by Alfred Lord Tennyson in *The Lady of Shalott* (1833): 'On either side the river lie long fields of barley and of rye, that clothe the wold and meet the sky.'

Our river now appears to flow gently – almost sluggishly – along this flat landscape, but looks are deceptive because it flows faster here than in the upper reach, despite the contrary impression. The river now flows down a gentle slope but in a very efficient channel, so velocity is relatively high.

When it reaches the sea, our typical river broadens out considerably into an estuary. Here the fresh water carried down the river mixes with the salty water of the sea, and flow is either downstream (when the tide is out) or upstream (when the tide is in). As Algernon Charles Swinburne described in *The Garden of Proserpine* towards the close of the nineteenth century, 'Even the weariest river winds somewhere safe to sea'. It is not uncommon to find major settlements on or near the estuaries of British rivers, where they can

A detail from an aerial view of the River Mersey at Liverpool dating from the 1850s. Rather than being excavated on the landward side of the riverbank, all of the docks in this view were constructed out into the river, beyond the original shoreline, in some places to such an extent that the width of the natural estuary has been reduced by as much as 25 per cent.

LIVERPOOL RECORD OFFICE

exploit the opportunities presented by both land and sea. Obvious examples include London on the Thames, Bristol on the Severn and Avon, Newcastle on the Tyne, and Liverpool on the Mersey. However, not all rivers in Britain flow directly into the sea – some flow into large natural lakes, and others have been artificially impounded and flow into reservoirs.

The Severn Estuary.
S. OWEN

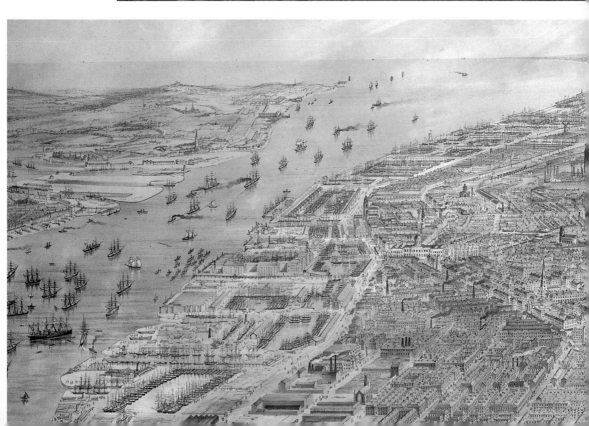

Regulated rivers

Throughout history rivers have been regulated and directly modified, for a variety of different reasons. The natural processes outlined above are thus mediated through human interference. For example, for thousands of years the Nile has been regulated to irrigate large areas of its floodplain and delta, and in China attempts to regulate flooding on the Yellow River, by building artificial levees, have promoted increased channel changes. The history of river regulation in Britain illustrates the changing pace and pattern of change. Rivers in Britain have been directly modified and controlled since at least the first century AD, when the Romans undertook land drainage schemes and river navigation improvements. Many small rivers were affected by flow control structures and water extraction to power watermills (of which there were more than 5,000 by 1086), and local regulation was common until the seventeenth century. From the end of the eighteenth century the scale of regulation increased a great deal, as large drainage schemes were implemented and many small water supply dams were built. During the twentieth century the pace of change grew faster, with the construction of large dams and large inter-basin water transfers and the adoption of large multi-purpose river management schemes. By the close of the twentieth century virtually all major rivers in the UK were regulated directly or indirectly by large dams, inter-basin transfers, pumped storage reservoirs, or groundwater abstractions. Human impact on rivers is dealt with more fully in chapters 5 and 7.

CHAPTER 2

Why do we have rivers in Britain?

Chris Park

Introduction

Put simply, we have rivers in Britain because of our climate, which provides precipitation, mainly in the form of rainfall, and because of our geology, which contains impermeable rocks into which water cannot soak. Some environments – like the Arctic and Antarctica – are simply too cold to produce rivers, because the ground is permanently frozen. Rivers are also rare in very arid places, which receive little precipitation and where most that does fall simply evaporates back into the atmosphere. So, compared for example with cold places beyond the Arctic Circle and hot places in the Middle East, Britain's climate is suitable for river development and capable of sustaining flows in river systems.

Because of the warming effect of the North Atlantic Drift (or 'Gulf Stream', a warm ocean current which sweeps up from the Caribbean past the shores of Britain), and the wetting effect of southwesterly winds, which bring moist air over Britain from a similar source, our climate is mild and temperate. Average temperature in London varies between 2° and 6° Celsius in January, and 13° and 22° in July. Rainfall varies across Britain, from around 1,600 mm in the more mountainous north and west, to less than 800 mm over central and eastern areas. Rainfall is spread fairly evenly through the year, but it is wetter in winter (September to January) and drier in early summer (March to June). See figure 2.1.

Rivers are also rare in places with permeable or porous rocks, because water can infiltrate into and move through such rocks, eventually carving out underground drainage systems. Consequently there are few rivers in parts of Britain which are underlain by chalk (such as the South Downs, or the North York Moors) or by limestone (such as parts of the Yorkshire Dales). But the story is much richer and more interesting than this summary would tend to suggest, because it is not simply a question of why we have rivers in Britain, but why

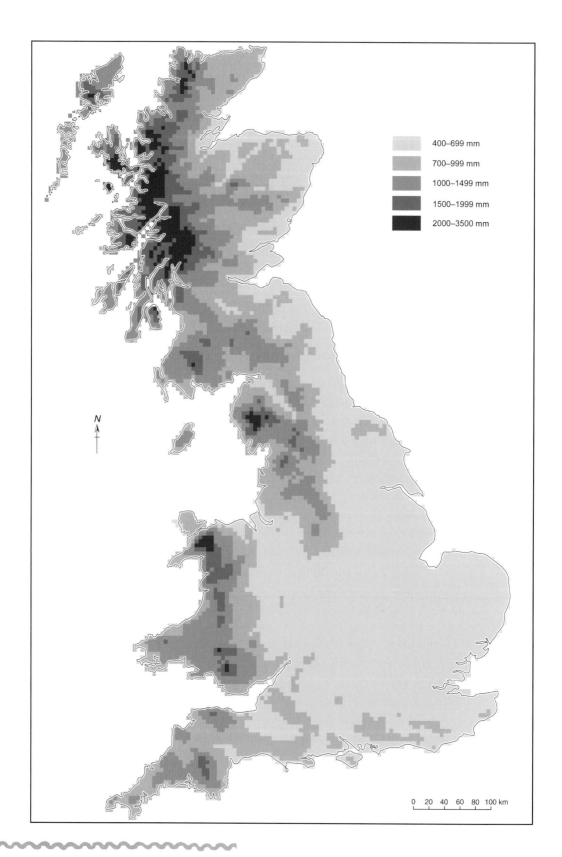

	400–699 mm
	700–999 mm
	1000–1499 mm
	1500–1999 mm
	2000–3500 mm

N

0 20 40 60 80 100 km

they are where they are, and why they are how they are. To understand this, we need to consider three main themes – how water moves through the environment (the water cycle), how rivers develop (and how they grow into networks), and how today's rivers are a product of interactions between different sets of processes that have shaped landscapes over very long period of time (particularly during and since the Ice Age). These processes are not peculiar to British rivers, but an understanding of them is necessary to appreciate the diversity and character of rivers in Britain.

left Figure 2.1. Rainfall map of Britain. Averaged yearly rainfall (mm) between 1961 and 1990.
DEPARTMENT OF GEOGRAPHY, LANCASTER UNIVERSITY

The water cycle

below Figure 2.2. The global water cycle.
(PARK, 2001)

Water supports all forms of life on Earth, and it occurs as standing water (in oceans and lakes), running water (in rivers and streams), and in the form of rain and water vapour in the atmosphere. The study of water on Earth is known as hydrology, and understanding of this water has increased a great

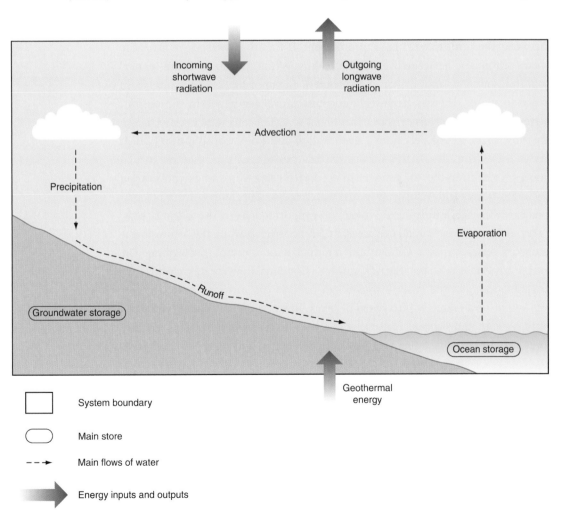

deal since the early interest of classical scholars. Aristotle suggested the basics of a water cycle, in which rivers were fed by water from multiple sources, including rain that soaks into the ground, condensation of air within the Earth and from the 'vapours' that rose on the mountains (Morisawa 1985). Much more recently, in 1580, Palissy connected the rain that soaks into the earth and springs with the origin of river water, and Perrault (1674) measured the discharge of the River Seine and found that it was comparable to the rainfall falling over the drainage basin.

The water (hydrological) cycle operates at a range of scales, the two most important of which are the global and the drainage basin cycles. It involves movements of moisture through the environment in its different phases (physical states) – as a liquid (water), a gas (water vapour) and a solid (snow and ice). These movements take place between the atmosphere, lithosphere (soil and rock) and biosphere (living plants and animals).

The global water cycle

At the global scale, the water cycle involves the continuous recycling of water between the atmosphere, land and oceans. Different processes redistribute water within and between these three realms. Within the atmosphere vertical and horizontal air movement and turbulent mixing transfers moisture from place to place, whereas large-scale currents move water within the oceans. Rivers and glaciers transfer water from land to the oceans. The cycle is driven by three main sets of processes – evaporation and evapotranspiration (which move water from the Earth's surface to the atmosphere), precipitation (which moves water from the atmosphere to the Earth's surface), and air movement, including winds and weather systems (which redistributes water from place to place within the atmosphere). Water is evaporated from the oceans, seas, lakes, rivers and vegetated land areas, and it becomes part of the atmospheric store of water vapour. Global and regional wind systems redistribute the water vapour across the Earth's surface. Condensation creates clouds and precipitation, and the latter brings water back to the surface where it enters the soil or flows directly into rivers or lakes. Rivers transport water from land surfaces into the oceans. Naturally, much of the precipitation falls directly over seas and oceans, effectively short-circuiting the land phase of the hydrological cycle (Figure 2.2).

The global cycle includes stores (groundwater, surface water, the ocean and the atmosphere) and processes that transfer water between the stores. Most of the water is stored in the vast oceans (Table 2.1). Rivers play a vital role in the global water cycle, because they drain water from land into the seas and oceans. River flow rapidly carries water downhill to the sea, but rivers store hardly any water at the global scale – water is typically resident in rivers up to about 2 weeks, whereas it can be stored for years in lakes, reservoirs and wetlands, and for thousands of years as ice in glaciers and ice caps, and in the oceans. In this sense rivers are rapid conduits rather than stores.

Table 2.1 Major natural stores of water within the global hydrological cycle

Store	Proportion of total (per cent)
Oceans	97.41
Ice caps and glaciers	1.9
Groundwater	0.5
Soil moisture	0.01
Lakes and rivers	0.009

Source: Park (2001)

The drainage basin water cycle

The fate of the precipitation which falls over land areas is determined largely by the ground surface conditions. Some precipitation falls directly into river channels, lakes and other water bodies. This is called *direct precipitation*, and it is rapidly transferred back to the oceans along rivers. Precipitation which falls over vegetated ground interacts with the vegetation in a number of ways. A certain proportion will land on the leaves and branches of the plants, as *interception*. This can be evaporated back to the atmosphere as water vapour. If the weight of collected water exceeds the supporting capacity of the leaves, they bend downwards and the water drips off them onto the ground below. Water can also be knocked off leaves by the direct impact of other water droplets. Another variable amount will trickle down the stems of plants as stemflow, and although this slows down the water most of it will eventually reach the ground surface below the vegetation. The rest of the precipitation will fall directly through the vegetation to reach the ground surface beneath, as *throughfall*. This fraction is clearly related to the type, density and structure of the vegetation it encounters. Relatively more precipitation will pass as throughfall in scattered woodland than in dense forest, for example.

Precipitation reaches the ground, either directly or after interacting with vegetation, and it can then have several fates. On a sloping surface with saturated soil, or on a surface with an impermeable horizon in the underlying soil, much of the water will flow across the ground surface as *overland flow* (or *sheet flow*), its path of travel being directed towards the lowest parts of the ground surface. In this way the water can reach the river channel and contribute to surface run-off. Not all parts of a basin produce overland flow, particularly if rainfall intensities are low and infiltration rates are high. Field studies have shown the importance of *contributing areas* within a basin (usually at the base of a slope, close to the channel) which can expand and contract during individual storms.

A stream with heavy bankside vegetation and trees: Clapham Beck, Clapham, N. Yorks.
S. OWEN

Much of the water which has not directly evaporated from the ground surface drains into the soil by *infiltration*, and it becomes part of the soil water store. This soil water store has great ecological and agricultural importance, because plants take in water (and nutrients in solution) from the surrounding soil via root osmosis. If soil conditions are suitable, much of this water will continue to move downwards through the soil horizons by *percolation*, and may eventually enter the underlying bedrock and contribute to the groundwater store (*aquifer*). Alternatively, and particularly on sloping surfaces, soil water will move downslope either through the pore spaces within the soil structure (*interflow*), or by flowing along impermeable horizons within the soil (*throughflow*). The water that moves downslope beneath the surface may appear in a seepage line or *percoline* (hollow) at the base of the slope.

Spring or resurgance,
River Greta.
C. PARK

Water can percolate into and through rocks which are porous (they have pores) and permeable (water can pass through them), such as sandstone, where it accumulates as groundwater (Figure 2.3). The layer of rock through which the water percolates is known as an aquifer, and humans can extract this water for use, usually by drilling wells. The water table is the upper level of groundwater in permeable rocks beneath the ground surface, below which the rocks are saturated. Springs appear where an aquifer outcrops at the ground surface, and these can contribute run-off to streams and rivers.

Most groundwater near the surface moves slowly through the aquifer while

below Figure 2.3.
Groundwater
percolation.
(PARK, 2001)

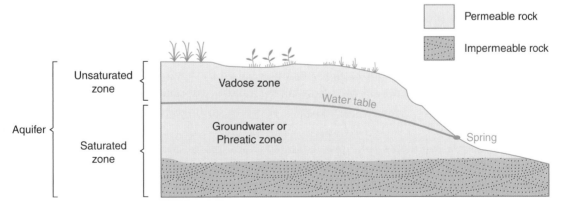

the water table stays in the same place. The depth of the water table reflects the balance between the rate of infiltration (recharge) and the rate of discharge at springs, rivers or wells. The water table usually follows surface contours and it varies with rainfall. Groundwater levels can vary a great deal over time, and this can create problems for the stability of deep building foundations and flood tunnels. This seems to be happening in the London Basin, in England, where plans are being made to control the rising groundwater within the chalk aquifer by abstracting water from selected sites.

River flow

The throughflow, interflow, percolation water and groundwater can be released into streams and rivers via springs, natural soil pipes and seepage through the bed and banks of the river channel. There are two important properties of river flow – velocity and discharge.

Flow velocity: this is the speed at which water moves along a river channel, and it is usually measured in m. s^{-1}. Velocity varies both through time and from place to place along a river, and it is controlled mainly by slope (water flows faster down steep slopes), discharge (velocity increases as discharge increases), channel shape (water flows faster through an efficient channel cross-section, and velocity is reduced by frictional resistance with rough channel beds and banks), and the size and shape of sediment in the channel bed and banks (smooth channels allow water to flow fast and rough channels slow down water movement by resistance caused by friction between the water and the channel).

Discharge: this is the amount or volume of water which flows through a given cross-section of a river in a given unit of time. It is usually expressed in $m^3 s^{-1}$ ('cumecs', short for cubic metres per second), and can be estimated by multiplying the cross-sectional area of the channel (width × depth in m^2) by flow velocity through that cross-section (in m s^{-1}). Hydrologists usually refer to discharge as Q. Discharge varies through time in a river system, and these patterns can be plotted as hydrographs, which are plots of variations in discharge through time (which show, for example, how the river responds to a storm event). British rivers, like most other mid-latitude rivers, usually have relatively low flows in summer and higher flows in winter, and this defines their annual flow regime or hydrograph. Superimposed on the annual cycles are the short-term responses of river flow to the rainfall associated with individual storms, and these can be plotted as storm hydrographs (see chapter 3).

Continuous measurements are now collected from many large river systems in Britain. The analysis of these streamflow records is important in the assessment of hydrological hazards (flood and droughts), in evaluating water resources, and in determining how climate change and land-use change are affecting river systems.

River flow is determined by a number of factors, including:

- The area of the drainage basin: all else being equal, larger basins have bigger average flows but they respond more slowly to storm events; larger basins have flatter storm hydrographs, because water arrives from tributaries in a more staggered manner.

- The shape of the drainage basin: long thin basins tend to have flatter hydrographs than more circular basins, again because water arrives from tributaries in a more staggered manner.

- Rainfall totals, which inevitably affect mean and peak flows; rivers that drain wetter areas have higher unit discharges (discharge per unit of drainage area, usually km^2) than those that drain dry areas.

- Rainfall intensity: when intensity is high the ground often cannot absorb all of the rain that falls, so a large proportion of it quickly drains off as overland flow, as a result of which the river responds quickly and has a shorter response time.

- Surface conditions within the drainage basin: vegetation intercepts rainfall and this slows down its movement into rivers and allows at least some to be evaporated before it ever reaches the river.

Discharge increases downstream in most rivers because of increasing drainage area. As a result, the erosive power of rivers tends to increase downstream; they can carry much larger sediment loads; they flow faster; and they flood more frequently.

How do rivers form?

The water cycle describes and explains how water gets into a river, and how various factors affect the flow of water in rivers, but it does not explain how a river forms in the first place. Here we explore how river networks develop, how they are affected by geological controls, and how they can be described and compared. As giant oaks grow from tiny acorns, so also do mighty rivers grow from small rills. Running water is an efficient agent of erosion, and overland flow running down a hillslope can dislodge particles of soil and sediment, start to erode simple small-scale channel-like features and transport sediment and deposit it downslope or down-valley. Vegetation cover can protect underlying material from erosion, and bare areas are much more susceptible to erosion by running water. Rills are small channels formed by soil erosion on hillslopes and gently sloping surfaces. They commonly develop on bare spoil

Gullies forming on
the hillside above
High House in upper
Borrowdale,
Cumbria.
S. OWEN

heaps and in recently ploughed fields, often at the end of summer when there
is no vegetation cover to protect the soil surface from erosion. Rills often form
very dense networks and they usually disappear in winter (either because the
soil is ploughed or soil creep and frost destroy the rills).

Once running water is confined within a channel, even a very small one like
a rill, it becomes much more effective and more efficient at eroding and transporting sediment and at shaping landforms. If rills survive long enough, they
promote further erosion and more and more water concentrates into the
linear depression to form gullies (deep, steep-sided channels). Gullies, in turn,
can grow into river channels, and if river channels continue eroding long
enough they can create river valleys.

River channels grow from rills and gullies by a chain-reaction of processes,
in which:

- Water flows towards the channel, because its bed is lower than the
  surrounding surface.

- The depth of water flowing in the channel increases, because it
  contains more water.

- Flow velocity increases: because it is deeper, so frictional resistance
  decreases.

- Erosion by flowing water is concentrated within the channel, because
  of the higher velocity.

- The base of the channel is lowered and it grows wider as a result of erosion.

- More water is encouraged to flow into the evolving channel, and the chain-reaction continues.

Flowing water usually concentrates into distinct watercourses or channels. Small channels tend to be called streams, and larger ones are called rivers. There is no particular size threshold, however, to distinguish a stream from a river.

River networks

Once a channel has started to form, it grows and attracts bigger flows of water and sediment. Across an area, rivers which start in this rather un-assuming way all drain towards the lowest point, so their paths inevitably converge on the lowest land. In this way, networks of streams and rivers form, like the veins on a leaf. Small streams (tributaries) join the main river, and as rivers develop more and bigger tributaries join them and so an integrated network, dominated by the main river, evolves within the drainage basin.

Until the nineteenth century, it was generally believed that all landscapes – including river valleys – were created suddenly, by short-lived but large-scale geological events. This pre-Darwinian interpretation, referred to by geologists as 'catastrophism' – often involved major floods, and was consistent with the

Figure 2.4. Drainage networks, showing (A) dendritic; (B) trellis; (C) radial; and (D) parallel drainage patterns.
DEPARTMENT OF GEOGRAPHY, LANCASTER UNIVERSITY

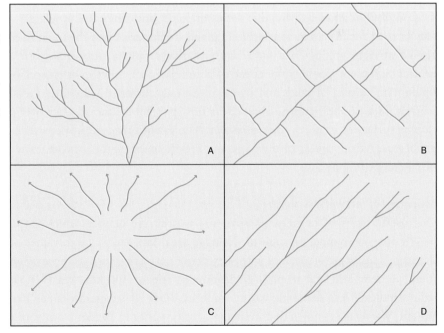

Biblical story of Noah's flood. An alternative interpretation, termed 'uniform-itarianism' (based on a more uniform operation of the types of geological processes we see today, but over very long periods of time), was proposed by Hutton (1795) and Playfair (1802) and gradually won widespread support because it seemed to fit the available evidence better. Playfair, for example, described how 'every river appears to consist of a main trunk, fed from a variety of branches, each running in a valley apportioned to its size and all of them together forming a system of valleys … having such a nice adjustment to their declivities, that none of them joins the principal valley, either on too high or too low a level; a circumstance which would be infinitely improbable, if each of these valleys were not the work of the stream that flows in it' (quoted in Morisawa 1985, p. 7).

Descriptions of network pattern

The most common drainage pattern for natural rivers is the dendritic network, which from above resembles the trunk and branches of a tree. Tributaries flow into the main rivers at quite sharp angles. Through time the network can grow by headward extension, in which the outermost tributaries extend by erosion into the hillslopes of the drainage divides. Geology often controls the overall shape of a river network, because it can strongly influence rates and patterns of erosion. Geologists have given descriptive names to the most common patterns. *Dendritic* patterns develop on uniform rock types where there is no strong structural control (such as fault lines or folds), but most patterns reflect geological influences. In a *trellis* pattern, which is common in areas which have rocks of different strengths (thus resistance to erosion) and in areas with regular series of folds (anticlines and synclines) – like parts of the Weald in south-east England – tributaries join the main river almost at right angles. In a *radial* pattern, rivers radiate outwards from a central high point, possibly the dome of a uniform rock outcrop or an area of uplift. The pattern of lakes and rivers in the Lake District is a classic radial pattern. In a *parallel* pattern, small rivers flow parallel to one another over a sloping surface of uniform rock resistance. The various river network patterns are best seen from the air or on maps, and they help create the local character of landscape (Figure 2.4).

Measures of network structure

One useful measure of network structure is drainage density, which is the length of river channel per unit of drainage area (km. km^{-2}). High values of drainage density are associated with very dense networks, such as those often found in semi-arid and tropical environments (up to 100 km. km^{-2}). Low values indicate less dense networks, such as those in temperate areas like Britain. Ward (1981) notes that drainage density varies in Britain from about

1.46 to about 0.02 km km^{-2}, with significant regional distinctions, for example high rates in north and south-west Scotland, Cumbria, Yorkshire, Mersey, mid-Wales, south Cornwall and east Devon. Stream frequency is a different measure of network geometry, based on the number of streams per unit of drainage area (no. km^{-2}). Dense networks tend to have high stream frequencies.

Both measures reflect the degree of dissection of a particular landscape. Fine-grained landscapes, with high drainage densities and high stream frequencies, tend to develop in areas with erodible soils and rocks and high rainfall. Badland topography, with dense networks of interlocking gullies and ridges – of the sort you will regularly see on the side of soil heaps and un-vegetated slopes – is a classic example. Coarse-grained landscapes, with low drainage densities and low stream frequencies, tend to develop in areas with resistant rocks and low rainfall.

Channel equilibrium and change

In 1899 the American geologist William Morris Davis proposed a *Cycle of Erosion* to explain how temperate landscapes, dominated by river activity, change over geological time-scales. Davis argued that all landscapes evolve from youth, to maturity and eventually to old age, and that different land-scapes are associated with and are indicative of each stage. He also proposed that all landscapes are a product of structure (geology), process (the geo-logical processes at work on it) and stage (age). The cycle idea was widely accepted until the 1950s, when hydrologists established that flow velocity increases downstream in most rivers rather than decreasing as Davis's model had assumed (in fact, required).

Since the 1960s geologists and hydrologists have preferred to view rivers as open systems, with inputs of water, transfers and storage of water and sediment, and outputs of water and sediment (ultimately to the sea). These open systems have the ability to adjust their form (morphology) – in terms of cross-section, pattern and slope – to reach and preserve equilibrium with the water and sediment load they carry, in order to maintain a balance of energy moving through the system. Equilibrium exists when the energy provided to do work (that is, to transport the sediment and shape the river landscape) is just enough to perform the work which has to be done. This state of equilibrium can be altered if any of the controlling factors change past critical thresholds. Such change is usually promoted by factors that are external to the river system, such as rainfall (associated with climate change), sediment load (perhaps associated with land-use changes) and slope thus velocity (perhaps associated with tectonic uplift or fault-line movements).

Rivers are open systems which can adjust their morphology to the throughput of water and sediment. Rivers can adjust over a variety of time-scales, and for convenience we can focus on short-term, medium-term and long-term changes, although these are obviously part of a continuous spectrum of change through time.

Short-term changes

Short-term channel changes occur over time-scales of years or less. They are caused mainly by variations in discharge, such as those associated with the

The effects of the flooding of the river Roeburn on Wray village, Lancashire, August 1967.
COLIN SHEARD

The Boscastle floods, August 2004.
PHOTOGRAPH: DAVID FLOWERS

passage of a storm across the drainage basin. Most flows in a typical river are small to medium in magnitude, and they remain well within the bank-full channel. But experience shows that the most dramatic channel changes are caused by less frequent large flows, including floods that overtop the banks and spill onto the adjacent floodplain.

The River Severn, which has a source in central Wales and flows into the sea at the Bristol Channel, is Britain's longest and best-studied regulated river (see chapter 8). It has long been regulated for water resource purposes and has a long history of flood problems. Demand for water continued to rise during the twentieth century, and an ambitious drainage basin management scheme was developed to augment low river flows, increase the amount of water that could be abstracted for supply purposes and decrease the flood risk. Clywedog Reservoir, a storage reservoir on the headwaters of the Severn, is an important element in the scheme. Water is stored at Clywedog under high flow conditions and released from it under low flow conditions. Since it was completed in the 1960s, low flows along the Severn have been increased by nearly a quarter, normal flows reduced by about half and the mean annual flood reduced by nearly a third. Detailed analysis of these flow changes, however, reveals that climate change has probably been a more important control than river regulation.

Extremely large flows can cause significant channel changes, but they are relatively rare. Catastrophic events of low frequency (particularly very large

Meanders and terraces, Howgill Fells, Cumbria. Here the relatively small headwater of the River Lune follows a braiding course through remnants of terraces along the valley floor. In post-glacial times there has been much reworking and redistribution by the river of fairly coarse gravel particles, most of which were washed here by fast-flowing meltwater streams over semi-frozen ground. The post-glacial river has transported and moved these particles under high flow conditions, but under normal conditions they lie stationary on the valley floor, too big for the river to move and too resistant to be worn down quickly by mechanical weathering. The river has cut a path through a major terrace (probably deposited by the meltwater streams), which now constrains further channel migration across this relatively steep upland valley floor.

C. PARK

floods) perform only a small proportion of the total work of a river. For example, the 1952 flood at Lynmouth in south-west England, which hydrologists predict was of a size that should be expected on average once every 150 years, caused extensive damage by destroying bridges and buildings, cutting new channels on the peat moorlands on Exmoor, depositing large boulders on the stream bed, diverting some channels and cutting off some meander bends. Since 1952 the River Lyn appears to have established a new equilibrium, and many of the features caused by the 1952 flood are left as residual or persistent elements in the landscape. A major flood in 1990 on the River Tay in Scotland, the third largest flood since 1800, caused widespread channel adjustments, damaged some artificial flood embankments, deposited some large gravel bars on the river bed and changed the location of many meanders. Even smaller rivers can have a devastating local effect, for instance the flash flood of the river Roeburn in Wray in north Lancashire in August 1967.

Flooding at Claughton, Lancashire, 1967.
COLIN SHEARD

Medium-term changes

Over the longer term, perhaps measured in thousands of years, channel changes appear to be controlled mainly by climatic change. Concern has been expressed about the implications of contemporary global warming for river management, although scenarios are difficult to establish because of the complexity of river response and because of limitations in current understanding of river equilibrium and adjustment. Over the past three decades a specialised area of research has developed, called palaeohydrology ('palaeo' simply means old or former), based on the study of past hydrological conditions and how river systems have changed through time.

Two of the most widespread indicators of medium-term channel changes are terraces and misfit streams, both of which illustrate channel adjustment to changing throughputs of water and sediment. A river terrace is a flat platform of land which lies above the level of the valley floor. Terraces are often remnants of an earlier valley floor higher than the present one, which has been cut into when the river's power to erode is increased. The terrace survives as a remnant of the abandoned floodplain.

Terraces represent adjustments of the river to changing circumstances, which might include sea-level fall (which creates a lower base level), uplift of the land (which increases river slope and thus velocity), decreased sediment load (perhaps associated with upstream impoundment of water and sediment behind a dam), or increased river flow (perhaps associated with the melting of upstream glaciers or with land-use changes within the drainage basin).

A misfit (or underfit) stream is a small meandering stream within a larger meandering valley, usually created as a response of the river to a significant reduction in discharge. Misfit streams indicate adjustment of channel pattern to changing climatic or hydrological conditions, such as a decrease in river flow since the end of the Pleistocene less than 10,000 years ago. The shrunken river reworks the floodplain material as best it can by sorting and redistributing sediment.

Long-term changes

Many river systems preserve evidence of their long-term evolution over geological timescales. A good example of this would be river capture or piracy, in which an actively eroding river might capture the headwaters of an adjacent river by eroding through the drainage divide and effectively stealing its flow. Evidence of such capture can often be found on maps and air photographs. Long-term river change is also apparent where there are signs of rejuvenation (renewed downcutting) (Figure 2.5). Evidence for this is often preserved in river long profiles, which sometimes display a step-like structure, with a series of concave-upwards segments indicating former base levels, usually related to falling sea-levels.

Dry valleys, which are common in areas underlain by chalk and limestone, also provide evidence of long-term change. These valleys, which now have no river running through them, are remnants of former active river systems which were eroded by very high meltwater discharges running over frozen ground during the Pleistocene Ice Age.

Figure 2.5.
Long profile of a
rejuvenated stream,
the River Ribble,
Lancashire.
(PARK, 2001)

Long-term environmental history

Although rivers are very common in the British landscape, they have not created much of the landscape of Britain that we see today. They have inherited and exploited pre-existing landscapes, largely shaped by the inter-

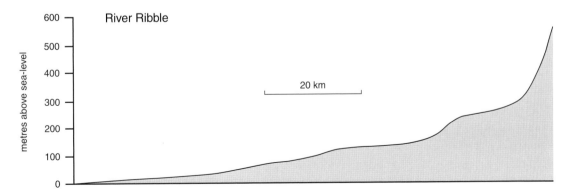

Misfit channel of an upper tributary of the River Rheidol, central Wales. A misfit or underfit channel is a river which is too small to have carved the valley along which it flows, and which provides evidence of long-term climate and environmental change. In this case, not untypical of much of upland Britain, the major size, shape and orientation of the valley have been determined mainly by conditions before and during the Pleistocene Ice Age, but much of the smaller-scale detail has been reworked and refashioned by smaller post-glacial rivers. Typical features include the wide, gently meandering valley, the large amount of particulate sediment deposited on the valley floor and its flat and relatively featureless appearance, and the relatively narrow present-day river which looks slightly out of place in this broad valley.

C. PARK

action of underlying geology and surface processes (weathering and erosion), under climatic conditions very different to those in Britain today. A quick summary of the geological evolution of Britain will show just how much our landscape is a palimpsest, with surviving fragments and remnants of by-gone ages and very different conditions. It will also demonstrate the relatively small and recent impact of rivers on landscape formation.

Geological background

The geological history of Britain is complex, reflecting the interplay of large-scale crustal plate movements, volcanic and mountain-building activity, and huge swings in climate and in the processes which create landforms and landscapes (Smithson *et al.* 2002). Few of Britain's rocks are older than the Palaeozoic era (590 m yrs BP – million years Before Present). In the early Palaeozoic (covering the Cambrian, Ordovician and Silurian periods) sediments were deposited in a broad geosyncline (regional-scale sedimentary basin) running from the south-west to the north-east of what is now Britain. During the Ordovician (515 m yr BP) there was much volcanic activity and extensive folding, and the major mountain chains of the north and west of Britain were formed during the Silurian (445 m yr BP).

Much of this landscape was eroded during the Devonian (415 m yr BP) and there was widespread deposition of sandstone across Britain, particularly in areas close to what was then mountains. Deposition continued through the Carboniferous (370 m yr BP), mostly under warm shallow seas (to form limestones and clays), in large coastal deltas (to form gritstones), and in swamps and deltas (to form coal shales). Towards the close of the Carboniferous there was also renewed mountain building (orogeny) and volcanic activity, in what are now Devon and Cornwall, and extensive land masses were pushed up (creating features such as Dartmoor and Bodmin Moor).

Climatic conditions in Britain changed dramatically during the Permian (280 m yrs BP) and the Triassic (240 m yrs BP) – the first period in the Mesozoic era – and the new land masses were eroded by dry desert conditions. Clays, sandstones and limestones were deposited in warm seas during the Jurassic (200 m yr BP) and Cretaceous (135 m yrs BP) periods, and chalk in the Cretaceous.

The Tertiary (65 m yrs BP) marked the beginning of the current geological era, the Caenozoic. Maritime sedimentation continued for a period in the

'A Frost Fair on the Thames at Temple Stairs', c.1684 by A. Hondius.

London and Hampshire basins, while at the same time volcanic rocks, particularly basalt, were being extruded (squeezed out as molten rock onto the land surface) on Skye and in Northern Ireland. In the Mid-Tertiary these areas were uplifted further during the Alpine orogeny.

By the Miocene epoch, within the Tertiary, the broad geological structure of Britain as we know it today was largely established. The land mass has since then been worn down by weathering and erosion processes (sub-aerial denudation). The deteriorating climate during the Tertiary increased the speed of denudation, so that today much of the former land surface of the Tertiary is lost. The key agent in this relatively rapid erosion was glaciation during the Pleistocene period (3 m yrs BP) in the Quaternary era (3 m yrs BP to present), when extensive ice sheets covered much of Britain and refashioned the existing landscape.

Seen in this long-term context of Britain's geological history, it can be appreciated that rivers have played a relatively small part in shaping the landscape and in the laying down of deposits. At different times, marine processes, tectonic processes and glacial processes have been the dominant forces. In this sense, Britain today is rather different to what it has been in the past. Over the long term, rivers are the exception rather than the rule in Britain. In post-glacial (Holocene, 0.01 m ys BP) times climate has been much milder, and weathering and erosion processes have continued to alter landscape, rework and redistribute earlier deposits, and create conditions suitable for the evolution of the river systems we see today.

The Quaternary

There have been at least six major changes in climate in Europe since the last major ice age, which covered most of northern Britain with ice (north of a line from the Bristol Channel in the west to the Wash in the east) as recently as about 15,000 years ago (Lamb 1972). Once the ice started to melt, with a warmer climate, sea level rose sharply (up to 100 metres within 10,000 years), and plants (particularly forest) and animals spread across areas of land which were left exposed when the ice retreated northwards. The gradual warming was punctuated by two much colder spells, known as interstadials. The first occurred between 11500 and 12000 BC, and it led to the regrowth of ice sheets over much of Scotland and Scandinavia, and the second lasted six centuries, from 8800 to 8200 BC, when ice again reappeared over western and central parts of the Highlands of Scotland, and in the valleys of the Lake District.

The last glaciers disappeared from Britain and Scandinavia between 7000 and 8000 BC, and by 6000 BC Europe was enjoying its warmest climate (during the so-called Climatic Optimum) since the Ice Age. During this warm period, which lasted until between 5000 and 3000 BC, mean annual temperatures over Europe were about 2°C higher than today. Sea level and the distribution of ice on land were somewhat similar to what we are familiar with today. Europe was then much wetter than before (and since). Forest disappeared from some areas and was replaced by peat bogs and expanded lakes. Climate changed again after the Climatic Optimum, becoming gradually drier and cooler between about 3000 and 5000 BC. This encouraged the return of forest cover, and trees even prospered on what are now the exposed western coast of Scotland and the Orkneys.

After about 900 BC climate worsened again (during the early Iron Age), becoming colder and wetter along much of Western Europe. Mean annual temperatures were up to 2°C cooler than today; evaporation rates were lower, and surface conditions were wetter in most places. Floods and storms became more frequent; valley glaciers grew and advanced in the Alps; peat bogs grew once again; large areas of the lowlands became marshy (and wooden trackways had to be built to cross them); many lakeside dwellings were abandoned as water levels rose. This stormy climate persisted in Britain until the early centuries AD, and was followed by droughts between AD 350 and 500, greater flooding between 550 and 590, and then a further period of droughts during the tenth century.

The early Middle Ages (roughly between about 1000 and 1200) saw a return to drier, warmer conditions not unlike today's climate in Britain. Mean summer temperatures during this co-called Little Optimum were perhaps 1°C higher than today. Trees grew at much higher altitudes than they do today, and pack ice in the North Sea was much further north than previously. This spell of hospitable climate was followed by two centuries (the thirteenth to early fifteenth centuries) of very unstable conditions. This period saw frequent floods and droughts (some very severe), some very mild winters, numerous great storms, and coastal floods. Historical evidence suggests that many rivers in England were deeper and more navigable during the Middle Ages than they are today, and some land in some farmed areas (for example in Cambridgeshire) had to be abandoned because of frequent flooding.

Things were to change again after about 1500, with a return to colder conditions, the coldest since the end of the Ice Age. This heralded the onset of the so-called Little Ice Age, which was to last in Britain up to about 1850. Climate was cold; parts of southern England were drier, but most of Britain was wetter and had higher river levels. By the late seventeenth century valley glaciers were once again advancing in the Alps; forests at high altitudes were in decline; and trees in exposed places (such as the Atlantic coast of Scotland) were dying. Between about 1550 and 1850 glaciers in Europe were further advanced than at any time since the Ice Age. The River Thames froze over in London on a number of occasions (because of the low temperatures but aggravated by the old bridges which restricted water movement), and frost fairs were regular winter occurrences through the seventeenth and eighteenth centuries.

Warmer conditions (similar to those of the Little Optimum of the Middle Ages) returned to Britain and much of Europe between about 1830 and the 1930s, with longer growing seasons and reduced rainfall. Since the middle of the twentieth century, temperatures have been rising, probably as a result of global warming associated with air pollution by greenhouse gases.

Over the last 10,000 years or so the rivers of Britain have thus adapted to numerous changes in climate, involving changes in both temperature and precipitation. Some of these adaptations are preserved in features such as misfit rivers and terraces, but much of the evidence is stored in floodplain and lake sediments.

Tower Beach, London 1952 by Henry Grant.
COURTESY OF THE MUSEUM OF LONDON

right Figure 3.1. Sloping surfaces with constant water depth: gravity pulls the water more strongly down the steeper channel (*b*) than it does down the less steep one (*a*).
DEPARTMENT OF GEOGRAPHY, LANCASTER UNIVERSITY

RIVERS AND THE BRITISH LANDSCAPE

CHAPTER 3

What rivers do: flows and forms

Andrew Folkard

A first approximation to a British river

Anyone who has taken even a casual glance at water flowing in a river will have noticed the fascinating multiplicity and complexity of patterns it makes. The aim of this chapter is to explain these patterns and the roles they play in the lives of British rivers. To do this, I will start by sketching out the simplest possible picture of a river, and then by adding layers of increasing detail, we will end up with a relatively realistic and complete idea of what the flow patterns in real British rivers are like. The broad framework of what a river is and why they exist has been covered in chapters 1 and 2. Chapters 3 and 4 focus on related themes but provide a more detailed exposition of some of the key physical features of British rivers, together with references that will allow readers to take these themes further if they wish.

At the simplest level, a river is a natural channel which carries water down a slope under the force of gravity. Why these natural channels exist has been covered in chapter 2. So, our first and simplest approximation to a river might be thought of as a channel with a perfectly rectangular cross section (vertical banks, flat bottom) which stays the same down its whole length (is 'constant'). This channel will extend down a slope at a constant gradient, carry water whose depth and speed are constant, and have a speed that is constant throughout any given cross-section of the river. The bed and banks of the river are impermeable. This crudest of approximations is illustrated in Figures 3.1a and b, which show slopes with a less steep and steeper profile with a constant

(a) less steep channel

water
hillslope
weaker gravitational force down channel

(b) steeper channel

water
hillslope
stronger gravitational force down channel

water depth. The question that this very approximate model of a river can be used to address is that of how fast water moves down a river. Slope angle is one of the things which determine how quickly water moves down river channels – all other things being equal, the steeper the slope, the faster the flow. The other factors are the processes which resist downwards motion, namely friction (the drag on the flow caused by the channel) and viscosity (the 'stickiness' of the water).

How much frictional drag there is on the water depends on two things: how rough the channel surface is, and what proportion of the water is in contact with it. The surface rough-ness of the channel is measured as the average size of the lumps that make it up. Thus sandy channels – commonly found in large estuaries such as the Humber or the Severn – have small roughness values, whereas cobble-bed channels – commonly found in upland streams – have large roughness values. The most widely used methods for deriving roughness values are those devel-oped by Nikuradse (1933), Gaukler (1867) and Strickler (1923) (Chadwick and Morfett 1998, Chanson 1999).

Grains Gill, the upper section of the river Derwent showing the coarse sediment bed channel.
S. OWEN

The effect of channel drag is to turn the water's downhill motion into eddies, which spawn smaller and smaller eddies, gradually dissipating the flow's energy and thus slowing the downhill motion. If water were not at all viscous, the drag from the channel would only affect those molecules of water in direct contact with it. Because it is, the drag has a significant effect on the movement of the water. We can think of the drag caused by the channel as extracting energy from the flow. Indeed, we can think of the whole process in terms of energy: the river turns potential (elevation) energy into kinetic (motion) energy, some of which gets turned into turbulent energy by the drag of the channel and thus dissipated.

The proportion of water in contact with the channel is measured using the 'hydraulic radius', which can be thought of as a number representing how free the water is from the drag of the channel. So the higher the hydraulic radius is, the higher the flow speed will be. It is calculated as the ratio of the

A typical babbly mountain brook. A tributary of Grains Gill, upper Borrowdale, Cumbria.

S. OWEN

cross-sectional area of the flow to the length of channel adjacent to water in the cross-section – the 'wetted perimeter' (Figure 3.2). A river with a large cross-sectional area and a simple channel shape – the characteristics found in the seaward end of any large river – has a large hydraulic radius. Conversely, a shallow mountain stream, with a complex bed, has a small hydraulic radius.

We can use all these factors to predict the flow speed in a river. Flow is faster if either the slope is steeper or the hydraulic radius is larger, and is slower if the channel roughness is larger. The most commonly used mathematical expression of this idea (which expresses it in a way which allows us to predict flow speeds) is known as Manning's (1883) equation – this is outside the scope of this book, but is covered in any standard hydraulics textbook (Featherstone and Nalluri 1982, Chadwick and Morfett 1998, Graf and Altinakar 1998). So, we have a model of the fundamental function of a river: to carry water down hills. We can think of this process in

Mature river channel, river Lune

CARNEGIE

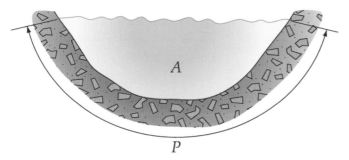

A cross sectional area of flow
P wetted perimeter

Figure 3.2.
Definition sketch of
area and wetted
perimeter.
DEPARTMENT OF GEOGRAPHY,
LANCASTER UNIVERSITY

terms of a balance of forces (gravity *versus* drag) or energy conversion from potential energy into kinetic and turbulent energy.

Introducing the first dimension: vertical variations

The description given above is as much like a real river as a quickly sketched cartoon is like a real person. To improve the likeness, we will now consider what happens if we drop our assumption that the flow is everywhere the same in any river cross-section. If we frame our thoughts within a strict three-dimensional framework, we can say that the first section gave us a zero-dimensional picture of a river (no variations in any direction). Here, we will add one dimension (the vertical one) to that picture.

Variations in the vertical direction are governed most strongly by the presence of drag effects at the bottom and top of the water body. Those at the bottom are caused by the solid bed, while those at the top are caused by the air above the water (which is unlikely to be travelling at exactly the same speed as the water, and will therefore be dragging it a little in one direction or another most of the time). The bed, being relatively immovable, will cause much greater drag than the air. The main effect that drag has is to reduce the flow speed, so flow will be slowest near the bed and gradually increase as we move up within the water body. The drag of the air above the water means that the water will not be fastest right at its surface. However, because of the relatively weak nature of the air drag, the maximum speed will be much closer to the top of the water than to the bottom.

left Figure 3.3.
Steamlines in laminar
flow.

right Figure 3.4.
Steamlines in
turbulent flow.
DEPARTMENT OF GEOGRAPHY,
LANCASTER UNIVERSITY

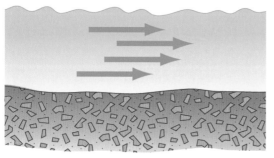

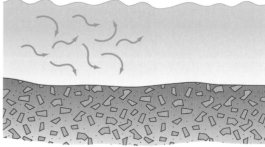

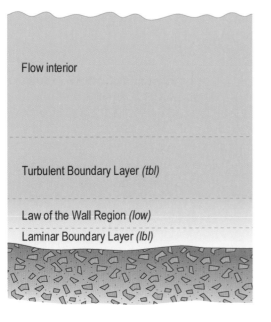

Flow interior

Turbulent Boundary Layer *(tbl)*

Law of the Wall Region *(low)*

Laminar Boundary Layer *(lbl)*

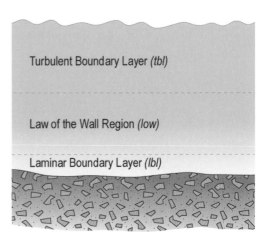

Turbulent Boundary Layer *(tbl)*

Law of the Wall Region *(low)*

Laminar Boundary Layer *(lbl)*

(a). Deeper water   *(b). Shallower water*

Figure 3.5.
Variation of flow
with depth.
DEPARTMENT OF GEOGRAPHY,
LANCASTER UNIVERSITY

left Figure 3.6.
Flow over a bed of
small particles.

right Figure 3.7.
Flow over a a bed of
large particles.
DEPARTMENT OF GEOGRAPHY,
LANCASTER UNIVERSITY

Within this general pattern, there are a number of regions whose distinction is caused by the detailed character of fluid flows. Very close to the boundary, the water is moving so slowly and its ability to move is so constrained by the presence of the boundary that its viscosity is strong enough to hold the fluid together so that it flows smoothly along parallel, stable streamlines (Figure 3.3). This state is known as 'laminar flow' and this region is known as the 'laminar boundary layer'.

Further away from the wall, the flow is faster and there is more space in which the flow can become unstable. Because the viscosity of water is very weak, it is no longer able to hold the flow in a nice smooth pattern in this region, so the flow becomes unstable and tends to roll around itself in turbulent eddies (Figure 3.4) However, the effect of the boundary is still felt in

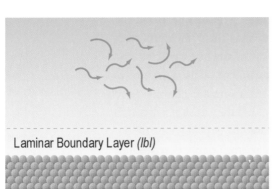

Laminar Boundary Layer *(lbl)*

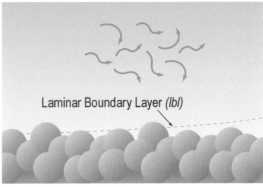

Laminar Boundary Layer *(lbl)*

River Derwent, a
typical small river
with clear water and
modest depth.
S. OWEN

this region, in that the flow speed of the water increases the further you get from the bed, so this region is called the 'turbulent boundary layer'. Whether flow is laminar or turbulent can be determined using a quantity known as the Reynolds number: this is fully explained in any introductory hydraulics or fluid dynamics textbook (Chadwich and Morfett 1998, Chanson 1999).

Finally, there is a region where the effect of the boundary is not felt at all. Because of this lack of boundary effect, in this region, the flow speed is the same at all depths. People tend to use terms in different ways, but this region is usually called the 'interior' of the flow. In many rivers, the water is not deep enough for this interior condition to appear, so that the flow speed varies throughout the whole depth (Figure 3.5a and b). This state is known as 'fully developed flow'. Furthermore, the role that the laminar boundary layer plays in the flow depends on its size in relation to the roughness of the bed. If the bed is very smooth, so that the particles which make it up are quite a lot smaller than thickness of these layers, they play a significant role in the flow, and the flow is referred to as 'smooth turbulent flow' (Figure 3.6). If, on the other hand, the particles in the bed are much larger than their thickness, they are only really a smearing of stickiness on the surface of the bed particles, and the body of flow that passes over the bed is all turbulent. This is known as 'rough turbulent flow' (Figure 3.7). Typically, British rivers are characterised by 'fully developed rough turbulent flow', meaning that they have fairly rough beds and modest depths. Fuller and more mathematical explanations of the terms described in this section can be found in many standard textbooks (including Graf and Altinakar 1998, Chadwick and Morfett 1998, Knighton 1998, Chanson 1999).

Introducing the second dimension: longitudinal variations

We will now consider the ways in which flow in a river varies down its length. There are various reasons why this happens. The most obvious is that the river channel gets larger and carries more water as it moves downstream. There may also be local variations in the channel – either natural ones such as waterfalls or rapids, or man-made structures such as weirs. As well as these changes in the channel, changes in the flow may be caused by changes in the water supply – such as floods or tidal surges.

The first section described the over-simplistic idea of gravity forces pulling water downhill, and the drag forces holding it back being in perfect equilibrium. Because of the causes just mentioned, this is not in fact the case: it will come closest to being true in straight river reaches where the cross-sectional shape, bed and bank material and channel slope are constant, and where there is no change to the flow rate due to rain. This state of affairs is known as 'uniform flow', and is the condition required to be at least approximated for the standard equations used to predict river flow rates to be valid (these include Manning's equation, as mentioned earlier, as well as the Chezy, Darcy-Wesibach and Colebrook-White equations, all of which are covered in standard textbooks on fluvial hydraulics). If there are factors causing the flow to vary significantly, we can categorise the flow as either 'gradually varying' or 'rapidly varying'.

Gradually varying flow results in the water depth changing along the channel. This is common and can be due to gradual changes in the channel's shape or slope, or in the water supply rate. It is usually not possible to see this gradual variation – you would have to measure the water depth quite

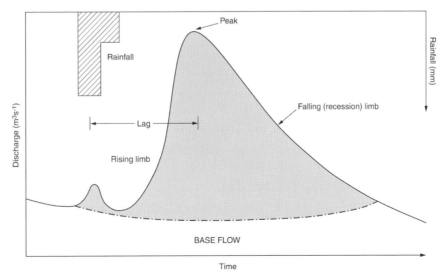

Figure 3.8. Storm hydrograph, displaying variations in river discharge through time, in response to the rainfall input from a specific storm event.
(PARK, 2001)

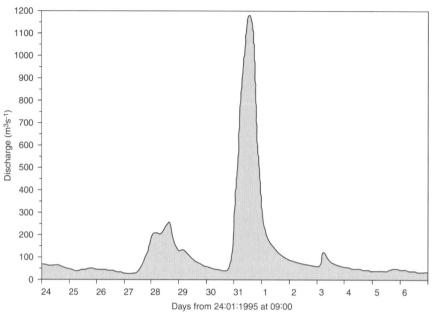

Figure 3.9.
A hydrograph from
the Caton gauging
station on the river
Lune.
© ENVIRONMENT AGENCY,
1995

carefully to discover it. A common way in which gradually varying flow occurs is through the passing of a flood down a river. Here, 'flood' means a significant increase in the flow rate due to rainfall, rather than the water overflowing the channel. The way in which the water level varies during such an event is shown in Figure 3.8: the rise of the floodwaters always tends to be more rapid than their fall. Often, several of these flood events can be super-imposed on each other. Figure 3.9 is a hydrograph from the Caton gauging

Fast-flowing section
and waterfall on the
river Kent, Cumbria.
S. OWEN

RIVERS AND THE BRITISH LANDSCAPE

left A hydraulic jump below a weir on the river Kent, Cumbria.
S. OWEN

right Hydraulic jumps over rocks, river Nith, Dumfries and Galloway.
S. OWEN

The Severn Bore
ENVIRONMENT AGENCY

station on the river Lune showing 15-minute interval data for one week either side of a flood event (31 January 1995). For British rivers, the pattern of flow over a year tends to be one of generally low flow rates interspersed by short-lived floods, giving the annual graph of flow rate a spiky appearance.

Rapidly varying flow is much more obvious to the naked eye. Its most common manifestation is the 'hydraulic jump'. This is the term used to describe the bubbling phenomenon seen at the bottom of weirs as water flows over rocks and boulders. Hydraulic jumps are transitions from 'super-critical flow' to 'sub-critical flow'. Both of these terms require some explanation.

If water is flowing at a particular rate (meaning that the same volume of water passes a fixed point every second), and has a particular amount of energy, then the way the flow depth, rate and energy are related implies that there are only two depths at which the water can flow. So the water can be in a relatively deep or shallow state. Because these two states move the same volume of water past a fixed point in one second, the deep one will

move more slowly than the shallow one. So we can have a deep/slow flow – which is called 'sub-critical', and a shallow/fast flow – which is called 'super-critical'.

When flowing water encounters an obstacle such as a weir or a large rock, it finds that the depth available for it to flow in is suddenly reduced, so it is forced into its super-critical state. As it passes over the obstacle, the steep downstream slope gives the water enough speed to maintain this state. On getting back to the main channel bed, however, it finds a relatively gentle slope, and is forced back to its sub-critical state. To do this, it has to get deeper and slower suddenly, which it is unable to do in a stable way. Instead, it achieves this transition through a hydraulic jump.

A hydraulic jump seen as you run past it is exactly the same as a breaking wave seen when you are standing still. We can use this analogy to provide another way of thinking about hydraulic jumps. The 'information' that there is this shallow slope beneath the downstream sub-critical flow is transmitted by waves caused by disturbances due to the bed roughness. The speed of water waves depends on the depth of the water they are passing over – in deeper water, waves are less hampered by the bed, so they move faster.

A key difference between sub-critical and super-critical flow is that in the former, the greater depth and slower flow mean that waves can move upstream. In super-critical flow, the waves are moving slower because the water is shallower, and the faster flow carries them off downstream. So the waves caused by the bed travel upstream until they meet the super-critical

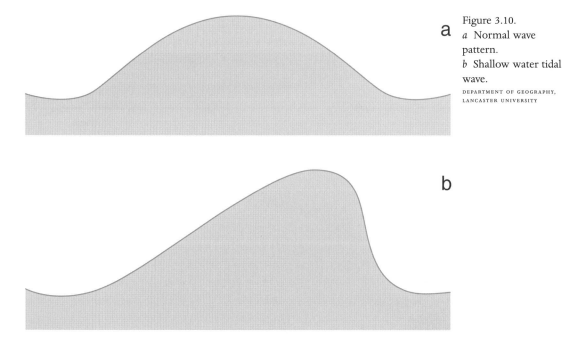

a

b

Figure 3.10.
a Normal wave pattern.
b Shallow water tidal wave.
DEPARTMENT OF GEOGRAPHY, LANCASTER UNIVERSITY

RIVERS AND THE BRITISH LANDSCAPE

flow coming over the obstacle, at which point they become unstable and break. Often downstream of a hydraulic jump, there is a train of 'standing waves' – waves coming upstream and getting more unstable as they approach the super-critical flow.

Another manifestation of rapidly varying flow is the tidal bore. These often spectacular phenomena are virtual step changes in water level that make their way up rivers. The best-known example in Britain is on the Severn, although good examples are also found on the Trent, the Mersey and the Kent.

Tidal bores are very rapid changes from tidal low water to high water. Tides (or 'tide waves') are just like normal waves, except that they take hours to go up and down, rather than seconds. So, just like normal waves, tide waves move more slowly when the water is shallower. As a tide wave approaches a coastline and the water gets shallower, the troughs (low tides) start to get pulled back by the drag of the bed much more than the peaks (high tides). Thus the peaks catch up the troughs, and the tide waves become asymmetric, so that there is a sudden rise from low to high tide and a slower drop back down (Figure 3.10).

In most situations, this simply results in an unspectacular asymmetry to tide times. At Preston, for example, where the tide has had to travel up the Ribble estuary for several miles, the time between low and high tides is about 2¼ hours, but the time between high and low tide is about 10¼ hours. In certain situations, however, the asymmetry becomes so extreme that the time between low and high tide is a few seconds. This is a tidal bore.

To summarise, we now have a picture of a river which, in addition to vertical variations in its flow, has longitudinal variations. These are caused by changes in channel shape and size, and changes in the water supply rate. The flow can vary gradually, as is the case when a flood passes down a river or its shape changes over a river reach, or rapidly as in a hydraulic jump or a tidal bore.

Introducing the third dimension: transverse variations

Now we can introduce the third and final dimension of flow variations within river channels – those which occur across the channel. Although it might seem sensible to look at this before the longitudinal variations (so that we cover all the variations in a cross section first, then extend that up and down-stream), I consider this to be the hardest of the variations to get a clear understanding of, so it has been left until last.

The key characteristic of tranverse motions in rivers is that they form a helical flow pattern. This only occurs where there are meanders in rivers, but since any river has slight bends in it, and the way in which the flow interacts with bends tends to cause them to grow, ultimately all river have bends (this is covered in more detail in chapter 4).

So, given that all rivers have meanders, let us now imagine water flowing down the river towards the apex of a meander. When the water gets to the apex, there is no reason for it to stop going in a straight line, until it hits the outside bank just downstream from the apex. So the water will tend to move across to the outside of the meander (Figure 3.11a). It then heads off towards the next meander, which bends in the opposite sense. So the water now all moves across the channel the other way, and piles up on the outside of that meander, which is on the other bank from the previous meander (Figure 3.11b). Thus, the water tends to move across the channel and back as it goes around first one meander and then the next.

The water on the surface will find this rather easier to do than the water at the bottom, because it is less trammelled up by the friction of the channel bed. So the strongest motion towards the outside of the bend will be at the surface. Although this will partially result in a slight slope in the water surface from the outside of the bend to the inside, it also tends to set up a cross-channel circulation flow in which the outward surface flow is complemented by an inward flow near the bed, with downward motion at the outside of the bend and upward motion at the inside of the bend completing the circulation (Figure 3.12). This circulation tends to carry on going (because friction is not strong enough to stop it) throughout the section between each meander apex.

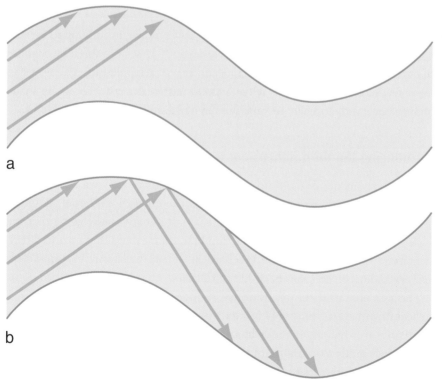

Figure 3.11.
Flow at a meander bend.
(AFTER KNIGHTON, 1998)

a

b

RIVERS AND THE BRITISH LANDSCAPE

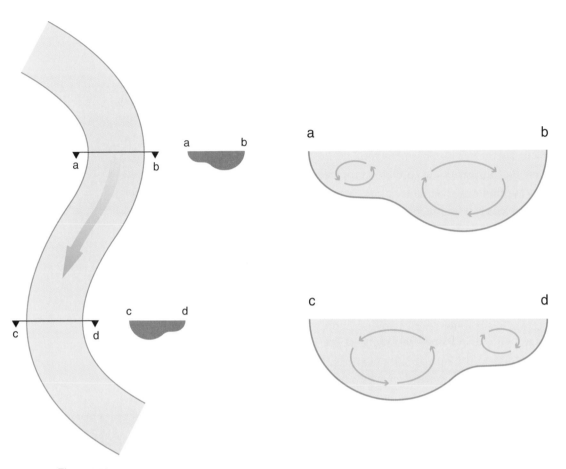

Figure 3.12.
Helical flow at a
meander bend.
(AFTER KNIGHTON, 1998)

However, it has to change its direction along the way, so we end up with a complex helical flow pattern at every point within the river. This helical flow pattern is particularly important for the development of the river channel shape, and these geomorphic effects on channel form will be covered in the next chapter. Until then, however, we continue to assume that the channel bed and banks are unerodible and permanent.

Flow complexities: waves, eddies, confluences, bursts, sweeps, boils and fronts

We have now moved some way from our simplistic idealisation of a river channel: the channel, though still unerodible and impermeable, has a cross-sectional shape and slope which varies up and downstream, receives varying amounts of water (leading to gradually varying flow), has obstacles such as rocks and weirs along its way which can lead to hydraulic jumps, has a flow of water within it which varies in speed vertically, and has a helical pattern associated with the meandering shape of the channel.

But if you look at a British river, these (except, perhaps, the hydraulic jumps) are not what you tend to see most obviously. Instead the aspects of the flow of the water which tend to catch the attention are rather smaller scale things: in small streams, it is the babbling flow. In larger rivers, upwelling 'boils' of water and fronts where the water has converged in on itself and thereby gathered together lines of foam and debris, are the most obvious features. At points of confluence, where two rivers meet, the mingling of their waters produces a menagerie of flow features. In this discussion, I am treating all these things as flow 'complexities' which are superimposed on the overall nature of the river. Thus, what has been covered so far is the over-arching context within which these features occur. In this section, we will look at them and see how they fit into this larger pattern.

The basis of all these complexities is the interaction of the river water with the channel bed and banks. There are several types of flow feature which arise from this interaction. Firstly there is the waviness often seen on the water surface when it is quite shallow. This is simply the result of weak standing waves and hydraulic jumps caused by the slightly super-critical flow over the large pebbles and small boulders on the bed. As the water gets deeper, the restriction in the flow depth caused by these obstacles lessens, so this wavy pattern disappears – which is why deeper rivers have smoother surfaces than

Smooth water surface in a deep section of the river Kent, Cumbria with boils and fronts of foam.
S. OWEN

shallow ones. Secondly there are eddies and regions of slack water caused by indentations in the river bank. These are important because they cause bank sediments, and the groundwater that seeps into the river through the banks, to mix with the main body of river water, and because the slack water areas are regions where pollutants in the river tend to get caught up and become concentrated. Thirdly there are regions of confluence, where tributary streams flow into larger streams. Often one of the streams is carrying more sediment than the other, so you can distinguish the water from each of them. Usually it is quite striking how distinct they remain quite a long way downstream of where they join. Often, too, you can see strongly whirling eddies which are formed by the shear – the difference in flow speed – between the two water bodies. One important effect of this process is that a lot of the power of the water to carry sediments in suspension is lost at these confluences, resulting in sediment deposition and the formation of bars of material. There is a lot of interest in what happens to the water at river confluences, partly because it is complicated and therefore has curiosity value, but also because the mixing which occurs there is important in determining how pollutants and biological organisms are distributed in the river downstream. Some examples of work in this area can be found in Gaudet and Roy (1995), Booij and Tukker (2001), and Biron *et al.* (2002).

In deeper rivers the water surface is smoother and is characterised by boils of upwelling water and fronts: lines of concentrated debris and foam. These are caused by a series of processes which, once again, originate where the water interacts with the channel. The initial process causing these motions is known as the burst-sweep mechanism (Figure 3.13). The faster flowing water away from the bed produces a series of roller-like motions in the slow water near the bed. These rollers are aligned across the channel, and are intrinsically unstable. By this I mean that if they are slightly disturbed by, say, a passing eddy in the main flow, they do not just settle back down again. Instead, the disturbance grows in a very specific way: the roller rears up like a striking python, and then breaks like a wave at the seashore. This process (known as a 'burst') carries slow water from near the bed up into the main part of the flow, often bringing bed material with it. It cannot just leave a gap in the water where it has come from, so it is replaced by a downward movement of relatively fast water from the main flow (known as a 'sweep'). This phenomenon is explained in more detail in Acarlar and Smith (1987a and b), Robinson (1991), Smith (1996), and Allen (1997).

These motions are quite small-scale things – only a few centimetres in size at most – but they appear to have a self-organising nature which causes them to group together and form much larger upwelling motions and associated downward sweeps. These larger upwelling motions are the cause of the boils of water to be seen at the surface of any relatively deep and reasonably freely

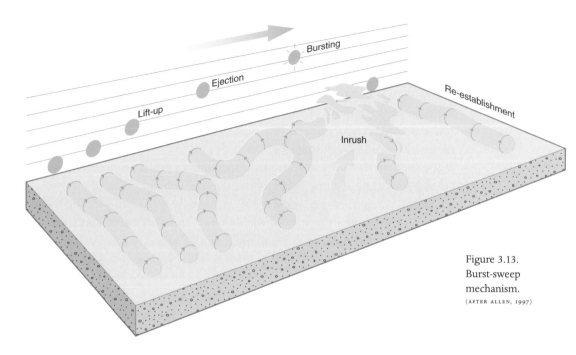

Figure 3.13.
Burst-sweep
mechanism.
(AFTER ALLEN, 1997)

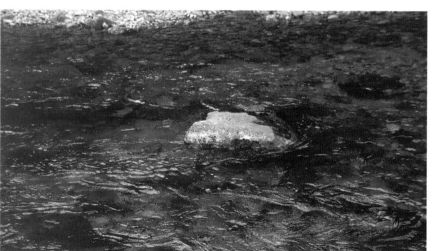

Eddies and boils on
the river Duddon,
Cumbria.
S. OWEN

Channelisation of
the river Lune at
Kelleth showing
eroded gravel bank
and meander.
S. OWEN

Bridge pier and evidence of deposition and scour downstream, river Duddon, Cumbria.

S. OWEN

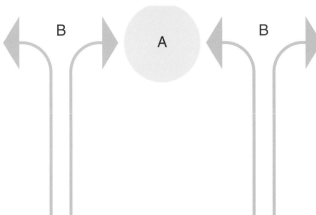

A = Zone of convergence
B = Boil

Figure 3.14. Zone of convergence between two boils.

DEPARTMENT OF GEOGRAPHY, LANCASTER UNIVERSITY

flowing river – the faster the river is flowing, the stronger they will be. More details about these features can be found in Matthes (1947), Jackson (1976), and Babakaiff and Hickin (1996).

Fronts of material are caused where these upwelling features cause the surface water to move out of their way. If two regions of boils are side by side, they will cause the surface water they displace to converge (Figure 3.14). This convergent motion will pull together all the foam and debris on the water surface in their path, producing a narrow region of high concentrations of this matter. These fronts will then be affected by the difference in the flow speed on either side of them, in just the same way as the front between the water from two confluencing rivers is, and will therefore become an unstable pattern of swirling eddying motions, before being broken up completely. These sorts of fronts are particularly common just downstream of a series of rapids, where the increased speed of the flow causes exaggerated upwelling.

River engineering structures

We have quite a detailed picture of what the natural flow in a river is like, except that we are disregarding, for the moment, any interaction the flow in the river channel might have with the world beyond its bed and banks (that is, that nothing can get through the bed and banks, and they cannot erode). However, as we shall see in chapters 5 and 7, the natural flow in British rivers have been adapted and exploited by human activity for many centuries, with the result that the character of many of these rivers is dominated by the engineering structures which have been built within or beside them. Many of these have an effect on the erosion of the river channel, as we shall see in the next chapter. We will now consider briefly the effects of those structures on the flow within rivers.

The most drastic form of in-channel river engineering is channelisation. This is a process whereby the whole channel of the river is defined, either by a concrete, drain-like structure, or by use of caged aggregations of large boulders, known as 'rip-rap'. This process is usually used to straighten inconveniently meandering rivers so that, for example, fewer bridges need to be built over them during the construction of a road, and there need be no fear that future meanders will make any bridges unstable. The wisdom of this purely mechanical approach to river management problems is considered in chapter 7. The main physical effect that channelisation has is to cause the slope of the channel to increase: getting from A to B via a straight path will always involve going down a steeper slope than getting there via a meandering path (Figure 3.15). This will cause the flow speed to increase, an effect which will extend both up and downstream of the channelised section of the

The Thames barrier in operation.
ENVIRONMENT AGENCY
THAMES REGION

RIVERS AND THE BRITISH LANDSCAPE

Figure 3.15.
The effects of
channelisation on
flow.
DEPARTMENT OF GEOGRAPHY,
LANCASTER UNIVERSITY

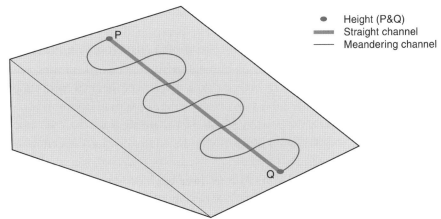

Height (P&Q)
Straight channel
Meandering channel

river. This faster flow speed will cause increased erosion. The flow within the channel will also gradually evolve into a meandering pattern as any small disturbance to the perfectly straight flow intended will be magnified by processes described in chapter 4.

The most common form of in-river engineering is bridge building. The main effect this has on the river flow is to restrict it – the need to build piers to support the bridge reduces the width of channel the water can flow in. This causes the water to speed up (due to the 'incompressibility' of water, i.e. it cannot be squashed or stretched, so if it is forced through a narrow gap it has to move faster through it), which again results in increased erosion. This erosion is especially strong on the downstream side of the bridge piers. Often this pier 'scour' requires special protective measures to be taken if it is not to cause the bridge to become unstable (Richards 1982a, Hamill 1999).

The hydraulics of weirs has already been discussed in the section on rapidly varying flow. The point of weirs is to produce a region of relatively deep, smoothly flowing water upstream of their position. Weirs have various uses. For example, they are useful technologically for regulating water flowing into millraces. The energy of the water flowing over Romney Weir on the Thames is also used to power networks to supply water and, potentially, electricity. Weirs are also used to facilitate flow measurement (which is of central importance to water management and flood defence). In the deep, slow (i.e. sub-critical) flows upstream of a weir, so long as they occur in a relatively straight section of the river channel (i.e. in uniform flow), there is a simple relationship between the flow depth and the volume of water flowing past. Thus a simple float device which can transmit measurements of the water depth (just like a petrol tank gauge) to a central monitoring office can be used to monitor flow discharge – the all-important measure of how much water the river is carrying. This simple relationship is different for all rivers (depending on the exact channel shape of each river), and is expressed as a graph called a 'rating curve', but if it has been measured once, it can be used many times to get the amount of flow from the depth measurements. Of course, channel shapes change, but if the relationship is measured occasionally, it can be used extensively in between.

The final type of in-channel engineering considered here is that which mitigates the effects of flooding. In coastal areas, tidal barriers can be used to protect against floods caused by surges of water driven up the river from the sea. Inland, relief channels are the most common 'hard' engineering method for mitigating floods – these involve the construction of a whole new river channel which fills only in times of flooding. More details of the effects of engineering structures on river flow can be found in textbooks on engineering hydraulics (for example Novak *et al.* 1996, Chadwick and Morfett 1998).

Estuarine flows and forms

The picture given thus far of flow in rivers pertains to the great majority of their length. In estuaries, however, where the rivers meet the sea, the character of their flow becomes so different from that found in the rest of the river that it requires special attention.

There are, of course, two competing flows in any estuary: the river and the sea. Whereas the sea comes and goes with the tide, the river just keeps on coming. The character of any estuary is first and foremost determined by the extent of the tidal motions: in some estuaries the tides are relatively small; in others they are relatively large, and in others, they are somewhere in between. Respectively these three cases are known as 'micro-tidal' (i.e. the tides are relatively weak, having height differences between high and low water of less than 2 metres),

left Figure 3.16.
A salt wedge.

right Figure 3.17.
A longitudinal front (with cross-section).
DEPARTMENT OF GEOGRAPHY, LANCASTER UNIVERSITY

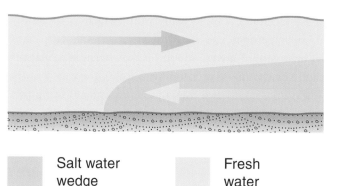

Salt water wedge   Fresh water

Salt water   Fresh water

'macro-tidal' (height differences of greater than 4 metres) and 'meso-tidal' (height differences of 2–4 metres).

These types of estuaries also tend to be different in other ways. One of these is the extent to which the salt and fresh water mixes within them. If there are only small tidal motions, the water does not have to move very fast to get up and down the estuary in a tidal cycle, so the mixing forces are relatively weak. So micro-tidal (river-dominated) estuaries are relatively weakly mixed. This tends to result in the salt water sitting in a fairly distinct formation which simply moves up and down the estuary over the tidal cycle. Because salt water is denser than fresh water, the seawater is forced to nose its way under the river water, so the shape of this formation is referred to as a 'salt wedge' (Figure 3.16). Because tidal heights around the British coastline are relatively large, salt wedges are quite rare in British estuaries. One example, which is only observed during neap tides, can be found on the Tweed.

Meso-tidal estuaries tend to be partially mixed: the boundary between salt and fresh water is less clearly defined than in salt wedge estuaries, but there is a distinct pattern of fresh water flowing seaward on the surface and salt water flowing landward on the bottom. These are quite common in Britain: the Thames, the Mersey and Southampton Water are all of this type.

Macro-tidal estuaries are 'completely' mixed, meaning that there is no vertical variation in salt content. However, this type of estuary tends to be relatively wide, with the result that the salt content does vary across the width of the estuary: the effect of the Earth's rotation causes the fresh water to be pushed across to the right of the estuary (if you are looking out to sea) and the seawater to come up the left hand bank. In between, there will be a region where the salt content of the water changes gradually as you move across the estuary. The Severn and Humber estuaries, the Firth of Forth and the Moray Firth are all examples of macro-tidal estuaries.

Just as with flow in the main body of rivers, there are complexities superimposed on this general pattern. These tend to cause fronts to form in

below Figure 3.18. A macro-tidal estuary at the initiation of an axial convergent front.

bottom Figure 3.19. An axial convergent front.

DEPARTMENT OF GEOGRAPHY, LANCASTER UNIVERSITY

Salt water   Fresh water

Axial convergent front

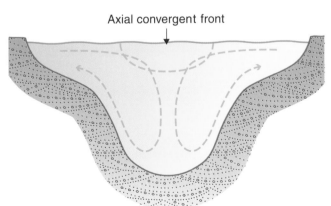

estuaries. The simplest form of front is that where the water changes from being sea water to fresh water. This is called the 'halocline' and is strongest in salt wedge estuaries and weakest in fully mixed estuaries.

There are also fronts caused by the effects of bed and bank friction on the flow of water. These are found particularly in macro-tidal estuaries. The first type is called a 'longitudinal front'. This occurs at points where the bed suddenly drops off from the relatively shallow mudbanks typically found at the sides of estuaries into a deeper channel. The flow in the deeper channel is less restricted by bed friction than that over the mudbanks, so it goes faster. This brings the salt water in the deeper channel section further up the estuary more quickly than that over the mudbanks. The result is that there is a sharp front formed between the saltwater which has advanced up the deep channel in the estuary, and the freshwater over the shallow mudbanks beside it (Figure 3.17).

This process also works in a vertical sense in macrotidal estuaries: as the salt water extends up the deeper parts of the estuary, the salt water at the surface moves ahead of the salt water near the bed (which is being held back by friction) (Figure 3.18). This is an unstable situation: salt water should flow below the less dense fresh water, not above it. Eventually this unstable situation breaks down, at which point the salt water which has advanced furthest up the estuary at the surface above the deeper part of the channel, plunges down to the bottom of the estuary. This plunging motion sets up two counter-circulations in the water around it (Figure 3.19). As the salt water makes its way further up the estuary, pushing fresh water out of the way, this counter-circulating motion is extended up the length of the estuary. This leads to a convergence zone at the surface of the water, which collects foam and debris. This is known as an 'axial convergent front'. The section seaward of the plunge point is referred to as a 'V-shaped intrusion' for obvious reasons. The Ribble estuary, being rather narrow, has a very clear single axial convergent front, whereas wider estuaries, such as the Tay, can have several at the same time. More details on the flow in estuaries can be found in McDowell and O'Conner (1977); Kjervfe (1988); Dyer (1997); and Lewis (1997). Examples of recent research into British estuarine fronts can be found in Ferrier and Anderson, (1997), and Turrell et al. (1996).

CHAPTER 4 # Rivers and their environment

Andrew Folkard

Introduction

In the previous chapter, I investigated how the water in a river does what it does. In doing so, I assumed that everything else associated with rivers did not change. This was done for convenience, to try to make the discussion clearer, but of course it is a simplification of what actually happens. From a purely material point of view, we can think of a river as being made up of three elements: the water, the sediment and bedrock which forms the channel, and the biological organisms which live in and around it. Having covered the first of these in chapter 3, this chapter will investigate the other two, and consider how all three interact with each other to produce the overall river environment. The mechanistic deconstruction in these chapters may seem to many readers to be at best necessary but perhaps a little dull. Yet to people like myself who study water and its place in the environment, it can give us a sense of being in the presence of huge and very gradually evolving phenomena. This sense of contact with something larger and longer lasting than oneself, and being able to understand how it works, can be fascinating and fulfils a very fundamental human urge.

Sediment movement

As well as moving water down slopes, rivers also carry sediments – from microscopic clay particles to massive boulders – eroding and altering them chemically as they go. From a sedimentary perspective, the role of a river is threefold: to erode, to transport and to deposit. One of the basic ideas of fluvial geomorphology is that these three roles can be spatially segregated to a large extent (e.g. Schumm 1977). Thus the river's path can be divided into regions dominated by erosion, transport and deposition, in that order from source to mouth (Figure 4.1). Within this basic pattern, there are in all rivers many smaller scale patterns of local sediment sources, transport regimes and storage sites, and the timescales of the processes that move sediment between these states vary greatly (e.g. Lewin 1981). For example, a landslide can supply sediment to a river in a few seconds, whereas storage of sediment within a floodplain occurs over periods of many thousands of years. Thus the role of a river as a sediment conveyor belt is a complex one both spatially and temporally. Catchment scale sediment supply has been discussed in more depth in chapter 2.

People who study this role of rivers – known as fluvial sedimentologists – distinguish between different types of sediment on the basis of how it is moved by the river, and where it came from. Some sediment is dissolved in the water so that it no longer appears as particles at all, but becomes part of the water itself. This is known as dissolved load. Globally, dissolved load makes up about one fifth of the total sediment carried within the river water, but it tends to be more prevalent where land is flat and arid, so on our relatively wet and hilly island, it makes up a smaller proportion. However, although the dissolved phase of sediment is rather unimportant in terms of the amount of physical material it carries, it is very important in terms of the chemical quality of the water.

Suspended sediment is the name given to sediment which is carried within the water, but which remains in particulate form. This is the stuff that makes the water look dirty, and is made up of clay, sand and other soil and rock particles. What keeps them suspended in the water is the vertical component of turbulent eddies within the water: if the speed of these vertical turbulent motions is less than the speed at which the particles tend to fall through the water (their 'fall velocity'), the latter process will win and the particles will tend to remain on the river bed. Since the fall velocity (as definitively

Figure 4.1. Schumm's zones of erosion, transport and deposition from source to sea. (SCHUMM, 1977)

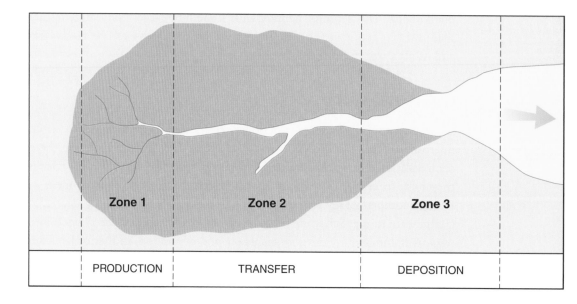

PRODUCTION TRANSFER DEPOSITION

described by Stoke's Law – see, for example, Bagnold 1966, 1988) depends on the size of a particle, bigger particles fall down, but smaller ones stay in suspension. Thus the spread of these particles within the water depends on their size: the smallest ones will be evenly distributed throughout the water, whereas the heavier ones will be concentrated near the bed.

Finally, the larger particles which sit on the river bed are moved along by the force of the water during fast flowing floods. Sediment thus moved is called 'bedload'. This can happen through rolling or dragging (sometimes called 'traction') or through 'saltation' – whereby individual grains are lifted temporarily into suspension, then return to the bed (for more details, see Pye 1994).

Whether a particle becomes freed from the bed and carried in suspension depends on whether the force on it is greater than the critical threshold required for suspension. How the size of this threshold force is related to the size of the particles is described by Hjulstrom (Figure 4.2) and Shields, two more of the pillars on which fluvial sedimentology has been built. In nature, things such as the tendency of small particles to be hidden underneath larger ones complicate the relationships represented by these theoretical diagrams.

Figure 4.2. The relationship between flow velocity, sediment size and transport. This widely used graph, based on the work of Hjulstrom, indicates the critical threshold velocities for the entrainment and deposition of sediment particles of different sizes.
(AFTER BUCKLE, 1978)

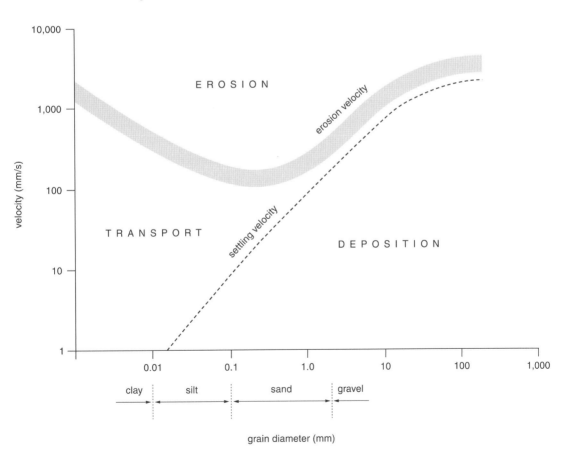

Sediments at a particular point in a river can also be distinguished according to whether they have been carried down the river from somewhere upstream – alluvial sediments – or washed into the river at that point (by water flowing either over the land surface or, more commonly, through the soil, picking up particles and dissolving chemicals as it goes) – these are called colluvial sediments. In some rivers, particularly in their mountain stream stage, there is no bed sediment in the river at all, and the bed is made up of solid rock: these are known as bedrock channels.

How much of each of these types of sediment load a particular river has will depend on the catchment characteristics, the amount of flow in the river, and the location within the river. For example, rivers in chalk lowlands, such as Dorset or Kent, tend to have small suspended loads (clean looking water) and quite coarse, gravely beds, whereas rivers in soft sandstone areas (Shropshire and Cheshire, for example) tend to have more suspended material and sandier beds. Rivers in flood will have more suspended material in them than during periods of low flow. Finally, rivers tend to sort the sediments out as they move downstream. Thus rivers tend to have coarse and poorly sorted material in their upper reaches, and finer and better-sorted sediment downstream (which is why estuaries tend to be muddy rather than pebbly). Since pollutants tend to attach themselves to the finest (clay) particles, this causes problems at the downstream end of rivers – where most major riverside towns tend to be located – and where pesticides and fertilisers washed off agricultural land upstream tend to become concentrated to hazardous levels.

Sedimentary bedforms

Anyone looking at a river bed anywhere in Britain will have noticed that sediments are not spread evenly over the river bed, but tend to bunch up into distinctive and easily identifiable features. Fluvial geomorphologists (people who study the shape of river channels and their associated floodplains, the processes that form and change these shapes, and their impacts on the wider environment) refer to these as 'bedforms' and categorise them using terms such as ripples, dunes, bars, riffles and pools. Leeder (1983) provides a framework for the investigation of these phenomena, by noting that water flow, sediment transport and bedform evolution all interact with and alter each other.

The most subtle of bedforms are the ripples commonly observed in fine, non-cohesive bed materials (silt and sand) and their larger counterparts, dunes. There is a strict dynamical distinction between the two (based on the orientation of the flow that separates from their peak, and their interaction with the water surface, see Bennett and Best 1996) but in essence, dunes are just big ripples. Their form is such that they are self-sustaining, i.e. they alter the flow over them so that the sedimentary erosion and deposition it causes serves to preserve their shape, although the material in them is constantly being carried off downstream and renewed from upstream and the features themselves also tend to move gradually. Their initial formation is a complex process (Muller and Gyr 1996) which involves a gradual spatial organisation by embryonic ripples of the eroding and depositing parts of disturbances in the flow caused by the riverbed. Ripple- and dune-like features can also occur in riverbeds made up of coarser material such as gravel (see, for example, Knighton 1998).

Bars are larger scale features which occur at localised sites of flow stagnation or convergence. They can be oriented along, across or at an angle to the main flow in the river, and can be attached to one or other bank or neither. When the flow slows, the vertical turbulent motions which keep sediment in suspension are reduced, so more of it falls out, and it is harder for the flow to drag bedload along. This occurs, for example, on the inside bend of meanders where the water becomes relatively stagnant as the flow heads for the outside of the bend, and as a result point bars are formed. Mid-channel, longitudinal bars are formed where the helical flow of the river (see chapter 3) produces convergent flow at the centre, which gradually drags bed material into the centre of the channel.

A point bar on the river Lune, Cumbria, together with block defences on the outer wall.

S. OWEN

Mid-channel bar,
river Lune, Cumbria.
S. OWEN

Pools and riffle sequences are perhaps the main feature of river channel bedforms. The details of their formation and their relation to other bed and channel forms, particularly meanders, is still a matter of some debate (e.g. Lane *et al*. 1999, 2002), but the basic idea is that they are quasi-stable features which result from the self-organisation of the flow-sediment system in river channels. Initially, the distribution of bed sediment in a river channel will be disorganised and non-uniform: in some places there will be more sediment, and in others there will be less. Where there is more, any sediment particles being moved downstream by the flow will tend to get caught up, thus enhancing the sediment levels in these regions. Where there is less, the flow will move more easily and be able to move the bed sediment along more easily, so these will become increasingly devoid of sediment. Because of the action of the water flow on them, the conglomerations of sediment will tend to move downstream, albeit very slowly. The small conglomerations will tend to move more easily, and therefore more quickly, than the larger ones. So the smaller ones will gradually catch up with the larger ones, forming even larger conglomerations. Eventually, there will be a relatively small number of

right Pool-riffle
sequence with
grazing cattle on
Scar Water, a
tributary of the river
Nith, Dumfries and
Galloway.
S. OWEN

right Riparian buffer
zone, River Keer,
Lancashire
H. ORR

Figure 4.3.
Flow and sediment transport over ripples or dunes.
DEPARTMENT OF GEOGRAPHY,
LANCASTER UNIVERSITY

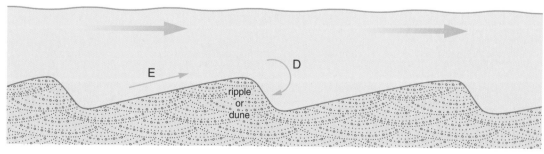

E = Erosion   D = Deposition

RIVERS AND THE BRITISH LANDSCAPE

relatively equally spaced large conglomerations of sediment, separated by regions relatively devoid of sediment. These features will, very gradually, be moved downstream as the river flow removes sediment from their upstream side and deposits new material on their downstream side (Figure 4.3). This is called a 'kinematic wave' and is exactly the same process whereby motorway traffic becomes lumpy: small clumps of traffic, usually seeded by a slow vehicle, are harder for cars to get through, so traffic tends to gather up at these points, leaving slightly emptier stretches ahead and behind them, which are easier for cars to pass through. As a result, the empty stretches get emptier and the busier ones get busier, until there is a series of clumps of traffic separated by relatively clear stretches, all moving at roughly the same speed.

In rivers, the 'busy' sections are known as riffles, and the 'empty' sections are called pools. Together, they create

the typical character of a river in which regions of shallow, babbling flow over riffles are interspersed by regions of deeper, more serene flow. These riffles do not tend to be perfectly uniform across the channel, but stronger on one or other side of the channel. This causes the flow to meander back and forth between riffles within the channel, as it flows preferentially through each riffle's weakest point. This meandering sets up helical flows within the river as discussed in chapter 3. Once again, these will tend to magnify the channel shapes which cause them, leading to an ever more accentuated meandering pattern in the flow. Some researchers posit that this is the cause of all river meandering, although others hold the view that the pool-riffle/meander relationship is weaker and more interactive than this.

In bedrock channels this sedimentary organisation obviously does not happen. However, a similar process of self-organisation does appear to be at work and results in the characteristic pool-step features whereby mountain streams do not descend in a smoothly sloping channel, but proceed by a series of steps over which the flow passes rapidly, and pools, in which it dawdles and deepens. Larger scale versions of this feature result in cascades, of which the Falls at Ingleton in North Yorkshire are a good example. Waterfalls are extreme examples of this phenomenon, where the position of the step is determined by the underlying geology and is caused by a discontinuous change from hard, uneroded rock to an eroded region.

The River Mersey in flood.
CHRIS E. MAKEPEACE

Channel shape and bank erosion

When viewed from above river channels in Britain vary considerably in shape. Most meander, but the extent of this sinuousity differs greatly. This variability is due to the hilliness of their catchments, the underlying rocks and soils, the weather and the past history of the area (see chapter 2). Rivers develop into different shapes in this sense by eroding their banks, a process which also provides or destroys a variety of habitats for riverine plants and creatures. As climate and land use change, rivers will contain more or less water and sediment and this will cause the shape of the channel to alter as the river becomes more erosive or depositional in character. Thus channel shape is a dynamic characteristic which responds to external forcing factors, and causes the river to reflect the nature of its surroundings. The rate of change can be slow, even in very sinuous channels – the Derwent in Derbyshire before its confluence with the Trent is very twisty, but has changed little since the Ordnance Survey map of 1836 (Walsh 1990). Similarly, the Lune doubles back on itself at Caton in Lancashire, but has changed little since the nineteenth century. Other rivers change more rapidly – for example, the Dane in Cheshire, and the Glass in Highland Region. Around many rivers, so called relict channels can be seen, showing where the river previously flowed under different climatic and sediment supply conditions (or, possibly, where it was before it was artificially straightened to some human end).

River bank erosion can result in a number of features, caused by the slipping, sliding, toppling or general collapse of the banks. These processes lead to stepping, cliffing or general re-shaping of the bank, which can be advantageous from an ecological perspective (for example, sand martins can nest in the vertical faces of river banks, and cattle, deer and other animals can reach the water to drink where the bank has slid away).

Bank erosion can be a problem in rivers: salmon and trout, for example, place their eggs in so-called 'redds' – structures they excavate with their tails in gravel-bedded rivers (Figure 4.4). They choose gravel, because it protects the eggs from predators while allowing oxygen-rich water to pass easily through, thus sustaining the embryonic fish. However, if there is excessive bank erosion, finer grained particles will get into the water and clog up the gravel, stopping the oxygen from getting to the eggs and stunting the growth of the fish. As a result, a number of fishing interests (usually local fishing associations and the Environment Agency) have come to agreements with local farmers whereby strips of land a few metres wide on either side of the river have been fenced off. This protects them from the erosive action of animals' hooves and stops grazing, thus allowing plants to grow which will consolidate the banks and further protect them against erosion. These so-called 'riparian buffer zones' are a preferable 'soft' engineering approach to this problem than the more traditional building of stone revetments, which replace the natural bank with much harder material. This tends to concentrate the flow near to the bank, leading to bed erosion and over-deepening of the channel, which is counter-productive for the fish, and which eventually leads to the under-cutting of the stone and heavily degraded river channels.

Classical descriptions of river channel form (e.g. Leopold and Wolman 1957) and much fluvial geomorphological work which has followed from this give an anthropomorphic justification for river meanders, stating that rivers 'are trying to adjust to the imposed variables' and change their form 'in order to transfer water and sediment as efficiently as possible', as though rivers were sentient entities with an agenda to fulfil. The process-based descriptions of the development of riffle pool sequences and meandering, helical flow given here are intended as an antidote to these descriptions. Thus rivers tend, through the repeated occurrence of small-scale processes, to form stable, self-organising bedforms, namely riffles and pools, through which meandering flow tends to develop. The preferential erosion and deposition caused by this flow then causes bank erosion, which over a long period of time will cause meanders to evolve. The extent to which this happens, and the rate at which it does, depends on the amount and variability of the water and sediment that arrives in the river channel, which in turn are determined by all the external factors present in the catchment, as discussed in chapter 2.

There have been many attempts to quantify the way in which characteristics of river flow are related to the overall shape of the river channel (see, for example, Leopold and Maddock 1953; Richards 1982a; Knighton 1998). Although some progress has been made in this respect, river systems are in general too complex for simple mathematical relationships to describe them

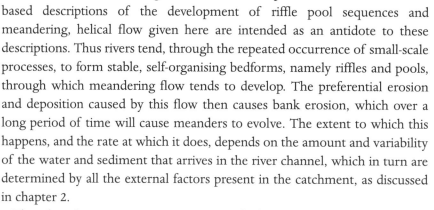

Freshwater shrimp.
STUART CROFTS

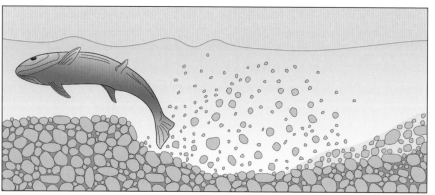

Figure 4.4.
Salmon excavation in gravel-bed rivers.
(AFTER ALONSO, THEURER AND ZACHMANN, 1996)

RIVERS AND THE BRITISH LANDSCAPE

adequately. As a result, fluvial geomorphologists are turning increasingly to the use of sophisticated computational models which simulate the behaviour of water and sediment in great detail to improve their understanding of the workings on the flow/sediment/bedform system (Lane *et al.* 2002; Bradbrook *et al.* 1999).

Riparian hydrology

As well as affecting the morphology of their own channels, and interacting with sediments within them, rivers also have an effect on strips of land to either side of them – the so-called 'riparian zone'. From a purely water-based perspective, this interaction manifests itself in two main ways: through the out-of-channel flow of the water during floods, and through the seepage of groundwater through the soil into the river channels.

The exchange of groundwater between the soil and the river through the river banks is the main way in which water gets into the river in the first place, and also the main route by which pollutants are exchanged between the river and its catchment. The rate at which water is exchanged will depend on the water pressure in the soil, the water depth in the river, and the permeability of the riverbank material. Quantifying these exchange processes, and relating our understanding of their small-scale details to catchment scale quantities of exchanges are topics of current research interest.

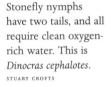

Stonefly nymphs have two tails, and all require clean oxygen-rich water. This is *Dinocras cephalotes*.
STUARY CROFTS

River floods are a major environmental hazard and have received much media attention in recent years. As well as their obvious social and economic impacts, the major scientific interest in them lies in the way in which they exchange material (sediment and pollutants in particular) between the river channel and its floodplain. They are also important agents of geomorphic change in the riparian zone, notably in their creation and re-working of levees.

River water chemistry impact on river ecology

The last of the three main material elements of rivers and their riparian zones is the collection of living organisms which depend on the various habitats provided by the river for their existence. The study of river and stream ecology has a relatively long history in this country, and British scientists at British sites did much of the pioneering work in this area. Many reaches of British rivers also have long histories of conservation of their physical and ecological constituents. Today these are often designated as Sites of Special Scientific Interest (SSSIs).

The living organisms found in British rivers consist of a wide variety of plants, animals, and bacteria and fungi. The distribution of these organisms depends on three main elements of the physical character of the river: the flow and temperature characteristics of the water, and the nature of the channel bed material, or substrate (for more details see, for example, Townsend 1986). The depth and shadiness of a river, which can vary across its width, can also influence the distribution of plants and animals. The chemical composition of the water also determines the ecology. In particular, dissolved gases are important for the ways in which all organisms deal with (metabolise) the material they take up. These dissolved gases can be taken up by the water from the atmosphere, or from water flowing into the river from the catchment, or via chemical processes within the water. Dissolved minerals are also found in river water, the mineral chemistry of the water being determined by the mineral nature of the catchment. For example, chalk bed rivers have high concentrations of minerals in their water, because chalk is easily eroded. Rivers flowing over very resistant materials, such as granite, on the other hand, will have low levels of dissolved minerals. The acidity of river water (i.e. the concentration of electrically charged hydrogen atoms in the water, measured using the pH scale) is also important for the ecology: this can change due to natural inputs, but usually only becomes damaging when anthropogenic pollution events change the water acidity significantly.

Water chemistry will clearly change over space and time within a river: recent rainfall has had less contact time with the rocks and soil in a catchment than groundwater, and thus will have lower concentrations of the chemicals which it takes out of the ground. So heavy rainfall tends to dilute the concentrations of catchment-derived chemicals in river water. Biological consequences of such chemical variation are not very significant when conditions are fairly close to the average. However, extreme changes due either to natural or human inputs can be of biological significance (for more details see, for example, Allan 1995).

Of the dissolved gases in river water, oxygen is the most ecologically important. Several water quality parameters are used to assess it, including DO (dissolved oxygen – the total amount of oxygen dissolved in the water), BOD (biological oxygen demand – the amount of oxygen in the water required by the biological organisms that use it) and COD (chemical oxygen demand – the amount of oxygen required for chemical reactions to take place between the chemicals in the water). A very low value of BOD, for example, implies that the water is clean to the point of being ecology-free, while a very high value usually implies a high level of organic pollutant (e.g. sewage) in the water. The ease with which water can absorb oxygen decreases as it gets warmer. Since water in the downstream section of rivers tends to be warmer than that upstream, and the flow in rivers is smoother downstream so there is less mixing of the oxygen in the air with the river water due to bubbling flows, oxygen levels tend to be lower downstream in rivers. This affects the distribution of ecology in rivers – for example, bloodworms (chironomid larvae) which dwell in the fine sediment found at the downstream end of rivers have haemoglobin in their bodies which allows the uptake of oxygen from the water even at low concentrations (e.g. Townsend 1986). Thus they are found in greater abundance in downstream reaches of rivers than organisms requiring more oxygen.

Similarly, mineral concentrations tend to increase downstream, as more of the minerals are washed into the river from the catchment, and these downstream variations affect ecological distributions. For example, molluscs require a certain minimum level of calcium in the water so only tend to exist in the downstream reaches of rivers. In view of the complex inter-relationship between these key factors, it is not surprising that habitats in streams and rivers are not usually homogeneous. Indeed, species distributions tend to be highly clumped at a variety of scales.

Plants in rivers

The distribution of vegetation in British rivers and streams is determined by the underlying rock type and structure, the shape and size of the river channel, the water supply system to the river and any human impacts on the river and the surrounding environment. Plants are the primary producers of

Table 4.1: Typical plants associated with in-stream habitats in upland, intermediate and lowland channels

Habitat	Uplands	Intermediate	Lowlands
Riffles	Alternate-flowered water-milfoil Bulbous rush Shore-weed *Hygrohypnum ochraceum* (moss) *Fontinalis antipyretica* (moss) *Solenostoma triste* (liverwort) *Chiloscyhus polyanthos* (liverwort)	Hemlock water-dropwort Brook water-crowfoot Stream water-crowfoot Canadian pond weed Intermediate water-starwort Blanketweed algae Rhynchostegium riparioides	Brook water-crowfoot Spiked water-milfoil Lesser water-parsnip Arrowhead Horned pondweed *Fontinalis antipyretica* *Rhynchostegium riparioides*
Runs	*Marsupella emarginata* (liverwort) *Nardia compressa* (liverwort) *Scapania undulata* *Hygrohypnum ochraceum* (moss) *Fontinalis squamosa* *Hyocomium armoricum* (moss) *Racomitrium aciculare*	Alternate-flowered water-milfoil River water-crowfoot Curled pondweed *Fontinalis squamosa* (moss) *Fontinalis antipyretica* Rhynchostegium riparioides	Spiked water-milfoil River water-crowfoot Common club-rush Fennel pondweed Unbranched bur-reed *Fontinalis antipyretica* *Rhynchostegium riparioides*
Slacks	Intermediate water-starwort Common water-starwort Floating sweet-grass Bog pondweed Floating club-rush Least bur-read *Sphagnum* moss	Perfoliate pondweed Broad-leaved pondweed Canadian pondweed Water-cress Branched bur-reed Curled pondweed Common duckweed	Yellow water-lily Flowering rush Shining pondweed Nuttall's ondweed Branched bur-reed Blunt-fruited water-starwort Fat duckweed

Source: Ward, D., Holmes, N. and José, P. (eds) (1994) *The New Rivers and Wildlife Handbook*. Sandy: RSPB: 41

The pollution tolerant mayfly *Baetis rhodani*.
STUART CROFTS

the river environment – they make living material from non-living sources (mainly the sunlight and substrate or water-derived nutrients). They can be divided into three categories. Periphyton live on or near the river bed and are found everywhere in British rivers, although they are most common in streams and small rivers. Phytoplankton are microscopic organisms that live within the water – they tend to develop in large lowland rivers during periods of relatively low flow rates, but do not dominate the ecological system as they do in lakes or ocean surface waters, because the flow of river water does not allow them sufficient time to develop large communities. Macrophytes –

Table 4.2: Typical plants of river banks/margins in upland, intermediate and lowland channels

Habitat	Uplands	Intermediate	Lowlands
Wet ledges within channel	Shoreweed Jointed rush Marsh spearwort Blinks Monkeyflower Ivy-leaved water-crowfoot	Indian balsam Brooklime Water forget-me-not Pink water-speedwell Creeping yellow-cress Water plantain	Marsh foxtail Common bulrush Blue water-speedwell Celery-leaved buttercup Great yellow-cress Great waterdock
Shallow waterlogged margins	Marsh violet Marsh stitchworth Bulbous rush Greater bird's-foot-trefoil Round-leaved water-crowfoot Marsh ragwort	Fool's water-cress Amphibious bistort Marsh yellow-cress Bittersweet Marsh woundwort Marsh marigold	Pink water-speedwell Fool's water-cress Water-cress Yellow flag Plicate sweet-grass Marsh horsetail
Reed/ sedge/ rush edge	Soft rush Sharp-flowered rush Bottle sedge Common sedge Floating sweet-grass	Reed canary-grass Hard rush Common spikerush Hairy sedge Slender tufted sedge	Common reed Greater pond-sedge Lesser pond-sedge Greater tussock-sedge Reed sweet grass
Steeper banks	*Pellia epiphylla* (liverwort) *Polytrichum commune* (moss) Purple moor-grass Mat-grass Tormentil Meadowsweet	Water figwort Water-mint Comfrey Butterbur Angelica	Great willow-herb Purple loose-strife Teasel Hemp agrimony Water chickweed Gypseywort

Source: Ward, D., Holmes, N. and José, P. (eds) (1994) *The New Rivers and Wildlife Handbook*. Sandy: RSPB: 41

A wooded river – Cairn Water, a tributary of the river Nith, Dumfries and Galloway.

S. OWEN

larger plants – are most abundant in mid-sized rivers, in backwaters and along the margins of larger rivers. The relative importance of these primary producers changes greatly with river size and conditions (for more details see, for example, Allan 1995, Haslam 1978, 1982).

The major groups of macrophytes are flowering plants, bryophytes (mosses and liverworts), lichens and a few large forms of algae. Most of these are members of botanical families which are primarily terrestrial, but which have made adaptations to enable them to live underwater at relatively low oxygen levels and with reduced light for photosynthesis. Many also have floating leaves which bring part of the plant into direct contact with the atmosphere. Like all the other groups of macrophytes, most of the flowering plants are 'benthic' – they attach themselves to the substrate. Some, like duckweeds, are free-floating and thus rely entirely on nutrients in the water for their survival.

Macrophytes tend to grow mainly where the water is relatively shallow and gently flowing – faster and deeper flows uproot them and deprive them of light and oxygen respectively. Four major categories of aquatic macrophytes can be identified: emergents found on banks and shoals, floating-leaved taxa on the margins of slow rivers, free-floating plants such as duckweed, and submerged or partially submerged taxa, such as reeds and water crowfoot which attach to the substrate. Their numbers and distribution are limited primarily by current speeds, light availability and the length of their growing season. Aquatic macrophytes do not tend to get grazed, although in autumn or early winter they die and provide organic material for other organisms to consume.

Macrophytes are important in several ways: they significantly alter the flow speed in rivers (they are agents of heightened hydraulic drag); they exchange many dissolved chemicals and nutrients with the river water; they act as regions of preferential sediment deposition; and they support often highly biodiverse epiphytic (near-to-plant) communities. Sometimes, they can become a problem in that they grow to dominate the river channel, blocking light and greatly increasing the drag on the flow. In cases where this occurs, they can be harvested to clear the channel and allow a wider variety of species to occupy it. Tables 4.1, 4.2 and 4.3 summarise the main species of plants to be found in or near British rivers, and the type of habitat within the river system that each prefers.

Table 4.3: Bankside trees and shrubs

Altitude	Species
Transitional	Alder Ash Common oak Common osier Native poplars
Lowland	Alder Common oak Common osier Alder buckthorn Native poplars
Throughout	White willow Goat willow (sallow)

Source: Adapted from Ward, D., Holmes, N. and José, P. (eds) (1994) *The New Rivers and Wildlife Handbook*. Sandy: RSPB: 39

Macro-invertebrates

The animals of lotic (flowing freshwater) ecosystems are generally categorized according to where in the water they live (Townsend 1986, Angelier 2003). For example, 'neustons' such as water boatmen (*Gerris* sp.) are associated with the water surface. Others prefer mid-water. 'Nekton' is the collective name given to creatures which can control their own motion through swimming, whereas 'plankton' have limited motility and are at the mercy of the current. However, the majority of the invertebrate biomass in rivers lives on or near the bed, and are known collectively as 'benthos' or 'benthic macro-invertebrates'. Of these, insects are the most numerous. Others, including sponges, flatworms, oligochaete (headless) worms, leeches, molluscs, crustaceans and mites, are less important, although in some habitats they can account for a high diversity of species or a large biomass. Together, these organisms form the first level of the food chain above the fundamental organic matter derived from the land, photosynthesis or dead organisms.

These benthic macro-invertebrates differ in their feeding strategies. They can be divided into shredders (which eat coarse particulate matter derived from the land); collectors (which eat fine particulate matter they filter from water and sediment); grazers (which eat algae attached to sediment surfaces); and predators (which eat other invertebrates). As a result of the distribution of basic food sources along a river, these types of benthic macro-invertebrates tend to prefer different reaches of rivers. Thus in the upper reaches, the basic food source is allocthonous (organic matter coming into the river from the catchment), favouring shredders. In the middle reaches, photosynthesis is the basic food source, favouring grazers. In lower reaches, photosynthesis is inhibited by turbidity, and the primary food source is fine-grained matter from upstream, favouring collectors. Predatory benthic macro-invertebrates will tend to thrive in all of these environments.

The flow speed of a river can significantly affect the spatial distribution of benthic macro-invertebrates. Where fast-flowing, turbulent water flows over shallow beds (in riffles, for instance), the stress applied to the bed means that only those invertebrates with the capacity to resist movement can exist. This can be achieved in various ways: through flattening of the body, hiding in crevices or under stones, by attaching to the substrate by means of hooks or threads (e.g. Blackfly larvae, *Simulium* spp.) or by weighing themselves down with large sand grains (e.g. Caddis larvae) (Townsend 1986).

The substratum can also influence benthic macro-invertebrate communities: some like stony, creviced stream beds, whereas others, such as the mayfly nymph, prefer fine particles. Many invertebrates are 'epiphytic' – they live on the leaves of aquatic plants, using them as stable sites from which to filter food from the passing water, or as sites for predating other invertebrates.

The other main group of invertebrates associated with rivers are those flying species whose eggs and larvae develop in the water and who then occupy habitats around the river channel. Common among these are mayflies, backflies, caddis flies and dragonflies. They tend to prefer shallow water (for their eggs and larvae), emergent plants (for resting on) and trees and shrubs to provide shelter from the wind and sun (for more details see, for example, Haslam 1997).

Vertebrates

The main form of in-channel dwelling vertebrates is fish (mammals such as water voles and otters are categorized here as bank dwellers, and are covered below). Once again, flow speed tends to determine the distribution of these creatures. Tables 4.4 and 4.5 summarise the preferred habitats within the river system of the main species of British fish. Some fish are clearly adapted for life in relatively fast flows – the brown trout (*Salmo trutta*) is a strong swimmer, and is streamlined, thus offering relatively little resistance to the flow. Other species, such as the bullhead (*Cottus gobio*) and stone loach (*Nemacheilus barbatulus*) spend their time in upland reaches close to the bed where flows are slower, or sheltered behind stones. Lampreys and catfish even sucker themselves to rocks with their large lips.

Substrate type is also an important factor in determining fish distributions, especially when spawning – the need for coarse gravel by salmonids to build their redds in, as discussed above, is a classic example of this relationship. Other species prefer to use large stones to protect their eggs. The variation of dissolved oxygen concentration along rivers, as mentioned above, also tends

Table 4.4 : Longitudinal zonation of fish in river systems

River system	Zone	Characteristics	Species
Upstream	Trout Zone – fast flowing brooks and streams	Very steep gradient, very fast flow rates, highly oxygenated, cool, silt free, oligotrophic	Trout, salmon, parr, bullhead, stone loach
	Grayling/Minnow Zone – medium fast streams and river reaches	Steep gradient, fast flow, well oxygenated, clean gravel	As above plus: grayling, to barbell, chub, dace
	Barbel Zone/Chub Zone – medium flowing river reaches	Gentle gradient, moderate flow, good oxygen content, mixed substrate (silt and gravel)	All above plus roach, rudd, perch, pike, eel
Downstream	Bream Zone – slow flowing/sluggish river reaches	Very gentle gradient, slow flow good oxygen content, variable temperature, silty substrate, turbid, eutrophic	Roach, rudd, perch, pike eel, tench, bream, carp

Source: Ward, D., Holmes, N. and José, P. (eds) (1994) *The New Rivers and Wildlife Handbook*. Sandy: RSPB: 73

Table 4.5: The status of British freshwater fishes

Native freshwater fishes	Extinct species	Threatened species	Significant extensions to range in last two centuries	Established introduced species – at least one self-sustaining population
Eel (breeds in the sea) Allis shad and Twaite shad (mostly estuarine) Barbel Gudgeon Tench Crucian carp Silver bream Bream Bleak Minnow Rudd Roach Chub Dace Stone loach Spined loach Pike Vendace Schelly Pollan (inland only) Salmon Trout Charr Grayling Three-spined stickleback Ten-spined stickleback Bullhead Perch Ruffe	Burbot	Allis shad Twaite shad Vendace Schelly Charr	Barbel Tench Crucian carp Bream Rudd Roach Chub Pike Perch	Rainbow trout Brook char Bitterling Carp Goldfish Orfe Wels Black bullhead Zander Rock bass Large-mouth bass Pumpkinseed

Source: Ward, D., Holmes, N. and José, P. (eds) (1994) *The New Rivers and Wildlife Handbook*. Sandy: RSPB: 80

Otters, *Lutra lutra*,
lying under a tree.
TONY HAMBLIN.
RSPB-IMAGES.COM

to play a role in determining the distribution pattern of fish. Thus oxygen rich upstream waters support brown trout, minnows (*Phoximus phoximus*), bull-head, grayling (*Thymallus thymallus*) and chub (*Leuciscus cephalus*) all of which require 5–11 millilitres of oxygen per litre of water to survive. Further down-stream, roach (*Rutilus rutilus*), ruffe (*Gymnocephalus cernau*) and pike (*Esox lucius*) need about 4 ml/litre, whilst carp (*Cyprinus carpio*), tench (*Tinca tinca*) and bream (*Abramis brama*) can survive with as little as 0.5 ml/litre (Varley 1967).

Finally, water temperature determines fish distribution – all species are restricted to a certain temperature range. Some – 'stenotherms' – such as trout and grayling can only occupy narrow temperature ranges, whereas others – 'eurytherms' – such as roach can occupy wider ranges. Different temperature ranges may be required for feeding, growing and reproduction.

Riparian ecology

Riparian plants are very important elements of the British river system, for many material reasons as well as their aesthetic value. They can vary from small grasses and mosses to the large trees and shrubs often found lining riverbanks, taking advantage of the ready and plentiful supply of water they support. They can also be seen as a hindrance – to anglers, boaters and water drainage for example.

Riparian plants stabilise the soil via their network of roots or rhizomes. They can thus help to prevent erosion of riverbanks, although uprooting of vegetation during floods can also provide sites for heightened levels of erosion. Vegetation also affects the chemistry of the river water: on plant death and decomposition, dissolved organic substances are released into the soil, and thence to the river water. Plants also oxygenate the water and influence the concentration of carbon dioxide and the water acidity. River animals and bacteria also use the oxygen released by plants. Finally plants help to neutralise the effects of organic effluents entering the stream and help purify the water.

Riparian vegetation also provides shelter and food for terrestrial and aquatic invertebrates, vertebrates and birds and, in doing so, provides food for fish. Dragonflies and caddis flies use emergent riparian vegetation to crawl up out of the water when they change from their aquatic larval stage to their winged adult stage. Birds and mammals can feed off fruit and shoots of riparian plants and derive shelter for themselves and their nests in the plant foliage. Riparian plants also provide nursery and sanctuary habitats for terrestrial birds and mammals.

Riverine waterbirds

Many species of birds use British river habitats either exclusively or during some part of their life cycle. There is only room for a small sample here and there are many books dedicated to this subject (notably Royal Society for the Protection of Birds 1994, Prater 1981). Most species of waterbirds prefer slow

Table 4.6: Status and habitat characteristics of major bird species associated with upland rivers

Species	Status	Habitat characteristics
Red-breasted merganser	Widespread north and west Scotland also Northern Ireland and spreading in North England and Wales. Absent during winter months when predominantly marine.	Well-oxygenated unpolluted upland rivers, with boulders, riffles and sand banks. Banks with dense vegetation such as heather, scrub and often woodland.
Goosander	In breeding season restricted to Scotland and North England but spreading in Wales. In winter widespread throughout Britain. Absent from Ireland.	Clear, unpolluted, upland rivers particulalry where close to mature trees during breeding season, more open waters during winter months.
Common sandpiper	Widespread in upland areas north of a line from Humber to Severn estuaries. Summer visitor only.	Water courses with shingle margins, banks and islands; rough vegetation on or mear to river.
Dipper	Widespread in north and west, absent from England east of a line Humber – Isle of Wight. Present throughout the year.	Fast-flowing streams and rivers with rocks, boulders, shingle, water-falls and rock outcrops with shallow water.
Grey wagtail	Widespread though absent in much of central and eastern England. Present throughout the year.	Turbulent streams with gravel bars; weirs, mill races. Favours wooded reaches.

Source: Adapted from Ward, D., Holmes, N. and José, P. (eds) (1994) *The New Rivers and Wildlife Handbook*. Sandy: RSPB: 61

Table 4.7: Status and habitat characteristics of major bird species associated with lowland rivers

Species	Status	Habitat characteristics
Great crested grebe	Widespread, mainly in lowland areas. Present throughout the year.	Open lake-like sections of 1 ha 0.5–5m deep, per pair during breeding season. Well-developed fringing emergent vegetation especially reeds.
Little grebe	Widespread and sometimes numerous especially in south. Present throughout the year on lowland rivers.	Shallow waters often < 1m deep and < than 1 ha extent. Luxuriant aquatic, emergent and marginal vegetation, overhanging branches, bushes and scrub.
Mallard	Very common and widespread on both lowland and upland rivers.	Waters with emergent vegetation, bankside scrub; rank vegetation and submerged aquatics. Very adaptable.
Tufted duck	Widespread, rather scarce but sometimes at high density. Present throughout the year.	Open lake-like sections with good marginal emergent vegetation. Depths in excess of 5m but usually less than 1m during breeding season.
Mute swan	Widespread in lowland areas; numerous in south. Present throughout the year.	Wide or open sluggish channels with islands, backwaters, spits or stands of emergent vegetation, eg reeds and abundant submerged aquatics in depths less than 1m.
Moorhen	Very common and widespread. Present throughout the year.	Prefers waters sheltered by woodland or tall emergent plants but utilises open bankside habitats for feeding.
Coot	Common, widespread in south, more scarce in north. present throughout the year.	Moderately wide but slow-flowing, open channels, with shallows and marginal emergent vegetation such as reeds and bulrushes. Overhanging and trailing scrub or branches important for feeding early in season.
Kingfisher	Widespread and quite common except in Scotland where scarce and absent in the Highlands. Present throughout the year.	Still or gently flowing rivers and streams with shallow areas of clear water, low overhanging branches or other perches essential.
Sand martin	Widespread; summer visitor Mar.–Sept.	Vertical earth and sand banks soft enough for burrowing. Open areas without woodland. Mainly along rivers in the north but artificial sites such as gravel workings in the south.
Reed warbler	Widespread but local in south; absent north England, Scotland, Ireland and much of Wales. Summer visitor Apr.–Sept.	Almost entirely restricted to areas with reedbeds or fringes, uses other bankside vegetation when feeding.
Sedge warbler	Widespread and numerous throughout lowland Britain. Summer visitor Apr.–Sept.	Low dense vegetation generally along water's edge, utilises reeds, willow carr, scrub and bushes.
Reed bunting	Widespread and common. Present throughout the year.	Marshy areas, reedbeds, fringing emergent vegetation, hedgerows and ditches, rank vegetation.

Source: Adapted from Ward, D., Holmes, N. and José, P. (eds) (1994) *The New Rivers and Wildlife Handbook*. Sandy: RSPB: 63 and 64

and quiet river waters, usually in lowlands, fringed by emergent plants within the channel and well-developed bankside vegetation, including trees. Beyond this, their habitat requirements are largely based on their feeding and nesting habits. For example, mallards (*Anas platyrhynchos*) and coots (*Fulica acra*) can

Ducks on the banks
of the river Ouse,
York, North
Yorkshire.
S. OWEN

dive up to 2m deep to reach benthic food sources, so require water shallower
than this, although they can also feed off the land. Most species are omni-
vorous: moorhens (*Gallinda chloropsis*) for example eat vegetation, seeds and
insects. Many, including mallards, teal (*Anas crecca*), goosanders (*Mergus
merganser*), common sandpipers (*Actilis hypoleucas*) and little grebes
(*Tachybaptus ruficollis*) get the majority of the animal part of their diet from
benthic invertebrates. As a result, they need the sort of shallow, productive,
nutrient-rich waters which support invertebrates in abundance. However,
invertebrates are difficult to come by in the winter, so most species adopt
more vegetarian diets at that time, with the exception of the little grebe,
which eats more fish. Other species have more varied diets: for example,
swans (*Cygnus olor*) eat aquatic plants along with all the epiphytes attached to
them and thus prefer moderately flowing, relatively shallow rivers which

Table 4.8: Status and habitat characteristics of major bird species associated with river floodplains

Species	Status	Habitat characteristics
Lapwing	Widespread but now scarce in lowland England and Wales. Present throughout the year.	A mosaic of arable and pasture with ploughed or open ground for nesting and grassland, preferably damp or with standing water for rearing chicks.
Redshank	Widespread but now very scarce in lowland England. Present throughout the year.	Damp meadows, marshland and estuarine marshes often with some standing water.
Snipe	Widespread but now scarce on lowland farmland, present throughout the year.	Wet meadows, rough grazing and upland bog with tussocky vegetation, needs wet or damp ground to probe for invertebrates.
Yellow wagtail	Widespread throughout England and Wales but declining, rare in Scotland, absent from Ireland.	Lowland flood meadows and damp grazing especially where vegetation low and near to shallow surface water.

Source: Adapted from Ward, D., Holmes, N. and José, P. (eds) (1994) *The New Rivers and
Wildlife Handbook*. Sandy: RSPB: 66

Kingfisher.

provide a sufficient supply of oxygen and nutrients to sustain the plant life; grey herons (*Ardea cinerea*) eat fish, invertebrates, amphibians, reptiles, small mammals and birds and thus seek out easily accessible shallow water with a good food supply; and species such as great crested grebes (*Podiceps cristatus*) and oyster catchers (*Haematopus ostralegus*) add molluscs, newts, and crustacea to the standard diet of plants, seeds and invertebrates.

The primary requirement for nesting for all these species is some protection from predators for their young. Some species, including mallards, teals and other ducks use tall bankside vegetation to achieve this. Others, such as moorhens and coots, nest on floating structures anchored in emergent aquatic plants or occasionally just above the waterline in overhanging or fallen trees or bushes. These nests are susceptible to flooding, although the birds build platforms for their nests to counteract this. Other species adopt more individual forms of protection: great crested grebes nest on mounds of vegetation in still waters separated from the bank; common sandpipers nest on shingle banks and grey herons nest in heronries in open woods or groups of trees close to rivers. Some species, such as oyster catchers and cormorants, although common along rivers in summer, return to the coast to nest during the winter.

Some species of waterbird prefer to stay away from the gently flowing waters preferred by most species. For example, the dipper (*Cinclus cinclus*) likes the stony-bedded rivers of highland Britain, especially those with turbulent flows in them. They feed on invertebrates taken from under stones on the riverbed. Tables 4.6, 4.7 and 4.8 summarise the preferred habitats within the British river system of the main species of river bird life.

Riparian mammals and amphibians

There is a very wide range of species of mammals and reptiles that use the river environment in one way or another, though relatively few that remain in the riparian zone throughout their life cycle. Among the occasional visitors are insectivores including hedgehogs (*Erinaceus europaeus*), common and pygmy shrews (*Sorex araneus* and *Sorex minutes*) and moles (*Talpa europaea*), the last of which are particularly attracted to worm-rich alluvial soils. Several species of bats, including whiskered bats (*Myotis mystacinus*), pipistrelles (*Pipistrellus pipistrellus*) and long-eared bats (*Plecotus auritus*) also frequent rivers because of the rich supply of flying insects available. Rabbits

(*Oryctolagus cuniculus*), rodents (for example grey squirrel (*Sciurus carolinensis*), wood mouse (*Apodemus sylvaticus*), yellow-necked mouse (*Apodemus flavicollis*) and brown rat (*Rattus norvegicus*)), carnivores (including red fox (*Vulpes vulpes*), badger (*Meles meles*) and domestic cats (*Felis* sp.)) and all species of deer are other generally terrestrial species that use river environments because of their rich diversity of sources of food and shelter.

Other mammals are more closely tied to rivers. Water voles or water rats (*Arvicola terrestris*) feed mainly on grasses and use the riverbank as a protected environment in which to build their burrows. Their ability to swim makes them well adapted to this habitat, and they tend to build tunnels for easy access to the water. They were once widespread in Britain, but are now in precipitous decline: their numbers have declined by 90 per cent in recent years, and they have almost disappeared in the south-west of England. This decline has been caused by habitat loss due to riverside development, pollution and predation by mink.

Otters (*Lutra lutra*) also remain within the riparian habitat for the large majority of their lives. They are territorial animals, the males requiring some 40km of river. They also need safe places such as tall bankside vegetation or riparian woods to rest and hide in. Male otters require this every 5–6 km (Haslam 1997). In areas used heavily for industrial, recreational and other human uses, this vegetation will need to extend some way onto the land. Otters feed on fish, eels and small animals, and being primary predators, are particularly sensitive to poisons that have increased in concentration as they pass up the food chain. They hunt using sight, so need relatively clean waters (Haslam 1997). Recently, otters have been successfully re-introduced to a

Saltmarsh on the river Dee at Kirkcudbright, Dumfries and Galloway.

S. OWEN

Table 4.9: Mammals, amphibians and reptiles and their UK river habitats

Mammal	Habitat	UK distribution
Otter	Rivers/wetlands and coastal areas (eg N and W Scotland). Needs cover of marginal vegetation, trees and reedbeds. Secure breeding sites essential.	Only abundant in NW highlands and islands of Scotland. Now largely absent from Central and S England.
Mink (non-native)	Rivers and wetlands, with cover of marginal vegetation and/or trees.	Became established in late 1950s, now wide-spread and expanding.
Water shrew	Clear, unpolluted streams and wetlands, with plant cover.	Throughout. Scarce N Scotland.
Water vole	Lowland rivers, canals, ponds and drainage ditches, particularly with good marginal vegetation.	Throughout, but declining rapidly.
Natterer's bat	Woodland adjacent to rivers.	Throughout, no longer common.
Daubenton's bat	Over open water.	Throughout, no longer common.
Whiskered bat	Open areas and woodland, especially with river and ponds.	Throughout, no longer common.
Noctule	Over rivers and lakes.	Throughout, no longer common.
Pipistrelle	Over or near water and grassland.	Throughout, common but declining.

Amphibian	Habitat	UK distribution
Smooth newt	Prefers still, hard water. Likely to be found wherever warty newts occur, though much more abundant. Will rapidly colonise sites, including urban sites.	Widespread, Britain and Ireland.
Great crested or warty newt	The most aquatic species, breeds in still or slow-flowing water above pH 5.5. A hard water species, rare in the north and west. Not very good at colonising new sites.	Rare in Britain, absent in Ireland.
Palmate newt	Rarest and smallest, found in still soft water but sometimes breeds in flowing water.	Widespread in Britain, absent in Ireland. Found in the west and north of Britain, but rare in central England and East Anglia.
Common frog	Typically breeds in warm, shallow (c 10 cm) edges. Spawn can be anchored to submerged vegetation and can survive substantial increases in water velocity or depth.	Widespread in Britain, not native in Ireland, declining.
Common toad	Perhaps most likely amphibian to be found in rivers. Wind strings of spawn around plants in water above 30cm deep.	Widespread in Britain, absent in Ireland.

Reptile	Habitat	UK distribution
Common or viviparous lizard	Often in moist well-vegetated habitats. Swims well.	Widespread in Britain and Ireland.
Slow worm	A legless lizard. Secretive; most often found by turning over stones in damp areas.	Widespread in Britain, absent in Ireland.
Grass snake	Most aquatic of reptiles, often swims. Hunts tadpoles and other amphibians in water. Egg-laying.	Widespread in England only. Absent in Ireland.
Adder	Quite often found on banksides.	Widespread in Britain, absent from Ireland.

Source: Adapted from Ward, D., Holmes, N. and José, P. (eds) (1994) *The New Rivers and Wildlife Handbook*. Sandy: RSPB: 48, 83

number of British rivers. Mason and Macdonald (1986) give more details about these evocative and attractive river mammals.

There are also many amphibious reptiles that occupy the British river environment. These include smooth newts (*Triturus vulgaris*), palmate newts (*Triturus helveticus*), common toads (*Bufo bufo*) and common frogs (*Rana temporaria*). Whereas toad tadpoles tend to be unpalatable to fish, and thus thrive in river waters, frog tadpoles are at risk of predation by fish, and frogs therefore tend to use pools or small drains for spawning, as long as they can develop sufficiently to leave before they dry up. Other, more terrestrial reptiles can be found in the riparian habitat, seeking food or shelter. These include common lizards (*Lacerta vivipara*), slow worms (*Anguis fragilis*) and grass snakes (*Natrix natrix*). Table 4.9 summarises the preferred habitats within the British river system of the main species of river mammal, amphibian and reptile life.

Riparian birds

As well as the ducks, wading birds and divers that use the river itself for feeding and nesting, there are many species of birds that use the riparian habitat in one way or another. Perhaps the most attractive are kingfishers (*Alcedo atthis*), which use riparian vegetation or anthropogenic structures such as fences as perches from which to spot food in the river. They catch small fish such as stickleback and minnow as well as small animals on the river banks, and thus prefer slow flowing, clear waters. Several other species, including sedge warblers (*Acrocephalus schoenobaenus*) and reed buntings (*Emberiza schoeniculus*) feed on plants, seeds and small invertebrates on riverbanks. As a result, they frequent lowland rivers with abundant riparian vegetation. Reed warblers (*Acrocephalus scirpaceus*) prefer reed beds backed by wet woodland and feed on insect larvae.

Grey and pied wagtails (*Motacilla cinerea* and *Motacilla alba*) are generally terrestrial birds, but are often found near fertile rivers lined by deciduous trees feeding on the rich supply of riverine insects and other invertebrates found in these habitats. Grey wagtails prefer fast-flowing rocky hill streams in summer and lowland rivers in winter. Pied wagtails tend to remain confined to lowland rivers. Sand martins (*Riparia ripariodes*) are not aquatic but will eat airborne insects over water and marsh. They are often found nesting in colonies where sandy cliffs form the riverbank.

Alien species

Alien species of plants or animals may have been introduced deliberately or may have escaped, and may alter the balance of the native community, as the coypu did during the 1960s in eastern England. Invasions can occur when foreign species are introduced, or when species from one part of the country are transplanted to another where they are not native. In contrast to chemical pollutants which can be eliminated at source, species introductions are usually impossible to undo: natural enemies are often lacking, and the impacts of the introduced species are unpredictable (Allan 1995).

The rainbow trout (*Onchorhynchus mykiss*) was once confined to the Pacific north-west of North America, but now has a worldwide distribution, including Britain, because it is easy to breed, appealing to anglers, and tasty to eat. Carp have been introduced to destroy noxious weeds. Japanese knotweed (*Polygonum cuspidatum*) and Hymalayan balsam (*Impatiens glandulifera*) are particularly invasive species of large plants that have become common on many riverbanks in recent years. The arrival of these aggressively invasive species can result in the decline of native species, changes in habitat use or habitat loss, the introduction of new diseases and parasites (Allan 1995).

Estuarine biogeography

Estuaries provide a wide variety of habitats for an immense diversity of plants and animals, including fresh, brackish and seawater, sandbanks, mudflats, saltmarshes and reed beds. They support both permanent residents and many species of visiting birds and fish, which use them as feeding and nursery grounds. The fine-grained, soft sediments that are deposited here as a result of the downstream fining process discussed above also provide habitats for a number of burrowing animals.

The main factors within an estuary that cause variations of species distributions within them are the temperature, salinity (saltiness) of the water, water current speeds, water depth and substrate type (which can vary from rock to sand to mud). Generally, a lower diversity of species, especially of benthos, tends to be found at the upper (freshwater) end of estuaries (e.g. Elliott and Kingston 1987, Warwick and Uncles 1980).

The bases of the food chain in estuaries, as in the open sea, are periphyton and phytoplankton. Crudely put, at the seaward end of an estuary, a marine ecology, based on plankton, tends to dominate, whereas at the shallower landward end, a freshwater ecology, based on periphyton and other benthic organisms becomes dominant. The majority of estuarine fish feed primarily on benthos, and thus lead a 'demersal' existence, living just above the bottom. The most abundant fish in estuaries are known as 'estuarine-opportunists' by ecologists and are present for only a limited period each year. Examples include plaice, whiting, cod, bass and mullet (Elliott *et al.* 1990). Other species, 'marine stragglers', freshwater species (e.g. rudd and roach) and migrants (e.g. salmon, lampreys and shads, which breed in fresh water, and eels, which breed in the sea) enter estuaries only irregularly, and are usually restricted to the seaward or landward end, or pass through during very limited time periods respectively. Permanently resident estuarine fish, such as gobies and flounders, comprise a relatively small number of species, but typically contribute a large proportion of the biomass (Little 2000).

As well as the aquatic ecology, estuaries also support a unique, fragile and highly biodiverse group of ecological communities via their sustenance of sandbanks, mudflats and saltmarshes. These comprise algae, microscopic plants, invertebrate animals (snails, crustaceans and insects), macrophytes, birds and larger fauna such as voles, foxes and otters (Little 2000) – even deer have been observed on saltmarshes, and cattle are often set to graze on their landward end.

On sandbanks and mudflats, which are too salty for macrophytes, the ecology is dominated by burrowing invertebrates, algae and wading birds, including curlew (*Numenius Arcata*), redshank (*Tringa tetanus*), and dunlin. At low tide seals bask on sandbanks: for example this is a common site by the famous railway bridge over the Tay estuary. Landward of these, there is then a succession of increasingly terrestrial macrophytes, beginning with the hardiest of halophytes (salt-resistant plants) such as cordgrass (*Spartina* spp.), moving through a wide variety of plants including glassworts (*Salicornia* spp.), puccinellia, rushes (e.g. *Juncus* spp.), sea lavender (*Limonium*), sea asters and samphire or sea fennel (*Crithmum maritimum*). Many of these have human uses – for example, the rushes have been used for centuries for weaving and thatching, and samphire makes a tasty alternative to more usual green vegetables.

CHAPTER 5

Rivers as an economic resource

Gordon Clark

Introduction

As outlined in chapter 1, Britain is a small country with many short rivers. Nowhere is more than about 110 km from the sea and the longest river, the Severn, flows for only 345 km, insignificant in length by European, let alone world standards (see Appendix 1). Yet these short rivers have always been an important element in the economic life of the country. This chapter explores the real economic value of rivers.

Rivers for water

The most obvious resource in the rivers of Britain is the water itself. Having a large population in a small country with short rivers, the UK has less river water per head of population than most other European countries, despite our climatic reputation for rain. The problem is exacerbated by the highest population densities being concentrated in the drier south-east of the country. It is not surprising that there is keen competition for river water from a wide variety of users. Two-thirds of the water used in Britain comes from rivers and lakes, and a third from groundwater. Figure 5.1 shows how the 45,000 registered abstractors of water used this resource in 2000. Perhaps surprisingly, water for cooling in electricity generating stations is the biggest use, followed by water for domestic purposes, fish farming and industrial uses.

Generating stations use river water to cool the steam that drives the turbines. The familiar 'pepper pot' shaped towers alongside coal- and oil-fired power stations cool the water until it is only 6–9°C above normal river temperature before discharging it into the river (minus the 10 per cent lost through evaporation). This warming effect on the river water can alter the plants and fish stocks downstream. The sequence of power stations along the Trent forms the largest concentration of river water users for cooling.

The second largest use of river water is for the public water supply. In Scotland, the Pennines and Wales, rivers have been dammed and lakes created or enlarged to regulate the supply of water to the cities across the seasons. Some of these, like Lake Vyrnwy supplying Liverpool, the Elan Reservoir for Birmingham and Thirlmere for Manchester, were major engineering feats of the later nineteenth century. They heralded a move to transfer water from the upland river basins where the rain fell abundantly, to the cities with their burgeoning demand from industry and for domestic uses. New reservoirs, like Rutland Water and Kielder (Northumbria), continue the tradition of flooding valleys to supply the cities. The London Ring Main, which re-distributes water all round the capital, is the latest in a long history of tunnels and aqueducts, trying to compensate for the fact that rivers follow the topography rather than the demand for drinking water. London and York are special cases because water is taken from the river directly for public use, supplemented by borehole water. The

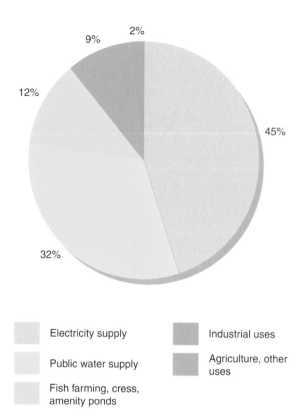

- Electricity supply
- Public water supply
- Fish farming, cress, amenity ponds
- Industrial uses
- Agriculture, other uses

Figure 5.1. Estimated abstractions from non-tidal surface waters in England and Wales, 2000. (WWW.DEFRA.GOV.UK/ ENVIRONMENT/STATISTICS/ INLWATER/INDEX.HTM)

Vyrnwy Dam, Wales. Still supplying water from Wales to the Midlands, it is one of many similar dams built in the late Victorian era to supply clean water to rapidly expanding cities across the UK.
VINCENT LOWE ARPS
WWW.LOWEFOTO.COM

The Sheffield flood, 1864. Faulty construction techniques at the Dale Dyke reservoir high above Sheffield led to a catastrophic failure of the embankment on the night of 11 March 1864. Two hundred and forty people lost their lives as the raging torrent made its way down the Don valley. Here lie the remains of a waterwheel washed away by the flood.

Thames and Lee provide 90 per cent of London's water. In a dry summer, these abstractions can leave only 20 per cent of the natural flow to reach the North Sea. The situation is not helped by the loss of water (20–30 per cent) through leaky pipes between the river or reservoir and customers. This wastage floods valleys unnecessarily and reduces river flows to no good public or environmental effect.

The industrial uses of water are numerous. Steel mills, breweries, paper makers and many other industrial processes use river water or groundwater for their trade. Along the Spey up to 33 distilleries can be abstracting water for whisky production. The decline of British manufacturing has seen the water table, lowered by industrial abstractions in many cities, rise again to near normal levels, which threatens to waterlog building foundations and rail/tube tunnels, particularly in London and Liverpool. The recent growth in inland fish farming, mostly for trout, has added a new demand for clean river water. Generally, the agricultural demand for river water is small (unlike, say, in the western United States and southern Europe). But in parts of the eastern counties and south-east Scotland, abstraction from small rivers during the high summer for the spray irrigation of field vegetables, particularly potatoes, could cause local shortages if not strictly regulated.

While industrial water needs are falling, domestic demand is rising, with more swimming pools, washing machines, lawns to be watered and power showers. Unsurprisingly only 11 per cent of British rivers have natural flow regimes; all the others have had their flow altered significantly by the removal and re-introduction of water for industrial or domestic users.

Rivers for power

As a river flows downhill to the sea, the momentum of the water has the power to do useful work before it reaches the sea. The earliest technology to harness the power of rivers was the waterwheel. Before the development of affordable steam engines in the nineteenth century, manufacturing and milling were usually powered by waterwheels. The Domesday Book of 1086 recorded 5,624 mills in England south of the Trent; indeed by the medieval period nearly every village had a mill. There were seventy on Anglesey alone, and along the Thames there was on average a waterwheel every 3 km.

Spray irrigation of potatoes, Jersey. This crop of Jersey Royal early potatoes will have its yield much increased by irrigation. In dry parts of the UK, agricultural irrigation can be a major user of water.
PETER DEAN — AGRIPICTURE IMAGES

The earliest recorded British waterwheels were Saxon. These were horizontally mounted wheels placed in the river which transferred power through a vertical shaft to turn, for example, stones for grinding corn. A small 2-horsepower horizontal wheel could grind as much corn as thirty people using querns (small hand-operated mills) and without sacrificing valuable arable land to growing fodder for real horse-power. Such simple waterwheels lasted well into modern times on small rivers in Ireland and Northern Scotland.

The next development was the vertically mounted undershot wheel. This was again placed in the river and the water-flow pushed the base of the wheel round. Water-flow might be increased and controlled by building a weir upstream and using sluice gates. The overshot wheel was more efficient still, because the use of gearing allowed the waterwheel to be alongside the river, not in it, and flumes could be used to direct water onto the top of the wheel. Vertical wheels could be used on larger rivers, but here the weirs conflicted with the need of bargemen for uninterrupted navigation. Overshot wheels, though more expensive to build, could deliver very significant amounts of power – the largest working wheel in the world is the 'Lady Isabella' at Laxey on the Isle of Man, with its wheel 22 metres in diameter.

The earliest water power was for corn milling but by the eighteenth century it was being used to pump water from mines, crush ore, smelt minerals, make paper, spin textiles and saw timber. Until well into the nineteenth century a water wheel was cheaper than a steam engine and more reliable, although summer drought and low river flow were weaknesses. By around 1800 there were 10,000–12,000 water mills in the UK. Eventually, however, the steam engine won out – capable of being installed even where there was no river, more powerful and eventually more reliable and cheaper per horsepower. Today the waterwheel is long obsolete, yet around the country they are being restored, either by enthusiasts for their intrinsic worth or as the centrepiece of a visitor attraction. Aberdulais Falls near Neath now generates electricity from its wheel. Other restored and working mills, often milling corn, can be found at Little Salkeld (Cumbria), Otterton (Budleigh Salterton), Dunster (Somerset) and the James Brindley Water Wheel at Leek (Staffs). Waterwheels for industrial use can be seen at sites such as the Abbeydale Industrial Hamlet in Sheffield.

The waterwheel generated mechanical power. The modern use of water power is to generate hydroelectricity. The first such public use in Britain was probably in 1890 near Fort Augustus in the Highlands. Although small run-of-

Lady Isabella Waterwheel, Laxey, Isle of Man. This is the largest water wheel ever built in these islands, just before steam fully replaced water power for pumping out mines. The wheel still turns and is a major Manx attraction in a village which has switched from lead mining to tourism.

COURTESY OF MANX NATIONAL HERITAGE

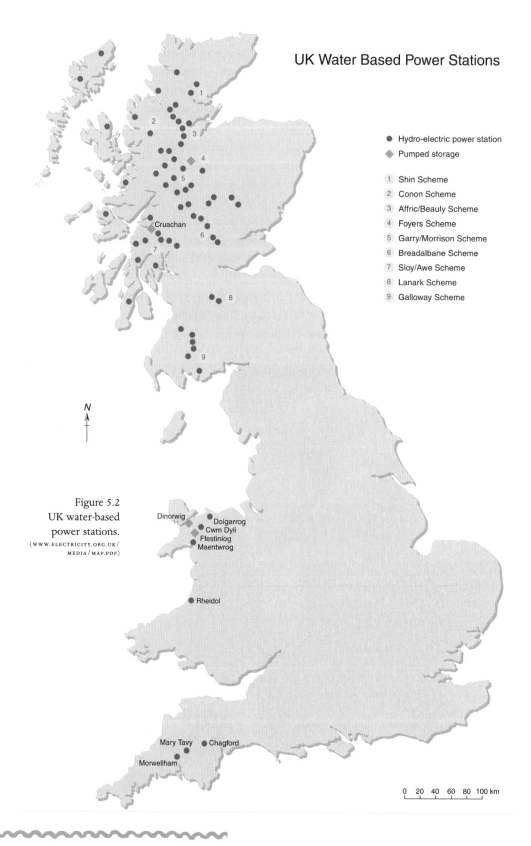

UK Water Based Power Stations

- ● Hydro-electric power station
- ◆ Pumped storage

1 Shin Scheme
2 Conon Scheme
3 Affric/Beauly Scheme
4 Foyers Scheme
5 Garry/Morrison Scheme
6 Breadalbane Scheme
7 Sloy/Awe Scheme
8 Lanark Scheme
9 Galloway Scheme

Cruachan

1
2
3
4
5
6
7
8
9

N

Figure 5.2
UK water-based
power stations.
(WWW.ELECTRICITY.ORG.UK/
MEDIA/MAP.PDF)

Dinorwig
Dolgarrog
Cwm Dyli
Ffestiniog
Maentwrog

Rheidol

Mary Tavy ● Chagford
Morwellham

0 20 40 60 80 100 km

flow turbines for electricity are available, hydroelectric generation is largely confined to mountainous areas. There have been a few examples in Devon, rather more in Wales and the Southern Uplands, but it has been the rivers of the wet western Highlands of Scotland which have been most assiduously tapped for electric power. Today the 65 hydro stations account for about 2 per cent of all UK generating capacity and about 1 per cent of actual output (Figure 5.2).

In the Scottish Highlands the development of hydro-electricity has acquired an almost mythical status as a force for economic development. It began in earnest with three hydropower stations at Foyers (1896), Kinlochleven (1909) and Lochaber (1929), which powered the aluminium smelters. After the Second World War the North of Scotland Hydro-Electric Board built dams and power stations from Argyll to Sutherland, employing 12,000 construction workers at the peak and 4–5,000 for many years. Hydro stations can be at full load in under two minutes, sometimes in seconds, so they are excellent for meeting temporary peak demand. Fortunately the summer period of low river flow in the Highlands coincides with the lowest season of electricity demand. However, with short, low-volume rivers, even in the Highlands, the electrical output of conventional hydro-stations is small. One solution is to construct pumped storage schemes,

Loch Sloy Hydro-Electric Power Station, Argyll. This is one of the larger conventional hydroelectric power stations in the Scottish Highlands, though in terms of output it is a small installation. In some senses this is 'green' electricity.

Tongland power station and overflow channel. Tongland is one of six, and the last, hydro-electric plants on the River Dee, Dumfries and Galloway.
S. OWEN

as has happened at Ffestiniog, Cruachan, Foyers and Dinorwig. The river water flows through turbines from a high-level reservoir and, instead of flowing on to the sea, is pumped back up to the high level reservoir, using spare generating capacity overnight from conventional power stations. The consequence is that the reservoir can be drained very rapidly, providing considerable power (1728 MW at Dinorwig) for a short period.

There are thought to be few more major opportunities to use British rivers for hydro-electric power, which may be fortunate as they are a controversial type of development: the reservoir floods a valley (albeit perhaps long de-populated); the initial capital cost is high; the dam is a massive use of building materials; and it is incongruous in a wild mountain landscape. On the positive side, hydro-electricity generation releases no direct pollution (no CO_2 or nuclear waste, for example), it is 90 per cent energy efficient, and the stations have very low running costs and a very long operational life of over fifty years.

In the 1970s, attention turned to dams or barrages across river estuaries. Schemes were proposed for the Severn, Mersey and Morecambe Bay among others, which would also incorporate roads along the top of the barrage, tidal power stations to harness the ebb and flow twice a day, and water storage and water sports on the artificial lake behind the barrage. None of these estuarine schemes has yet been built (despite the lure of pollution-free electricity) because of concerns over the economics of such massive constructions and the environmental effects of the lake on riverine and coastal ecosystems. What have been built are the flood barrages at Woolwich (London) and Hull, and barrage schemes at Stockton-on-Tees and Cardiff Bay (on the Taff and Ely rivers). These control water levels behind the barrage, opening up leisure uses of the lake, removing the eyesore of inter-tidal mudflats and allowing prop-erty development along the river/lake-side. The latter is probably the real incentive for such schemes.

Rivers and fish

Fishing in British rivers and canals is the nation's favourite pastime; about 1.1 million anglers are licensed in England and Wales and there are around 5,000 angling clubs. Anglers have thirty-two native species of freshwater fish and over ten imported ones to choose from. Coarse fishing – along canals, rivers and lakes – is a major activity, but one it is hard to measure in terms of time spent or fish caught. But the range of equipment on sale in every town's fishing-tackle shop shows the spending power fishermen are willing to invest in their hobby (Environment Agency 2002a).

Interesting things can be found in British rivers – the occasional sturgeon, freshwater pearl mussels in the Spey and Tay, lamprey and oyster beds in

Valley floor of the River Dee, north-east Scotland.
C. PARK

below Haaf-net fishing on the River Lune, 1934. Salmon and other fish were caught by the simple device of standing in the river near its mouth with a wide net into which they swam. It was a very cold way to earn a living. Today wild salmon are caught all along the River Lune by rod.
COURTESY OF LANCASTER CITY MUSEUMS

the Thames estuary. Some species are relics of the Ice Age – the vendace and Arctic char in some of the Cumbrian and Scottish lakes and lochs, for example. Better known, however, are the commercially valuable fish – the salmon, trout and eel. Fishing for eel is mostly concentrated in the tidal reaches of the Severn and the rivers of Somerset and South Wales (glass eel and elvers) and in East Anglia for yellow eel. Annual catches are believed to be about ten tonnes of elver and a few hundred tonnes of yellow and silver eel.

N

left Figure 5.3.
Major salmon and
sea trout rivers and
fisheries in England
and Wales.

(ENVIRONMENT AGENCY
FISHERIES STATISTICS, 2001)

0 20 40 60 80 100 km

1	Coquet	18	Plym	35	Loughor	52	Conwy
2	Tyne	19	Tavy	36	Tywi	53	Clwyd
3	Wear	20	Tamar	37	Taf	54	Dee
4	Tees	21	Lynher	38	Cleddau	55	Ribble
5	Esk (Yorks.)	22	Fowey	39	Teifi	56	Wyre
6	Itchen	23	Camel	40	Aeron	57	Lune
7	Test	24	Torridge	41	Ystwyth	58	Kent
8	Avon (Hants.)	25	Taw	42	Rheidol	59	Leven
9	Piddle	26	Lyn	43	Dyfi	60	Crake
10	Frome	27	Severn	44	Dysynni	61	Duddon
11	Axe	28	Wye	45	Mawddach	62	Esk (Cumbria)
12	Exe	29	Usk	46	Artro	63	Irt
13	Teign	30	Taff	47	Dwyryd	64	Ehen
14	Dart	31	Ogmore	48	Glaslyn	65	Derwent
15	Avon (Devon)	32	Afan	49	Gwyrfai	66	Ellen
16	Erme	33	Neath	50	Seiont	67	Eden
17	Yealm	34	Tawe	51	Ogwen	68	Esk (Borders)

right Figure 5.4.
Active fish farming
sites, 2000 –
Scotland.

(ASTRON CARTOGRAPHIC
CENTRE, 2001)

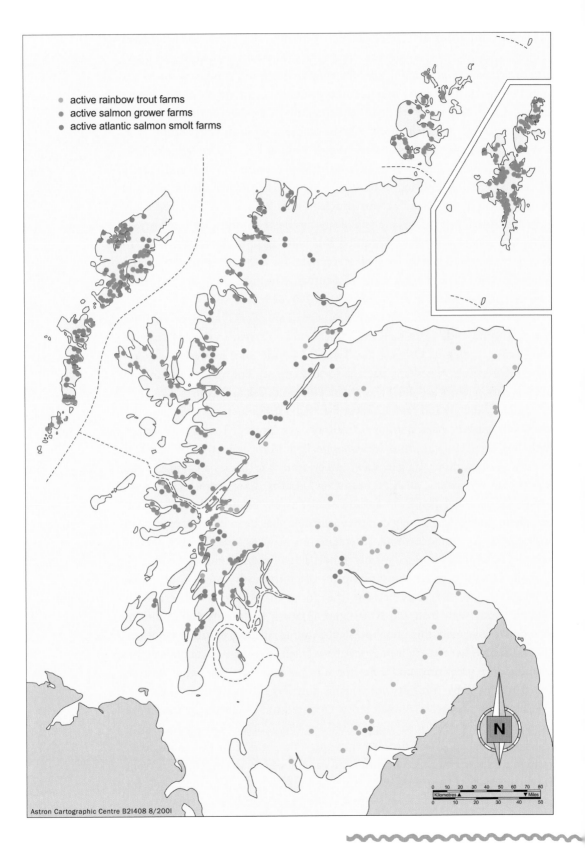

- active rainbow trout farms
- active salmon grower farms
- active atlantic salmon smolt farms

N

| 0 | 10 | 20 | 30 | 40 | 50 | 60 | 70 | 80 |
Kilometres ▲ ▼ Miles
| 0 | 10 | 20 | 30 | 40 | 50 |

Astron Cartographic Centre B2I408 8/200I

Salmon and trout are the most economically significant river fisheries (Figure 5.3). Originally they were caught for subsistence and were cheap and plentiful throughout Britain. Like the medieval fishponds built in the water meadows alongside rivers, they secured a supply of affordable fresh protein during the winter months and for Lent and Fridays. By the nineteenth century the right to fish a stretch of river had become a separate legal property in most non-tidal rivers, lakes and reservoirs. Fishing had moved from subsistence to a leisure activity but one with a real economic value and closely associated with landowning interests. There are around 400 salmon rivers in Scotland and about 68 in western England and Wales. The declared catch varies each year but in England and Wales has been around 15,000 fish a year (about 60 tonnes), of which around a half is released back into the river. In Scotland about 75,000 fish a year are caught by rod – over 10,000 on the Tweed in 2002. The market value of Scottish salmon angling is about £400 million. A beat with an average catch of 100 salmon a year might sell for around £600,000. Around 3,400 jobs (full-time equivalents) are dependent on Scottish salmon fishing and anglers add £70 million a year to the economy. In some areas – such as Orkney, the Tweed, Deeside and Speyside – salmon fishermen are an important part of local tourism. The main English and Welsh salmon rivers are the Tyne, Eden, Derwent, Usk and Wye.

Salmon fishing by rod catches fewer fish than salmon netting. Even into the twentieth century haaf netting for salmon was practised in several rivers, including those flowing into Morecambe Bay. More recently conventional netting is on a much bigger scale, either from the river bank (as on the Tweed) or as trawling offshore near river mouths. The number of salmon caught by net has fallen from around 80,000 a year in the mid-1980s to half that figure today. This purely commercial fishery has been hit hard by the fall in prices due to salmon farming. Several netting licences have been bought out recently by angling interests, mainly in north-east England and on the Tweed.

In the last thirty years the farming of salmon, mostly in north and west Scotland (Figure 5.4), has become the dominant source of supermarket salmon, along with Irish and Norwegian imports. In 1986 10,000 tonnes of salmon were farmed; this grew to 130,000 tonnes in 2000, which is 430 times the rod-caught harvest. Salmon prices have fallen (though rod-caught salmon commands a premium) and consumption has risen, so that what was an expensive, exclusive fish forty years ago is now less expensive than cod.

Fishing for trout tells a similar story. Declared rod catches of sea trout are around double those for salmon; netted sea trout catches have halved since the mid-1980s; and river fish face growing competition in the shops from farmed rainbow trout. Brown trout are caught widely in British rivers from the Hebrides to Hampshire, where a 1,400-metre trout beat might sell for £450,000.

River fishing is full of odd contrasts. Intensely commercial netting and fish farming interests sit alongside the lazy riverbank experience of the hobby fisherman. Fishing can be simple fun, or it can be the rough world of poachers versus water bailiffs and police. River fishing relies on a natural asset (the wild native fish), but intensive management is often used to increase the fish available, through restocking, riverbank management and water pollution controls. On some rivers the return of salmon and trout has served as an

indicator of the quickening recovery in river water quality, and nowhere more so than on the once heavily contaminated Thames and Mersey, where salmon were plentiful 200 years ago. On other rivers escapees from fish farms are blamed for the decline in wild fish stocks.

Improving the rivers

So far we have looked at the commercial uses to which the natural resources of British rivers have been put – the water and fish. In both cases managing the river can improve its value. Another obvious use of rivers is as highways for navigation and traffic, but this soon revealed the shortcomings of rivers in their natural state and the need for further improvements.

The Spey demonstrates the simplest way to use rivers for transport – from the sixteenth to the nineteenth centuries logs from the Strathspey forests were floated down to the river mouth, shepherded by men in coracles. More orthodox was the way in which Romans, Saxons and Vikings used rivers like the Severn and Trent to penetrate England for raiding missions and trade. However, British rivers are too short, meandering or shallow to form high-capacity inland waterways comparable to the Rhine or Danube. Yet on a lesser scale they were used extensively for transport because the economics were so compelling. A packhorse can carry 150 lbs and a carthorse may pull a tonne on a good level road, but when pulling a barge, a horse can move 30

Windermere in the English Lake District. C PARK

tonnes on a river and at least double that on a canal. In the eighteenth century it was cheaper to supply York with sea and river-borne coal from Newcastle, 320 km away, than from the West Yorkshire pits only 32 km by road. A few lakes – notably Windermere and Coniston – were important for navigation, too.

Although few places in England were more than 24 km from a navigable river, these did have serious drawbacks as a means of communication. The river might freeze in winter or have too little water in a dry summer. Meanders made haulage slow and a pilot might be needed to guide boats because shifting shoals were a danger (notably on the Trent). Fishing traps and weirs for mills could also hinder traffic. It became increasingly obvious that improving on the natural state of British rivers could improve their navigability. Straightening out the river channel would increase scour and make navigating gravel bars easier. Haulage would be simpler if a towpath were provided. From the fifteenth to the late eighteenth centuries numerous schemes were implemented to improve rivers for navigation, especially in their lower reaches – few major rivers remained in their natural state along their entire length. Probably the first improvement scheme approved by Parliament was on the River Lee in 1425; Elizabethan schemes took place on the Trent and in the seventeenth century the Thames, Warwickshire Avon and Wey were straightened and embanked. Of course legal authority was needed to rebuild a river and usually this was granted to a city corporation or the Commission of Sewers (basically the major riparian landowners). The Fens were a special case. Records at Ely show people using the waterways as their normal means of transport. And it was in the Fens that the biggest river remodelling took place as part of Vermuyden's plan to drain the marshes. The Nene, Welland and Great Ouse were all extensively 'rebuilt'. A common tactic was the 'cut', digging out a new river channel through or past a twisty section – on the Kennet and Waveney, for example, in the eighteenth century.

Not all such schemes were welcomed. For nearly a century, until 1720, Nottingham fiercely resisted Derby's plan to improve navigation on the Derwent, feeling this would have an adverse effect on the town's trade. Liverpool also vainly resisted schemes to improve navigability into Manchester in the eighteenth century, as the city was to do again over the Manchester Ship Canal in the late nineteenth century. The pace of change was rapid. Schemes on the Yorkshire Ouse, Trent, Dee and tributaries of the Severn added 440 km of extra navigable rivers between 1660 and 1700. Another 320 km had been opened up by 1730, mostly through schemes in northern England on the Weaver, Mersey, Douglas, Irwell and Don (Rolt 1950) (Figure 5.5). This northern shift reflected the emerging industrial economy of the region based on coal, ores, salt and brick clay, all of which benefited greatly from the cheapness of river transport. The greatest of the medieval rivers for traffic was the Severn, helped by a tidal limit well inland and numerous improvement schemes which extended navigation up as far as Shrewsbury and later Welshpool. The fact that the Severn was declared 'The King's High Stream' deterred the riverbank owners from crippling traffic by levying tolls (see also chapter 8). With these improvements rivers supported the carriage of coal from Newcastle to Cambridge, and of Cheshire cheese and Yorkshire butter to London. A partial nationwide transport network had been fashioned out of an unpromising drainage system, much to the benefit of traders and consumers.

Rivers and canals

The problem with relying on rivers (however 'improved') to provide a means of cheap transport is that one's journeys are limited to those directions in which the topography directs the rainfall to the sea. Canals (wholly artificial rivers) opened up the new routes that the merchants wanted between producers and customers. Not only that, but canals are straighter and more consistent in depth and water flow than rivers, which increases the efficiency of barge traffic. Canals are rivers designed by accountants. In many ways the canal network grew out of the river system and they are inextricably linked in terms of water supply, routes and traffic (Boughtey 1998). It is possible to identify four types of canal – spurs, parallels, linkages and free-standing. Spur canals are short canals leading off from a river to connect a port more effectively to the sea. Examples include the canals at Ulverston, Ripon, Aylesbury, St Helens, Driffield and Market Weighton. Many of these fell into disuse once the town's modest port trade dried up and today alternative leisure uses are limited because of their short length.

Parallel canals are those built alongside a river but which follow a different route, allowing commercial traffic on an otherwise un-improvable river route. Examples of parallel canals include the Sharpness Canal to Gloucester, the Bridgewater & Taunton, the Manchester Ship Canal, the Monmouth & Brecon, the Erewash, the Old and New Bedford Rivers on the Fens and the Aberdeenshire. In each case there was a clear demand for trade along the route but the river was incapable of taking large enough barges by virtue of its shallowness, natural obstructions or meanders.

The third type of canal, the linkages, includes some of the major engineering feats of the canal age. The problem with the British river network is that, by and large, the rivers flow from the higher heart of the country to the sea. This radial pattern makes it hard to use rivers to travel *across* Britain from coast to coast; somewhere in the middle of the country the rivers become too small to be navigable and then they stop because of some topographical barrier such as the Pennines. In the eighteenth century major schemes were

River and canal. A detail from an aerial panorama of Liverpool, *Illustrated London News*, 1865. On the far right can be seen the pair of warehouses flanking Stanley Dock (the only Liverpool dock excavated from the riverbank rather than built out into the estuary). Stanley Dock connected the main dock system on the river Mersey to the Leeds and Liverpool Canal, an extension of which can just be seen climbing landward via a short series of locks from Stanley Dock. The Liverpool terminus of the main canal was a mile or so to the right (south). The stretch of canal which can be seen running along the top of this image is just beginning its journey through the industrial heartland of Lancashire and across the Pennines as far as Leeds on the river Aire.

developed to link separate river systems by building a canal across their head-waters. The Kennet & Avon Canal (137 km) linked the navigable parts of the Thames at Reading and the Avon near Bristol. Numerous locks were needed to surmount the watershed. The Thames & Severn Canal (now disused) made a similar east–west link from the upper reaches of the Thames to the Severn near Stroud. In this case the watershed was dealt with by digging the Sapperton Tunnel (1789; 3482 m) under the Cotswolds. The Forth & Clyde Canal linked those rivers across the narrowest point of Scotland.

The final type is the free-standing canal. In this group the canal builders finally untied themselves from the rivers and built canals on routes they believed would be profitable. The Grand Union Canal linked London and Birmingham with a directness none of the rivers could match. The Leeds & Liverpool Canal linked the Mersey and the Aire, albeit by a circuitous route (203 km) and with locks and two tunnels to get up over the Pennines. This had never previously been possible, yet northern industrialisation was creating new traffic. In Scotland, the Crinan and Caledonian Canals were similarly new routes.

The development of the canals was an important part of British history (Hadfield 1981). They emerged from the uncoordinated activities of

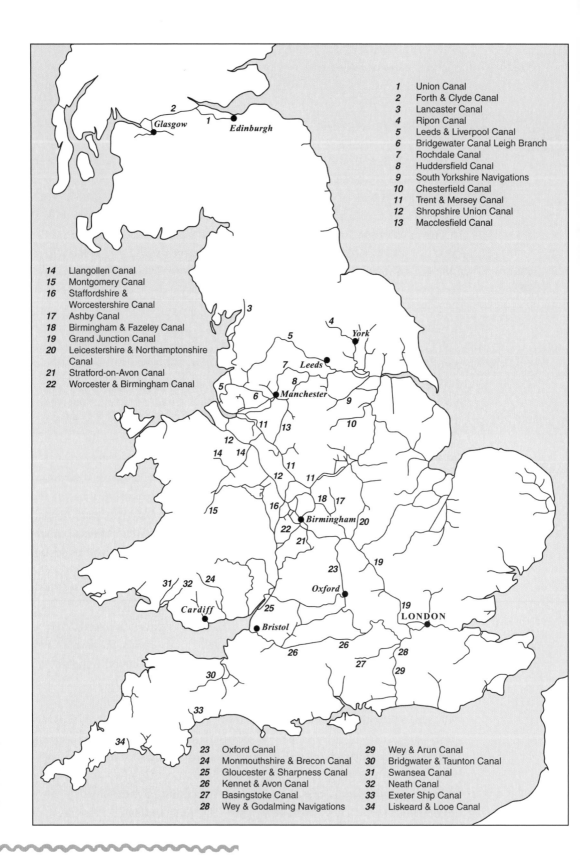

1 Union Canal
2 Forth & Clyde Canal
3 Lancaster Canal
4 Ripon Canal
5 Leeds & Liverpool Canal
6 Bridgewater Canal Leigh Branch
7 Rochdale Canal
8 Huddersfield Canal
9 South Yorkshire Navigations
10 Chesterfield Canal
11 Trent & Mersey Canal
12 Shropshire Union Canal
13 Macclesfield Canal

14 Llangollen Canal
15 Montgomery Canal
16 Staffordshire & Worcestershire Canal
17 Ashby Canal
18 Birmingham & Fazeley Canal
19 Grand Junction Canal
20 Leicestershire & Northamptonshire Canal
21 Stratford-on-Avon Canal
22 Worcester & Birmingham Canal

23 Oxford Canal
24 Monmouthshire & Brecon Canal
25 Gloucester & Sharpness Canal
26 Kennet & Avon Canal
27 Basingstoke Canal
28 Wey & Godalming Navigations

29 Wey & Arun Canal
30 Bridgwater & Taunton Canal
31 Swansea Canal
32 Neath Canal
33 Exeter Ship Canal
34 Liskeard & Looe Canal

numerous independent companies and investors. Yet they created a national inland waterway system of canals and improved rivers which allowed un-interrupted barge traffic anywhere between the Thames and Lancashire/ Yorkshire with the ports of Hull, London, Bristol and Liverpool forming the four corners of an 'inland waterway box' of canals and rivers. By 1830 the canals and rivers in the core of Great Britain matched the roads – they were a network. Of the seventy largest British cities by 1841, only Luton had no river or canal links to the sea (Figure 5.6).

It is interesting how quickly this system emerged. The earliest British canal was probably the Fossdyke Navigation, built by the Romans in AD 120 to link the River Witham to the Trent, and the Exeter Canal dates from 1563/67. However, most of the canals were built in just seventy years between about 1760 and 1830. The Sankey Canal from St Helens to Wigan spearheaded the modern canal era in 1755. Growing industrialisation created a rising demand for bulk traffic around Britain; road transport could double the cost of such products after just 20 km. This was the heyday of canal investment and in the 1790s 'canal mania' gripped investors – no fewer than 81 Acts of Parliament authorising new canals were passed between 1791 and 1794. Of the 163 Canal Acts between 1758 and 1803, 90 were principally to serve collieries and another 47 for ore and metal traffic. These canals lubricated the early Industrial Revolution. They were also a significant source of temporary employment during their construction – this is the era of the 'navvy' (navigator) travelling the country between canal sites. Canals employed large numbers working the barges and at inland ports such as Wigan, Manchester,

Caen Hill Locks on the Kennet & Avon Canal.
BRITISH WATERWAYS
PHOTOLIBRARY

A drawing of Chisenhale Street bridge on the Leeds and Liverpool Canal in 1802.

LRO, DP 175, REPRODUCED BY PERMISSION OF THE COUNTY ARCHIVIST, LANCASHIRE RECORD OFFICE

Selby, Stourport and Birmingham. In 1841 about two per cent of UK employment was associated with the 6,832 km of canals and improved river navigations.

Nonetheless, the canals had their limitations. They offered improved transport compared with the roads, but only up to a point. The speed of movement was limited to around 6 kph in order to prevent erosion of the banks. Lack of water in the Midlands meant that the canals there were narrow, especially at the 7-foot (2.13m) wide bridges and locks. Since the Midland canals were at the heart of the system, only narrow boats of limited freight capacity could participate in national canal trade. The lack of a standard gauge for canals among their builders was a serious flaw, and one which most of the future railway companies were to heed. Journey times were lengthened by the slowness of passage through locks. The Grand Union Canal has 159 locks between London and Birmingham via Blisworth; London to Avonmouth has 125; and the Leeds & Liverpool 147. Tunnels could avoid the need for locks but, if only one boat wide (which was cheaper to build), this again slowed traffic. Building the canal along the contour of the land was sometimes an option for avoiding locks, but the penalty, as on the Lancaster Canal, was a circuitous route round the hills. Passage through a flight of locks could be designed for one-man operation, but in many cases locks required two people, which raised crewing costs and freight rates. The canal system was a huge improvement but its weaknesses show why, when the railways came, they rapidly came to dominate freight traffic with their far greater speed, loads and geographical coverage.

The canals of Britain have left us a major architectural and engineering legacy. The five-kilometre long Standedge Tunnel (1811) took 16 years to build but in its day was one of the longest tunnels in the world. The flight of locks at Bingley on the Leeds & Liverpool is much photographed. The aqueduct at Pontcysyllte on the Llangollen Canal is an amazing experience to cross, while the Caledonian Canal, one of very few canal projects to be publicly financed over its 19-year construction period, was notable for the size of vessels that could use it.

Finally we have to note that the last century of the canals has been one of decline and then renaissance. By 1888 only eleven canal companies were regularly profitable because trade had been captured by rail and then road. In fact few canals regularly paid dividends much greater than the 4–5 per cent available from a savings account. Canals closed and became derelict; tunnels collapsed; locks rotted; and the new motorways severed the canals. The nationalisation of most of the canals under the Transport Act of 1947 was really a process of managed retreat (see Appendix 8). Yet the formation of the Inland Waterways Association in 1946 and the River Avon restoration trust in 1952 heralded the campaigning groups who sought to revitalise the canals both for their intrinsic preservation value and as leisure facilities. The advent of EU, Lottery and local authority funds since the 1980s has allowed the British Waterways Board to accelerate the process of restoration (see www.britishwaterways.co.uk). Notable highlights are the partial or complete re-opening of the Kennet & Avon Canal, the Forth & Clyde and Union Canals, the Rochdale and the Huddersfield Narrow. The Lancaster Canal is now directly linked to the national network for the first time. The Anderton Boat Lift near Northwich has been restored and the stunning new Falkirk Wheel links the Scottish canals in as innovative a piece of engineering as any seen in the canal era.

Today the canals, and the rivers with which they link, are again vibrant (Figure 5.7). Property development by British Waterways on urban canal-side sites is fuelling repairs and enhancements to the system. There are 100,000 registered canal anglers, 25,000 registered boat owners, innumerable walkers and cyclists, and a fibre-optic IT network under the towpaths links the major cities as the barges did 200 years ago.

The canals grew because of the inadequacy of much of the natural river systems for freight traffic and the canal system is inextricably linked with the rivers and their ports. Today one can still travel almost seamlessly from river to canal and eventually to a port.

The Falkirk Wheel. Stunning design and clever engineering link the boats on canals at two levels, the canals themselves having been reopened fully to traffic. The Wheel is itself a major visitor attraction for this part of central Scotland.

Rivers as ports

Ports do not have to be at the mouth of a river (witness Dover and Holyhead) but most British ports are. A river mouth provides sheltered anchorage from the sea without the need for costly breakwaters, and smaller ships can progress upstream well inland, as the Romans and Vikings did in their shallow-draught boats up the Ouse to York, for example. The simplest river ports saw ships at anchor mid-channel with goods ferried ashore by small

right Figure 5.7. Major inland navigable waterways, *c.*1999.
(AFTER ROBERTS, 1999)

Major Inland Waterways

Inverness

Fort William

Glasgow

EDINBURGH

N

Lancaster

Ripon

York

Kingston upon Hull

Preston

Leeds

Manchester

Doncaster

Liverpool

Sheffield

Lincoln

Chester

Nottingham

Llangollen

Stoke-on-Trent

Welshpool

Leicester

King's Lynn

Norwich

Peterborough

Birmingham

Coventry

Northampton

Cambridge

Worcester

Bedford

Brecon

Oxford

Bishop's Stortford

Swansea

Pontypool

Bristol

LONDON

Bath

Newbury

Reading

Maidstone

Guildford

Tonbridge

Bridgwater

Taunton

0 20 40 60 80 100 km

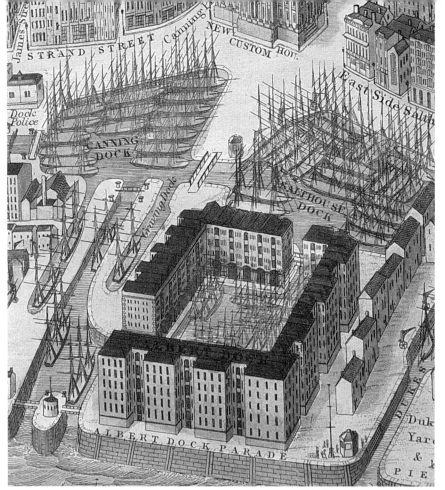

Albert Dock, Liverpool, built in 1845 by Jesse Hartley, Chief Engineer to the Port of Liverpool from 1824 to 1860, from an aerial view of Liverpool by Ackermann, 1847.

boats or porters – Aberdeen's Shore Porters' Society (1498) is the oldest firm in the UK. Even today many a small river will have a modest port for a fishing fleet, some coastal traffic in timber or fertiliser and some pleasure craft; Eyemouth and Berwick-upon-Tweed are examples straddling the Scotland/England border.

The next stage saw the building of quays along the riverbank so that loading could be directly from ship to shore. Close by, warehouses of ever more storeys and area would store goods, protected from weather and thieves. As ships got bigger, the water depth along the quay became inadequate to keep the ships afloat at all states of the tide, so new ports were developed even closer to the river mouth, as happened at Port Glasgow on the Clyde and with Glasson Dock on the Lune below Lancaster. Eventually ports were built well down the estuary, like Tilbury, Avonmouth and Immingham. If migration downstream still yielded inadequate depth or the quays became congested, a solution was to build a dock (fed by river water) which maintained a constant water depth irrespective of the tide or river flow – Blackwall (1661) on the Thames was probably the first wet dock in the UK and Liverpool got its first in 1715. The disadvantage of the dock is that access might be restricted to the hours around the twice-daily high tide. Docks, of course, are major feats of engineering which only the wealthiest ports or investors could afford. A secure future for trade would be needed to justify such an investment. This could be based on a multitude of trades (as at Liverpool and London) or focused on a key commodity such as cotton to Salford Docks (56 km) up the Manchester Ship Canal (1894) or coal at Cardiff.

While the nineteenth century saw new ports established and older ones expanded, it also witnessed the final demise of many up-stream ports such as Chester on the Dee, Gainsborough on the Trent, and Beverley on the Hull. Larger ships and silting of the river removed their trade. Other 'lost river ports' declined when their key cargo ceased, such as at Laxey when the Manx lead mines closed.

Although the early river ports were small operations, by 1900 the largest ports had totally transformed their river mouths. Eventually the Liverpool docks extended for 17 km along the right bank of the Mersey, with 43 km of quay frontage. Dock buildings like Liverpool's Albert Dock (1845), or London's West India Dock (1802) and St Katherine's Dock (1826/28) were major pioneering structures. Trade grew rapidly in the free-trade Victorian era as industrial production grew by 20–30 per cent each decade throughout the nineteenth century. The national economy was 3.4 times bigger in 1901 than in 1841, and the UK population increased from 16 million to 41.5 million between 1801 and 1901. Raw materials flooded in for the textile industries, as did ores and foods, while coal, fish and finished manufactures sailed out. Initially the Irish and North Sea trades were dominant; the trans-Atlantic and Imperial trades followed. The flows through each port reflected the industries ashore and gave the town some of its character (as, for example, the tobacco trade in Glasgow or coal trade in Whitehaven). This would be reinforced by the processing of imported goods in the town – cotton goods in the Manchester area, Gillow furniture from hardwoods imported through Lancaster, refining sugar in Liverpool, flour milling in Gateshead. Then the road and rail operators who served the port would be joined by ship repairers and shipping companies who owned local fleets (like the Cunard, Harrison and Ellerman Lines in Liverpool or Denholm in Glasgow). Taken overall, the port and its ancillary activities created a wealth of jobs (skilled and unskilled) which stimulated terraced house building and the general growth of population in Newcastle, Sunderland, Hull, Liverpool, Glasgow, London and many other cities. It is fitting that with so many people earning a living from port freight, the river ports of Britain were perhaps the last part of the country seen by British emigrants to the New World and Australia. And the Thames was probably the first part of Britain sighted by East European immigrants in the nineteenth century and Caribbean ones after the Second World War (the MV *Windrush* – named after a river – docked at Tilbury in 1948). River ports were one of the key growth areas of British cities throughout the nineteenth and early twentieth centuries.

After about 1960 two very significant changes took place in the ports which had then been repaired after their heavy wartime bombing. The use of, first, pallets and then containers massively increased labour productivity in cargo handling (not to mention reducing pilfering), so five or ten crane operators could move the tonnage previously requiring a hundred stevedores. The large container ships (and the ever-larger bulk carriers of oil and ores) outgrew the Victorian ports and new container ports sprang up at Seaforth, Greenock, Felixstowe, Tilbury and Southampton – nearly all estuary ports rather than river ones. New oil terminals were developed at Stanlow (the Mersey), Fawley (the Solent) and Hound Point (the Forth) (Appendix 8). Old docks and warehouses became redundant for trade – they will re-appear later in our story as a new type of riverside resource.

The second change, which accelerated in the 1960s, was the realignment of UK trade patterns from the Americas and Commonwealth to a uniting Europe. The ports with the highest growth rates were situated on the east coast, particularly in the booming economy of the South East. In 1965 the five largest UK ports in terms of tonnage were London, Liverpool, Milford Haven (oil imports), Southampton and the Medway ports. By 2001 the five largest were Grimsby and Immingham, Tees and Hartlepool, London, the Forth ports and Southampton (Department of Transport, annual). Felixstowe was the largest container port and Dover the largest road vehicle shipping port. Not surprisingly the Mersey Docks and Harbour Company now owns Sheerness and Chatham in order to tap into this east-coast trade. Europe-wide firms are concentrating production on one or two pan-European factories with consequently ever-longer distribution hauls across the transparent frontiers of the EU. The east-coast ports are well placed to handle these cargoes. In effect the major river-mouth ports for UK trade are now Europoort on the Rhine/Waal and Antwerp on the Schelde, with smaller feeder vessels running back and forth to the UK ports.

River mouths were not only the basis of ports; many also developed shipbuilding industries, which developed out of chandlery and repair work. Most rivers had a firm making dinghies or fishing boats, but the real concentrations were on the Thames, which was soon overtaken in the late nineteenth century by the yards on the Mersey, Clyde, Tyne and Tees. River mouths allowed spectacular launches of naval or merchant vessels yet were sufficiently sheltered so that ships could be fitted out after launching. Up to the 1960s shipyards dominated these river mouths both in terms of the skyline and the multiplicity of skills in the shipbuilding and support trades.

All in all, the mouths of British rivers were dynamic economies providing a livelihood for many families and the basis for urban expansion. All this was achieved only by repeated investment to transform river mouths into reliable deep-water channels.

Rivers as barriers

So far in this chapter we have looked at rivers as routes – long thin channels for the flow of water, fish and boats between their source and the sea. Looked at another way, every river is also a barrier to communication; how to get to the other side of a river is a problem that needs to be solved.

The simplest solution is the ford – you wade, ride or drive across at a point where the river is shallow enough to permit this in safety. Fords were previously found even quite far downstream when rivers were much wider and shallower at low tides than they are today. There was a Roman ford across the Trent at Littleborough and perhaps one on the Thames at Westminster. Centuries of embanking have tended to make rivers narrower as they pass through cities, deepening them to the point where fording is now impossible.

People and cargo can be shuttled back and forth across a river by a ferry, preferably flat decked and 'roll on, roll off', which can be of a size and with a frequency of crossing to suit the traffic. Several river ferries were found across the Forth from Fife to Edinburgh before the Kincardine and Forth road bridges were built, and also across the Thames. They can still be found in Liverpool as *The Ferry Across the Mersey*, across the Fal estuary, at Plymouth and Dartmouth, at Felixstowe across the Orwell and Stour, and across the Clyde to Dunoon. The weakness comes when road traffic exceeds ferry capacity; then delays may become lengthy.

The high capacity solution for a river crossing is a bridge. The one-horse-wide packhorse bridge was easy to build. The Romans built many wider bridges – examples include those over the Thames close to the present London Bridge, one at Newcastle and another over the Tees at Piercebridge. A bridge over a narrow river is technically simple once you have mastered the stone or brick arch – the early medieval wooden bridges tended to be washed away by rivers in spate, so stone or brick were preferred.

By the eighteenth century, flat-surfaced arched bridges had been developed, e.g. Skerton Bridge over the Lune at Lancaster (1788) and, most impressively, Brunel's bridge over the Thames at Maidenhead (1838) which has a very long flat-arch design which crosses the river in a single span. If the river is wider than the arch, then the bridge can be made long enough by a sequence of arches. This creates a road crossing but at the expense of impeding navigation – none but the smallest vessels will be able to pass through the narrow and low bridge arches. The multi-arched bridge is really only feasible where the river is shallow enough to allow the construction of the numerous bridge piers. The development of the railways in the nineteenth century increased the need for long flat-surfaced viaducts over rivers and valleys.

Maintaining river traffic under a bridge was a serious problem. A city on a river needs bridges, yet if the city's wharves and other ports are upstream, how can one allow ships to pass? An expensive solution, used at Carlisle Bridge (Lancaster), the Menai Straits Bridge and recently at the Queen Elizabeth II Bridge over the Thames at Dartford, is to build a very tall bridge with a single broad span across the river itself so that even tall-masted ships can get to the quays upstream. The transporter bridge – there was one across the Mersey at Runcorn and still is one over the Tees at Middlesbrough (1911) – solved the problem by suspending a short section of roadway from a very high steel framework. The transporter road section shuttles back and forth when there are no ships passing, and the bridge structure is high enough not to impede navigation. The limitation is its low carrying capacity; as traffic increases, the queues become intolerable. The vertical-lift bridge (again one over the Tees at Middlesbrough and another recently at Salford Quays) simply hoists the whole road section upwards for a ship to pass.

The bascule bridge and swing bridge are effective compromises. In a bascule bridge (London's Tower Bridge, 1894, is the best known example) the road deck has a counterweight at one end and can be swung up till the roadway is vertical. A tall ship can then pass through, and at all other times the road is open to traffic. The swing bridge – Kincardine Bridge (1936) across the Forth is the biggest and the one at Newcastle (1876) is on the line of the Roman bridge – solves the problem by pivoting the road at its central point in the middle of the river. When a ship needs to pass, the bridge is swung through 90° until it lies parallel with the river, leaving room for the ship to proceed.

None of these types of bridge can cope with a deep river. Ferries lack road-traffic capacity and are slow. Many bridges restrict the size of vessels that can pass under the bridge. Crucial events were the development of the motorway network, the growth in road traffic and the need to avoid lengthy detours upriver to the lowest bridging point (Goole on the Humber, Kincardine on the Forth, and Gloucester on the Severn). Britain needed estuary rather than river bridges, which could cross deep, broad channels in a single span while allowing sea-going vessels to pass beneath. The problem was first tackled on the Tay with a technically simple, multi-arched rail bridge – the boats on the Tay were quite small. The bridge's collapse in a storm in 1879 reminded bridge designers of the extent to which estuaries were subject to far stormier conditions than urban bridges. The Forth Rail Bridge (1890) solved the problem by using a massive three-cantilever structure. But from the 1960s the dominant technology for estuary bridges has been the suspension bridge which uses cables, supported by towers on or near the river banks which are tall enough to keep the roadway suspended far above the waters so ships can pass. Early British examples were a wrought-iron suspension bridge over the Tweed as early as 1741 and Telford's suspension bridges at Conwy and Menai Straits in the 1820s. Britain pioneered improvements to suspension bridge technology with the Forth Road Bridge (1964), the first Severn Bridge (1966) and the Humber Bridge (1981) (Figure 5.8). With a central span of 1410m the Humber bridge was the largest in the world when it was opened and is still the third longest. The cable-stayed design used for the second Severn road bridge (1996) and the Queen Elizabeth II Bridge at Dartford (1991) also allows long central spans for busy estuaries.

An alternative way of crossing British rivers is through a tunnel. This is the favoured method of crossing the Thames for the London underground and has been used at the Blackwall, Rotherhithe and Dartford road tunnels. Pedestrian-only tunnels are found at Greenwich and Woolwich (which also has one of the two remaining ferry crossings on the Thames). Tunnels are also found under the Tyne at Jarrow, and twice for road and once for trains under the Mersey between Liverpool and Birkenhead. The Severn tunnel (1886) is the best known mainline railway under a major river estuary. The second phase of the Channel Tunnel Rail Link will use a new rail tunnel under the Thames to reach St Pancras. Around £200 million a year is charged in tolls for bridges, tunnels and ferries. The biggest concentrations of river crossings are where an urban area straddles a river. There are no fewer than 47 crossings of the Thames between Kew and the North Sea (Table 5.1). A huge amount of investment is needed to cross a major river flowing through a large city like London.

Figure 5.8. Comparative lengths of British tunnels and bridges.

DEPARTMENT OF GEOGRAPHY, LANCASTER UNIVERSITY

The final type of river crossing is the flood barrage. The one across the Thames at Woolwich is the largest of its type in the world. A much smaller one is found where the River Hull joins the Humber. Both were built to

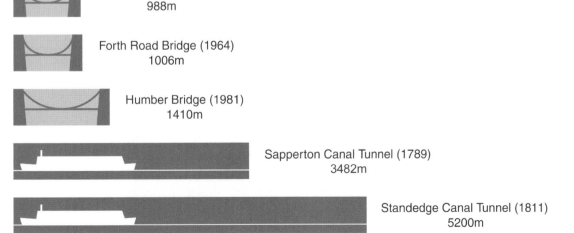

1st Severn Bridge (1966)
988m

Forth Road Bridge (1964)
1006m

Humber Bridge (1981)
1410m

Sapperton Canal Tunnel (1789)
3482m

Standedge Canal Tunnel (1811)
5200m

Table 5.1: Thames crossings by type and mode below Kew*

	Tube	Rail	Foot†	Road
Tunnel	10	2‡	2	4
Bridge	2	6	2	17
Ferry*				2

* Excludes ferries *along* the Thames
† Pedestrian-only bridges and tunnels
‡ Includes the Channel Tunnel Rail Link under construction in 2003

protect the valuable real estate of a major city from catastrophic flooding when spring high tides, low air pressure and high winds can combine to push a 'storm surge' up the river from the open sea. The 1953 storm surge on the east coast killed 307 people. The fact that south-eastern Britain has been slowly sinking since the end of the last glaciation (independently of any sea-level rise due to global warming) makes such flood defences all the more timely.

Getting across rivers has always been a financial and engineering challenge. Fortunately, solving this problem has produced some major advances in bridge design which have enhanced the skyline. Examples include the railway bridge at Berwick-upon-Tweed, Derby's Ironbridge at Coalbrookdale, the 'coathanger' bridge at Newcastle-upon-Tyne, Tower Bridge and the Forth Rail Bridge. The celebration of the Millennium saw National Lottery money used

Gateshead Millennium Bridge over the River Tyne, Newcastle. This bridge – the world's first rotating bridge – opens like a blinking eyelid, which tilts the whole structure upwards and away from the river, to allow the passage of ships. It is the first opening bridge to be built on the Tyne in over a century and cost £22 million to build. The main structure was fabricated off-site and lifted into place by one of the world's largest floating cranes, Hercules II. The bridge links Newcastle Quayside, on the north bank of the Tyne with Gateshead Quays on the south bank, which in recent years has undergone a major renaissance with the development of buildings such as the Baltic Centre for Contemporary Art.
C. PARK

to create some new pedestrian-only bridges which seemed destined to become architectural icons, notably the Millennium Bridge between St Paul's and the Tate Modern Gallery in London, the Gateshead Millennium Bridge and the one over the Lune at Lancaster.

At leisure on the river

Strolling across the bridge or messing about on boats are fine dreams. The angler, birdwatcher, casual stroller and dog walker can watch the canoeing and boating. With freight traffic now a rarity on most rivers and canals in

Punting on the River Cam at Cambridge.
© FOTOGENIX.CO.UK

Britain, their main function is for leisure. Measuring how much use is made of rivers for pastimes is difficult. So much is informal, unregulated and not recorded – people just 'doing their thing'. You cannot continually survey 8,640 km of navigable waterways, but sample surveys do indicate the scale of activities. Some 10 million people make 160 million visits to a British Waterways' river or canal each year. No fewer than 100,000 boats are licensed for use on canals and in total around 2 million boats are owned. Over a million anglers are licensed with the Environment Agency and perhaps two or three times that number fish on an occasional basis.

Angling is arguably Britain's most popular sport, apart from walking in the countryside. Motorboats are common on the broader rivers and canals, the Norfolk Broads especially. Rivers like the Thames, Trent, Ouse and Lune attract rowers and the National Water Sports Centre at Holme Pierrepoint near Nottingham is an extension of the Trent for rowers and canoeists. For the latter, quiet canals and rivers provide a good training ground, but the white waters of fast streams in the mountains are the real challenge. Gorge walking and gill scrambling, where you climb up and abseil down waterfalls, similarly test one's nerve. The bigger waterfalls, like the Aysgarth (Yorkshire), Grey Mare's Tail (Dumfriesshire) and Corrieshalloch (Ross & Cromarty) are small by world standards but impressive enough to be much visited and photographed by tourists. Photographers can find much to capture as light plays on the water and the spray generates small rainbows. Long-distance footpaths along the Thames and Severn and urban riverside walks along the Mersey, Tyne and Clyde have opened up the riverbank to the casual stroller and the serious rambler alike. Sometimes they will see classic spectacles, like the Boat Race or punting on the Cam. There is the chance of a lucky glimpse of yellow iris, dragonflies or the flash of a kingfisher hunting. It is not surprising that eight per cent of rivers are protected as Sites of Special Scientific Interest. Rising water quality and the decline of heavy industry have allowed nature to flourish along many a riverbank, even where staithes once loaded coal barges or outfalls discharged effluent.

The popularity of rivers has never been greater. About three per cent of day leisure visits make some use of inland water (often near people's homes) and a similar percentage of the population regularly participates in a water-based sport or recreation, often travelling considerable distances. At times these activities co-exist less than harmoniously. The anglers may object to the rowers and canoeists disturbing the fish, as on the Wye. The water-skiers may be a threat to the swimmers and rowers and may annoy walkers seeking tranquillity. The sheer number of canal boats on the popular stretches can cause delays, and the popularity of the Norfolk Broads may harm the river ecosystem and undermine people's enjoyment of the area. Despite 200 km of navigable rivers and broads – the broads are lakes formed when medieval peat workings were flooded – a million visitors and 5,100 boats can cause queues and pollution which are far from *The Wind in the Willows* image of boating. Yet the economic power of holidaying on the Broads (3,000 jobs and £147 million a year turnover) has encouraged a complex management plan to be developed. Areas are cordoned off for repair, sewage and oil discharges are controlled and access to sensitive areas for wildlife is restricted. British rivers are now a major recreational resource for many people throughout the country. That poses challenges – between different activities and different interest groups – and also offers great opportunities for development, as the next section shows.

Riverside development

In their natural state lowland rivers tend to have low, marshy or tidal fringes; in cities this creates difficulties. Bridges have to be longer; you cannot build close to the river without the danger of flooding; loading boats is slow. It is far better to encroach on the river and build artificial embankments to clearly separate the river from the city. Such embankments could include a riverside road, built high enough above the water to stop flooding inland. An embankment can also operate as a quay alongside which warehouses can be built to store goods. With enough money to invest in embanking, riverside properties can become valuable real estate. From fish processors next to the fishing quays to flour and sugar mills by the docks, processing, storing and trading in goods has long been a key activity in ports.

Building a port is easier if the breakwaters, quays and docks are built out into the deeper water of the river channel. The London docks were excavated from marshland; those at Leith, Avonmouth and Immingham by pushing out into the estuary, as were those at Southampton and Felixstowe. The Liverpool docks were constructed out into the Mersey channel, to the extent that between Pier Head and Birkenhead, the Mersey was narrowed on both banks by about 500 metres, leaving the river nearly a third narrower than it originally was at this point. Such narrowing by riverbank development makes the river flow more quickly and leads to greater susceptibility to flooding unless embankment walls are raised high enough. In London the Thames was constricted upstream of the docks by the embankments from Battersea to Blackfriars. At the Victoria Embankment 15 hectares was gained from the river to provide space for the new London Main Drain and Underground lines in the 1860s and 1870s.

In the last fifty years the vast areas of docklands and associated industrial sites made redundant by the growth of container ports has opened up urban redevelopment sites. Those in London (with large docks and intense property pressures) are the most spectacular. Using the London Dockland

The meandering Black Water, tributary of the Water of Ken, Dumfries and Galloway.
S. OWEN

Development Corporation to unify landownership, a master plan for offices, hotels, apartments, public space and London City Airport was drawn up, with the Docklands Light Railway and Jubilee Line to provide increased accessibility to the City. Between 1993 and 2002 the workforce at Canary Wharf grew from 7,000 to 55,000 – almost as many jobs as were lost in the area during the 1960s and 1970s. However, the character of the new jobs is very different from those that preceded them and such areas have changed from working-class to gentrified; from manual work to office and professional occupations; from traditional East End to global financial centre; from cheap terraced house to upmarket apartment. The river that was a working highway has become a desirable backdrop to rooms with a view.

In other cities the transformations have been smaller in scale but similar in style. The Albert Dock in Liverpool has flats, shops and museums. Hull too has a museum (The Deep) while the Royal Yacht *Britannia* is the centrepiece of Leith Dock's redevelopments. Former naval port areas in Chatham and Portsmouth have similarly gone upmarket. Even small ports like Whitehaven, Hartlepool and Lancaster have seen riverside regeneration. At Swansea and Cardiff the barrages have improved the outlook (from tidal mudflats to perpetual bay). Riverside walkways have become commonplace, opening up formerly private land into safe, attractive, public spaces. Tree planting, seating and public art are often found and with information boards to help guide visitors along the riverside. The cleaner water, and the possibilities of seeing fish or even otters (now reported on the Tyne at Newcastle), make these attractive places to stroll. These previously functional areas have become places of vistas, the picturesque and even of spectacle.

Riversides are (and always have been) prime areas for key, even iconic buildings. The Houses of Parliament and the Liver Building are obvious Victorian examples. Recently the Scottish Exhibition Centre by the Clyde and the Baltic Centre for Contemporary Art at Gateshead have continued this tradition of important public buildings on the riverside. The redevelopment of urban

Royal Dockland,
London, 1955.
© SIMMONS AEROFILMS

canal-side sites tells a similar story, notably in central Birmingham, Gloucester, Nottingham and the Port Hamilton financial district in Edinburgh. Paddington Basin in west London could be the next 'hot spot'. The Salford Quays development at the east end of the Manchester Ship Canal has spearheaded the renaissance of the whole city, with new museums (the Lowry and the Imperial War Museum North), shops, offices and flats. Overall the former dockland river sites in many British cities are being transformed into areas of cultural interest and economic regeneration.

London City Airport. This photograph shows the rapid transformation from an area of ship berths and cargo handling seen on the previous page to one with an airport, new housing and offices.
© SIMMONS AEROFILMS

CHAPTER 6 # Rivers as a cultural resource

Colin Pooley

Introduction

Most people in Britain live or work within at least a few kilometres of a river or stream, and the presence of water in the landscape plays a major role in how we develop associations with place. Although rivers are likely to be a much stronger landscape feature in rural than in urban areas – and it can be argued that rivers form a key element in the classic image of a rural idyll – many cities are also strongly defined by the river which flows through them: Glasgow and the Clyde; Liverpool and the Mersey; London and the Thames. This chapter examines the place of rivers in British landscapes and town-scapes, assesses the contribution of such landscapes to the evolution of national and regional identities, and explores ways in which rivers contribute to the construction of both individual and collective cultural identities within Britain.

Association with place is a central theme of this chapter, and it is suggested that to some degree we are all shaped by the places in which we have lived and with which we associate. Most readers could probably create a personal biography of their identity with place in which rivers and streams form an important part. This can be illustrated by a brief, generalised account of this author's residential history.

I was born and lived until the age of ten in the flat and featureless fenlands of Eastern England. This was the landscape and culture depicted so effectively in Graham Swift's *Waterland*: a landscape of open spaces filled with rich agri-cultural land divided by a dense network of rivers and dykes. Some were entirely artificial, and most had been strongly influenced by human activity through drainage of the Fenlands. They formed a regular network of land-scape features on the doorstep of a child growing up in rural eastern England. Very early memories include fishing for minnows and sticklebacks with a net and jam jar in a local stream, exploring the fields and dykes around the village, and, of course, falling in the water and returning home covered in oozing mud. Exploration of and contact with water were key elements of the process of learning through play and exploration as a child growing up in Fenland England. Some activities were more structured. I recall frequent fishing trips with my father to the larger rivers and drains. We would sit for hours on the usually grey riverbank catching perch, tench, bream, eels and occasionally pike. We would weigh our catch at the end of the day before returning it to the water. At the age of eight such activities seemed very grown up, giving both power and responsibility to the young fisherman. It could be argued that such association with the landscape through rivers aided the transition from childhood to adolescence.

From the age of eleven I lived, first, just outside and then in a small market town in the East Midlands. This period coincided with growing independence and the ability to explore beyond the immediate locality. Rivers and streams continued to play an important role in everyday life. One house in which we lived had a long garden with a stream at the bottom. The stream formed both a barrier which had to be crossed to reach the open fields that I explored and in which I created imaginary kingdoms, but also a focus for activity in its own right. At various times the stream was dammed, bridged, excavated, defended and manipulated in a variety of ways. Rivers form one of the most creative

A view of The Wash, Gedney Drove End in the Lincolnshire Fens. Water is an important feature of the flat fenland landscape. Rivers and dykes add variety to the landscape as well as providing essential drainage, forming routes for water-based transport, and the sites for leisure activities.

FENS TOURISM GROUP

natural environments for childhood play. I attended secondary school in the nearby town, and most lunch times I went with friends to the local park to talk and pass the time. A moderately large river flowed through the park and, again, this often became the centre of activity. On frosty winter days we would tentatively test the ice, often ending up with wet feet; herd the stranded ducks by lobbing small stones at them; or crash through the ice with large bricks or logs scavenged from the parkland. On lazy summer days we might play 'Poohsticks', racing pieces of wood between the bridges, or simply lie by the relaxing water in the sun. At times the park would be the site of conflict between rival groups of boys from different schools. Then, the river could become a barrier behind which we might retreat as each group established a degree of territoriality.

I attended university in Liverpool, my first encounter with a large city. While the choice of destination was in part determined by the quality of the academic course, Liverpool as a city was attractive both because of its reputation as a centre of popular culture in the late 1960s, and by its urban form structured around the Mersey. Liverpool's cultural identity was, and still is, strongly linked to the river and the waterfront. Through my adolescence the dominance of the 'Mersey Sound' in popular music and the vibrancy which

The Crook of Lune near Lancaster. This large meander loop in the river Lune has long attracted attention. Turner painted a well-known view of the Lune valley from here and today it provides a well-used picnic site, leisure area and start for riverside walks.

PAUL MULLINEAUX

the city projected made it an attractive destination. This was reinforced by first-hand experience of the majestic waterfront, and of a growing realisation, through academic study and personal experience, of the role of the Mersey in the creation of the city's distinctive past and present. Long before the redevelopment of the Albert Dock complex as a tourist destination, the Mersey waterfront was a focus for leisure and recreation as well as a (declining) source of employment and a continued focus for political protest. In an age of student protest most marches started or ended at Pier Head.

For most of my adult life I have lived in or near the small university city of Lancaster in North Lancashire. Like Liverpool, this too is a city focused around the river which flows through its heart. The Lune forms both a focus for activity, with an attractive waterfront and striking new Millennium pedestrian bridge, but the river also acts as a barrier, with the two road cross-ings frequently congested and contributing significantly to Lancaster's perceived traffic problems. However, the Lune is undoubtedly a key feature of the townscape and is one of the factors that made Lancaster an attractive place for me to live. In the countryside around Lancaster the Lune forms an important landscape feature and recreational resource. From my current home I look out across the Lune valley and can observe its daily moods; its rapid regime changes, as after heavy rain when the river can rise quickly and cover the entire flood plain; the wild fowl that fly along the river; and the agri-cultural activity taking place on its banks. It is central to the economic, social and cultural life of the surrounding countryside, and observation of the state of the river and activities related to it form a regular part of the weekday rhythm of my journey to work.

There is nothing in the least remarkable about the above story, but that is precisely why it is important. Although most of the time our association with landscape, and with the streams and rivers which form an essential part of both rural and urban areas, is taken for granted, we can probably all relate similar experiences and senses of association with water in landscapes and townscapes. It is precisely these images and associations that this chapter now explores in more detail.

We begin by looking at the nature and meaning of culture, focusing on the development of cultural identities within Britain and the role played by land-scape (and especially rivers) in this process. These themes are illustrated by case studies which examine the ways in which rivers influence both individual and collective daily lives. We then explore the role of rivers in the British creative arts, focusing on the representation of rivers in novels, poetry, art and music, and assessing their contribution to the creation of a distinctive British culture. Finally, the chapter examines the significance of rivers for contempo-rary belief systems, and concludes by assessing the likely future role of rivers in the dynamic cultural milieu of the twenty-first century.

Rivers and culture

The concept of culture can be defined and manipulated in a variety of ways. Hall (1995, 176) defines culture as 'the system of shared meanings which people who belong to the same community, group or nation use to help them interpret and make sense of the world'. He argues that culture is thus produced by both the 'material and social world', and includes the practices that produce meanings as well as those regulated by shared values. Our collective 'maps of meaning' produce a common identity, and he concludes that 'culture is thus one of the principal means by which identities are constructed, sustained and transformed'. Taking this definition as a starting point, it can be suggested that if contact with rivers and streams in British landscapes and townscapes forms a key part of the everyday and formative experiences of most people, then it follows that these experiences will also contribute to the creation of collective cultural identities.

This connection between rivers and culture can be achieved in a variety of ways and may change significantly over time. Rivers may contribute to material culture through the ways in which people are connected via the common experience of work that relates to or is dependent on rivers. For instance, in the past this was especially significant in large river ports such as Glasgow, Newcastle, Liverpool, Bristol and London, where a substantial proportion of the population were either directly or indirectly dependent on the river for their livelihood through dock work or associated manufacturing, processing and transport. Increasingly, with the decline in manufacturing and port-related activities, employment opportunities have shifted to the tourist sector, but the relationship between material culture and rivers remains. Rivers can also contribute to social culture through their association with leisure and associated creative artistic activities. Thus not only are rivers a site for relaxation and enjoyment, but also they may form the focus of new creative activities, for instance the development of major new galleries in various British cities on waterfront sites (the Tate Modern in London and the Tate Liverpool for instance). Both concepts of culture can be linked on the same site, though their relative importance may change over time. Thus in the eighteenth and nineteenth centuries the Severn at Ironbridge was an important focus for material culture, at the heart of the industrial revolution and providing employment for thousands of people. However, even at this time it was also creating a new social culture as the wonders of the iron bridge itself, and the raw power of the iron industry, became a focus for contemporary artistic representation. Today, Ironbridge and Coalbrookdale are principally tourist destinations where the twenty-first-century heritage industry reproduces past landscapes and cultures. It thus contributes significantly to the creation of one sort of contemporary social culture, albeit one based on nostalgia for a particular representation of industrial heritage, but it also contributes to present-day material culture through the creation of significant local employment in the tourist industry. The River Severn, however, is central to all these representations of culture (see chapter 8).

This chapter concentrates mainly on the links between rivers and non-material culture within Britain: those aspects of identity and ideology which help to bind individuals and groups together with a common sense of belonging. They go beyond the materiality of (for instance) common workplaces or leisure activities and embrace shared values and belief systems. These, however, may interact with and be reinforced by the material world. The most obvious and immediate representation of culture for most people is that of national or regional identity. Concepts of Britishness, Englishness, Scottishness, Welshness and various regional identities have received considerable attention in recent academic and popular debate. Awareness of such national and regional identities has been heightened by the impact of political devolution within the United Kingdom, and by the increasingly multicultural society in which we live. We now investigate the extent to which there are values which are shared by everyone in Britain, or in particular parts of the island, and the degree to which these values relate to the British landscape, including rivers.

Storey (2001) suggests that national identity is composed of five key elements which can be summarised as: consciousness of forming a community; cultural sharing; territorial attachment; common history; and the right to self-rule. All debates about the construction of Britishness emphasise the role of history in constructing national identity. Some argue that a British cultural identity emerged in the medieval period (Hastings 1997); others place it later, in the eighteenth or nineteenth century (Hobsbawm 1990; Colley 1992). Following a detailed analysis of the emergence of Britishness from dissimilar regions Colley (1992, 327) summarises British national identity as being based on 'a broadly Protestant culture, on the threat and tonic of recurrent war, especially with France, and on the triumphs, profits, and Otherness represented by a massive overseas empire'. This largely military and imperial concept of Britishness excludes concepts of landscape, but as Graham *et al.* (2000, 60) suggest, 'concepts of Englishness are rather different'.

Geographers such as Lowenthal (1991) and Rose (1995) argue that sense of place is a key component in the construction of Englishness, and that in particular the southern English landscape as represented in the paintings of Constable or the music of Elgar, came to represent all that was quintessentially English. Cosgrove *et al.* (1996, 536) expand this notion suggesting that notions of an English landscape are dominated by what they term 'Deep England', which consists of 'the cultivated lowland regions of scarps and wide river valleys with small, hedged fields, tight villages and occasional country houses set in parkland ... overwhelmingly located in an arc of lowlands around London, with outliers in such areas as the Vale of York and the Cheshire Plain'. This idea of Englishness is neither universally accepted nor complete. It ignores, for instance, northern landscapes of rugged hills and industrial towns, but it does chime with popular notions as espoused by the British Prime Minister, John Major, who in 1993 characterised Britain as consisting of 'a country of long shadows on county grounds, warm beer, invincible green suburbs, dog lovers and pools fillers' (quoted in Storey 2001, 85). This raises a further area of debate: that concepts of Englishness are often taken to encompass Britishness, 'with the term British used in effect as an English surrogate' (Matless 1998, 19).

Not surprisingly, the extent to which British identity has become associated with Englishness is strongly contested by the Welsh and Scots, each of whom have a strong tradition of asserting their own identities through language, culture, politics and heritage. In both Scotland and Wales it can be suggested that landscape plays a significant (though not dominant) part in the construction of identity. For instance, Storey (2001) argues that 'in versions of Welsh nationalist discourse the mountains are seen as the heart of the nation, somehow symbolising a Wales untainted by outside, specifically English, influences.' Plaid Cymru uses a symbolic representation of Welsh mountains as its logo, and both the Scottish Tourist Board and the Wales Tourist Board use landscapes (including rivers) as major selling points in all their advertising. For instance the Wales Tourist Board includes the following on its website: 'The landscape is laced with clear-flowing rivers and streams. There's water everywhere, from reed-fringed pools to dramatically beautiful lakes deep in the mountains. And activities, too, exciting watersports and superb fishing.' Similar phrases, backed up with appropriate visual images also abound in the publicity material of the various tourist boards that promote the English regions.

Rivers and the self

So far we have concentrated mainly on group identities, and have explored the ways in which landscape in general, and rivers in particular, contribute to the construction of national and regional cultures. However, we all also have an individual identity which may in part be related to a sense of group consciousness, but which also is constructed through our images and perceptions of the self. This section explores the role of rivers in the production of such individual identities.

Most simply, the concept of self-identity relates to the system of beliefs, principles and commitments through which we lead our lives (Greenwood 1994). All humans require such principles to make sense of themselves and the lives they lead, although for most of us these are mostly implicit rather than explicit. Rodaway (1991) identifies three recurring themes within concepts of the self: the self as consciousness and identity; the self in relationship to the physical and social world; and the self as biography located in a place of meaningfulness. Thus self-identity is constructed within ourselves (the embodied self); in relation to family, friends and neighbours through social interaction and social performance; and through our relationship with place. It is this latter aspect which is of relevance here. Geographers have a long tradition of exploring personal attachments to place, and Tuan (1974a and b) used the term 'topophilia' to mean the affective bonds which develop between people and places. Thus places, including rivers, can become centres of personal meaning which help to fashion our identity. Constructions of the

In the nineteenth century the river Mersey lay at the heart of Liverpool's economy. The port and port-related industries employed a large proportion of the male population. This engraving shows St George's Dock as a hive of activity.
BOYDELL GALLERIES, LIVERPOOL

self are also usually produced in opposition to the 'Other': those aspects of wider society and landscape that generate negative reactions (Philo 1991).

Landscape, and rivers in the landscape, can contribute to the construction of 'self' in a number of ways. Whenever we come into contact with a particular landscape feature it has the potential to contribute to the formation of identity. Thus Cosgrove (1984, 15) argues that 'landscape represents an historically specific way of experiencing the world developed by, and meaningful to, certain groups'. This will occur most readily when the landscape forms a particularly significant role in an individual's life, for instance through work, leisure activities or associations with friends and family. Studies of workers in a range of industries including farming, fishing, and transport have shown how they develop an identity with their employment and the environment in

which it is situated. The extent to which farming is not just a job but a 'way of life' is well documented, and it can be suggested that rural restructuring, and specific events such as the 2001 foot and mouth outbreak in Britain, have required farming families to reconstruct their personal identities (Saugeres 2002). Those who work on or with rivers may develop similar relationships with the places which are significant to them.

Historically, one of the largest groups of workers depending on rivers for their livelihood was dock workers. From the late nineteenth century various social surveys expressed concern about the working and employment conditions of the British dock labour force. Employment was not only dangerous and relatively unregulated, but also largely casual, with no certainty of work from one day to the next. The nature of the work tied individual workers and their families to the dockside community and, in doing so, helped to create a strong sense of personal identity within the dock labour force.

Although precise conditions of employment varied from port to port, the key characteristics of dock employment in the first half of the twentieth century were similar in all parts of Britain. Dock work was divided into a number of specialist branches ranging from those who worked in the ship's hold, loading and unloading cargo, to those employed as porters on the quayside who were responsible for moving goods for onward transport by rail or road. The work of the dock labourer was governed by a number of cycles. There were seasonal variations in trade but, more importantly, the flow of ships was affected by short-term variations in weather conditions and by the state of the tide. Thus there would be periods when ample work was available, but other times when many dock workers (especially those engaged in loading and unloading boats) were unemployed. Dock labour was recruited on a casual basis at hiring stands along the dock system, with those known to be regular and reliable workers recruited first. Others gained only occasional employment. Thus the income of a dock worker was erratic, and a prolonged slack period in the port could produce acute poverty. It was these problems that various enquiries into the dock labour force tried to tackle (Lascelles and Bullock 1924; Hanham 1930; Caradog Jones 1934; University of Liverpool, Department of Social Science 1954; Lovell 1969).

Employment as a dock worker, and the daily, weekly and seasonal rhythms of work on the river could permeate all aspects of a dock worker's life. Knowledge of when work was available could only be gained by living close to the dockside (usually in very poor quality housing), and by being part of the dockland community. Working on the docks was thus more than a job, but became a way of life. Choice of home, patterns of recreation, and friendships were all bound up with work in the port, and only those who became part of the dockland community could survive. It is thus reasonable to suggest that the self-identity of dockworkers in the first half of the twentieth century was largely constructed through their engagement with work on the river. These points are well summarised by Caradog Jones (1934, 136) in his wide-ranging social survey of Merseyside:

> The great majority of dock labourers live as near as they can to their work ... The reasons for this preference are fairly obvious and by now well accepted. To begin with, the river frontage of docks on the Liverpool side is about seven miles in extent. Even a worker living immediately behind the line of docks may have to make a long journey to reach the stand where he is most likely to gain employment, and he will not wish to make it still longer if he can avoid it ... Moreover, the docker who fails to find employment in the morning is obliged to appear again at the afternoon stand ... A third reason of some importance is that it is essential for the docker to pick up information and rumours about the probable demand for labour at different stands. If he is isolated from the public-houses and places where dockers normally congregate, he is likely to miss many good chances of work.

Although work is a dominant factor in the lives of most people, contact with or location by a river can help to fashion self-identity in a number of other ways. For some, rivers can be a threat, and coping with flooding on a regular basis (for instance along parts of the River Severn) can itself become a way of life. Rivers are also an important source of recreation, and contact with a river can provide moments of contemplation and relaxation. Angling is one of the country's most popular pastimes, and a major part of its attraction for many is simply the ability to sit quietly by a river, to think and to escape the bustle of everyday life. This quality of fishing is stressed by Izaak Walton in his well-known seventeenth-century book in praise of angling: 'And first I shall tel you what some have observed, and I have found in my self, That the very sitting by the Rivers side, is not only the fittest place for, but will invite the Anglers to Contemplation'. (Walton 1653 (1983 edition, 70)). It can be suggested that for Britain's many fishermen and women a few hours spent by a river is an important part of their personal identity.

The role of water, and of waterways, in creating a peaceful and restful ambience is also stressed in publicity produced by present-day companies promoting canal and river holidays. Material on the website promoting Hoseasons boating holidays in Britain is typical: 'Remember how holidays used to be? ... Easy and unhurried; the endless freedom of long, lazy days ... and not a care in the world. That's the feeling you get on a Hoseasons boating holiday'. For some, therefore, association with rivers can link biography and place. Work or recreational activities which bring people into regular contact with rivers can enable individuals to develop and express themselves more effectively, and to construct distinctive identities of the self.

Rivers and creativity

Cultural identity may be expressed not only through a group association with region or nation, and through conceptions of the self, but also through a society's creative art. This section examines the ways in which landscape in general, and rivers in particular, play a central role in British creativity, and the ways in which rivers have been represented and used in the creative arts. In his foreword to a collection of some 180 poems focusing on 'The River's Voice', Roger Deakin highlights the centrality of water in general, and of rivers in particular, to the creative process. He writes: 'I know of few people and no poet for whom water is not a first love … we are forever water babies, responding playfully to the least drenching; singing in the rain or in the bath, thinking or dreaming wild thoughts as we are borne weightless in the swimming pool, the river or the sea'. He asserts that rivers are a 'measure of our civilisation' and that 'water is the most poetical of elements, allowing of no awkward sudden movements: even a stone dropped in sinks gracefully' (King and Clifford 2000, 15–18).

The most obvious link between British rivers, creativity and culture is through the use of art, music and literature to represent and project particular landscape images which conform to notions of Englishness or other identities. Thus, the poems of Wordsworth and the other Lakeland poets, the music of Elgar, Delius and Vaughan Williams, and the paintings of Constable and Turner among many others are often associated with typically idyllic notions of the English landscape. This use of creative art to convey particular images of landscape, and the role of rivers in this process, is explored later. First, however, we examine some specific ways in which rivers have been used to represent and convey particular cultural concepts. These include representations of the personality of rivers, the use of rivers as playgrounds, the role of rivers as barriers, the extent to which rivers are threats, and the use of rivers as resources.

The personality of rivers

Most people are fascinated by the sense of fluidity and movement embodied in a river or stream. Watching water flowing under a bridge can produce an almost hypnotic effect, and the range of movement and responses that water produces as it negotiates obstacles in a stream can remind us of human behaviour and personality. This is a theme taken up by many writers who, to a greater or lesser degree, endow flowing water with human characteristics representing and reflecting the vitality of nature. Those writing for children, especially in stories where animals are also given anthropomorphic characteristics, have done this particularly effectively. Thus A. A. Milne writes of the landscape in which Christopher Robin and his friends live:

By the time it came to the edge of the Forest the stream had grown up, so that it was almost a river, and being grown-up, it did not run jump and sparkle along as it used to do when it was younger, but moved more slowly. For it knew where it was going, and it said to itself, 'There is no hurry. We shall get there some day.' But all the little streams higher up in the Forest went this way and that, quickly, eagerly, having so much to find out before it was too late. (A. A. Milne, *The House at Pooh Corner*, chapter 6).

In a similar vein, Kenneth Grahame repeatedly gives his river human characteristics in *The Wind in the Willows*, perhaps the book that first springs to mind when linking literature and rivers. For instance, the description of Mole's first encounter with the river and Rat's enthusiasm for its charms:

The Mole was bewitched, entranced, fascinated. By the side of the river he trotted as one trots, when very small, by the side of a man, who holds one spellbound by exciting stories; and when tired at last, he sat on the bank, while the river still chattered on to him, a babbling procession of the best stories in the world, sent from the heart of the earth to be told at last to the insatiable sea.

… [The river is] brother and sister to me, and aunts and company, and food and drink, and (naturally) washing. It's my world, and I don't want any other. What it hasn't got is not worth having, and what it doesn't know is not worth knowing. Lord! The times we've had together! (Kenneth Grahame, *The Wind in the Willows*, chapter 1).

Both Milne and Grahame gained much of the inspiration for their writing from experiences of the rural landscapes of southern England. Grahame was born in Edinburgh, but was sent as a small boy to live with his grandmother at Cookham Dean in Berkshire. Here he gained familiarity with and a love of the Thames and riverside life and, although he lived much of his adult life in London, his childhood experiences strongly influenced his later writing. Similarly, the landscape Milne created for his stories of Winnie the Pooh was inspired by the Ashdown Forest in East Sussex, close to the home in Hartfield that he moved to in 1925 following the birth of his son, Christopher Robin (Drabble 1979).

Writers of adult fiction may also endow rivers with human personalities to emphasise the life and vitality of nature and to provide context for their narrative. Thus in his influential novel, *Waverley*, Walter Scott describes a romantic encounter in the Highlands against the backdrop of the headwaters of the Tay. Here he not only uses the river to emphasise the natural surroundings, but gives the streams personalities which to some extent reflect the feelings of his characters:

These streams were different also in character. The larger was placid, and even sullen in its course, wheeling in deep eddies, or sleeping in dark pools; but the motions of the lesser brook were rapid and furious, issuing from between precipices like a maniac from his confinement, all foam and uproar. (Walter Scott, *Waverley*, chapter 22)

Some writers also reverse the process, using the characteristics of rivers to describe and illuminate aspects of the human form and individual personality. In such instances the writer recognises the distinctive features of a natural form and reflects this back in the human condition. This is seen in an extract from the work of the Welsh poet R. S. Thomas:

> I am Prytherch. Forgive me. I don't know
> What you are talking about; your thoughts flow
> Too swiftly for me; I cannot dawdle
> Along their banks and fish in their quick stream
> With crude fingers ...
> (From *Invasion on the Farm*)

Rivers as playgrounds

Rivers are not only the site of organised leisure activities, but also the setting for much informal recreation, especially for children. This is borne out by recent research examining the role of rivers in the lives of children growing up in London today. Although, in part, rivers were perceived to be polluted, neglected and potentially dangerous places (see below), they also offered significant opportunities for creative and challenging play and relaxation. In particular the liminality of rivers, providing a threshold across which children could cross into another world with different behavioural norms and activities, was seen to be important (Tapsell *et al.* 2001). Similar themes are also represented in creative literature, where rivers are often the sites for both adult and childhood play that may also be associated to some degree with life-changing experiences.

Melvyn Bragg captures this well in his novel *A Son of War*, set in north Cumbria. It is summer and the Wiza river is traditionally dammed by local children to provide a pool for swimming. The central character, Joe, joins a group of older boys in a dispute about who should build the dam and where it should be constructed. It is a battle over territory between rival gangs that begins with friendly banter and play, but ends with a battle where stones are thrown and Joe is injured. Before conflict occurs Bragg illustrates well the diversity of challenging play that took place in one small pool:

> Word went out. It became a little resort, a spa, an adventure. Speed and
> some bigger boys made a raft. Smaller boys braved the trickle of water on

the wrong side of the dam and hopped across stones on the river-bed. One or two of the bigger boys ran hard across the grass and leaped and bombed the water. Joe loved swimming and was developing pace in the front crawl. Here he was reduced to the breast-stroke, more sedate, but more able to look around and avoid being bombed.' (Melvyn Bragg, *A Son of War*, chapter 22)

Joe's mother, Ellen, also recalls similar activities in the same spot when she was a child, emphasising the timeless quality of rivers and the way in which similar activities have been recreated by succeeding generations of children:

She herself had swum there, in years before the war and she sheltered from the heat of the glowing hot day, she remembered with affection that tang of river water, the coolness of it after lying on the grassy bank, the free amiable anarchy of the boy-made pool. (Melvyn Bragg, *A Son of War*, chapter 22).

In her Green Knowe books for children Lucy Boston makes extensive use of the river as a site for play and adventure, especially in *The River at Green Knowe*, and rivers in winter, especially when frozen, provide very different but equally challenging environments for play. These, too, are captured in creative writing. For instance, in *The Prelude*, Wordsworth describes his experiences of skating on frozen lakes in the English Lake District, and the novel *Tom's Midnight Garden* by Philippa Pearce provides a vivid account of children skating on the river Ouse to Ely:

They skated on and the thin, brilliant sun was beginning to set, and Hatty's black shadow flitted along at their right hand, across the dazzle of the ice. Sometimes they skated on the main river; sometimes they skated on the flooded washes. Only the willows along the bank watched them: and the ice hissed with their passage. (Phillippa Pearce, *Tom's Midnight Garden*, chapter 23)

Adult 'play' on rivers typically takes one of two forms. In some writing it is represented as an adventure which often turns into comedy or farce; alternatively it provides a setting for a romantic encounter. Sometimes the two may be combined. Although the classic tale of adult misadventure on a river (the Thames) must be Jerome K. Jerome's *Three Men in a Boat*, where the river forms an integral part of what is essentially a comic study of human nature, similar themes are also explored by other authors. The Thames was an important feature in many of the novels of Charles Dickens (see below), but he also used it extensively in some of his shorter and lighter pieces to provide an amusing commentary on aspects of human character and behaviour:

This is the most amusing time to observe a regular Sunday water-party. There has evidently been up to this period no inconsiderable degree of boasting on everybody's part relative to his knowledge of navigation; the sight of the water rapidly cools their courage, and the air of self-denial with which each of them insists on somebody else's taking an oar, is perfectly delightful. (Charles Dickens, *Sketches by Boz*, chapter 10)

Philip Larkin's novel, *A Girl in Winter* includes an excursion in a punt on an Oxfordshire river that combines elements of romance, amusement and mild danger, using activity on the boat to symbolise the growing relationship between the two main characters:

Katherine, summoning all her determination, poised the pole and slid it ... down into the river at exactly the right angle. Cheered she hauled on it with all her might. It suddenly grew rigid in her hands. Carried on by the impetus of the stroke, she tugged wildly for a second, then at the last moment overbalanced by trying to improve her grip. Robin ... took a step forward, caught her neatly round the waist, and pulled her upright again. She stumbled and put her hands on his shoulders ... Katherine sank down on the cushions, trembling from rage, fright and embarrassment. (Philip Larkin, *A Girl in Winter*, 1947, part 2, chapter 4).

Rivers as barriers
Rivers are linear features in the landscape and, as such, form natural barriers. Many long-standing administrative boundaries follow rivers, demarcating counties, parishes and individual properties. The fact that rivers may change

their course over time can then cause problems as boundaries and footpaths have to be re-aligned, but the symbolic value of the river as a permanent marker in the landscape is substantial. Rivers may also form physical barriers inhibiting movement. In the past, where there were no convenient bridges, or when people wished to avoid paying a bridge toll, rivers would often be forded. But, depending on the state of the water this could be dangerous and it was not unusual for lives to be lost. Today, river crossings cause substantial traffic bottlenecks in many towns and continue to create a barrier to movement. In urban areas, rivers can also continue to act as symbolic barriers as local gangs might demarcate their territory using natural barriers such as rivers. Such territoriality is well established in the academic literature (Sack 1986), and also finds representation in British creative writing.

The river Mersey bisects the Merseyside conurbation with the river separating Liverpool from Birkenhead and other settlements on the Wirral. Liverpool and Birkenhead form very different and distinctive communities, with the residents of each having a strong sense of local identity that is strengthened by the barrier effect of the Mersey. Much the same could be said for the significance of the Tyne in creating the distinctive identities of Newcastle and Gateshead, and rivers play a similar role in other cities including Glasgow and London. In her somewhat sentimental account of life on Merseyside during the 1930s, Helen Forrester highlights the role of the Mersey as a barrier to movement for those with limited resources:

> It used to cost twopence to cross the river on the ferry-boat from Liverpool to Birkenhead. Twopence is not a very large sum, but if one has no money, the river is a real barrier, and, during the Depression years, was an impassable one to many of the poverty-stricken people of Liverpool. (Helen Forrester, *Twopence to Cross the Mersey*, 1974, chapter 1).

Rivers as barriers also occur quite frequently in children's literature, where the barrier to be crossed can introduce elements of danger and adventure. A scene in the popular children's novel *The Animals of Farthing Wood,* by Colin Dann, typifies this. An unlikely group of assorted anthropomorphic British wildlife has to cross a substantial river during the course of a journey from one home to another. The more nervous animals enquire about the width of the river and Toad reassures them that it is easy to cross. Inevitably, a drama ensues and the leaders of the group, Fox and Badger, come close to drowning. The drama of the river crossing and its immediate aftermath fills two chapters of the book and creates considerable dramatic tension for a young reader.

Rivers as threats
Rivers may be regarded as places of danger, either because of the behaviour and volatility of the river itself, or due to the foolhardiness of those living by

or trying to cross it. Flooding is the major threat posed to human life and property by rivers and, as indicated in chapter 7, regulating rivers to minimise this threat is a major preoccupation of modern water management. Many writers have used floods as a source of dramatic inspiration, creating not only a sense of danger but also emphasising the way in which the natural power of the river is, for the most part, beyond the control of humans. The volatility of a river, which can rise and fall and change its mood very quickly, can be seen to reflect the unpredictability of human personality, thus producing a cultural bond between people and the natural world.

In *The Mill on the Floss*, George Eliot draws on her personal knowledge of midland England to recreate places, customs and relationships with which she was familiar (Drabble 1979). The livelihoods of the characters living in the mill and its surroundings are bound up with the water that drives the mill, and the flood which eventually destroys the mill also creates the tragic drama that claims the lives of the central characters. In almost the last lines of the book Eliot enacts the final drama, emphasising the way in which human existence is entwined with nature as the small boat is swept away by flood debris:

'It is coming, Maggie!' Tom said in a deep hoarse voice, loosing the oars and clasping her.

The next instant the boat was no longer seen upon the water, and the huge mass was hurrying on in hideous triumph.

But soon the keel of the boat reappeared, a black speck on the golden water.

The boat reappeared, but brother and sister had gone down in an embrace never to be parted, living through again in one supreme moment the days when they had clasped their little hands in love and roamed the daisied fields together.

(George Eliot, *The Mill on the Floss*, 1860, book 7, chapter 5).

The writing of D. H. Lawrence is similarly deeply embedded in the East Midland landscape, and rivers often play a prominent role in his writing. In *The Rainbow*, Lawrence begins by emphasising the location of the Brangwen's farm adjacent to water that at first is non-threatening:

The Brangwen's had lived for generations on the Marsh Farm, in the meadows where the Erewash twisted sluggishly through alder trees, separating Derbyshire from Nottinghamshire. (D. H. Lawrence, *The Rainbow*, 1915, chapter 1).

However, after heavy rain the character of the river changes and a somewhat intoxicated Tom Brangwen perishes in the swollen river. The writing again emphasises the natural power of the water and the inability of humans to control unpredictable natural elements:

Fear took hold of him. Gripping tightly to the lamp, he reeled and looked round. The water was carrying his feet away, he was dizzy. He did not know which way to turn. The water was whirling, whirling, the whole black night was swooping in rings. He swayed uncertainly at the centre of all the attack, reeling in dismay. In his soul he knew he would fall. (Chapter 9).

In an urban area floods can wreak particular havoc, and some artists have both recorded such events and represented them as deeper visions of urban decay. L. S. Lowry painted the Irwell in Salford on several occasions, recording a literal representation of its characteristics in flood in his pencil drawing *The River Irwell at the Adelphi*, and exaggerating this into a devastated industrial landscape overwhelmed by water in his oil painting *The Lake*. Howard (1991,

L. S. Lowry, *The Lake* (1937), oil on canvas.

L. S. Lowry, *The River Irwell at the Adelphi* (1924), pencil.
THE L.S. LOWRY COLLECTIONVG

154) argues that this is the painted equivalent of T. S. Eliot's *The Waste Land*, 'producing a tragic definition of modern existence as a spiritual wasteland'. Again the artist emphasises the inability of humanity to control water, and suggests that nature may take retribution for harm inflicted by the processes of industrialisation and urbanisation.

Many writers also use rivers as the vehicle through which a character attempts to take their own life. Thus in George Eliot's *Daniel Deronda*, Mira is saved from drowning by Daniel; but in Thomas Hardy's novel *The Return of the Native* the fated Eustacia Vye takes her own life in a swollen stream on Egdon Heath in Wessex. Here there is a strong sense that the natural world is reclaiming a character who appears doomed from the start of the story. What is common to many of these representations of the dangers of rivers is that they are used to some degree as a retribution for the failings of either human character or society.

Rivers as a resource

The role of rivers as an economic resource was discussed in chapter 5, and this central function of rivers has also been portrayed in British literature and creative art. As Drabble (1979, 195) notes, in the early years of the industrial revolution, 'it was considered proper to admire industrial architecture, feats of engineering, the glories of man's triumphs over nature. The early mill owners, far from retreating out of sight of their mills, proudly overlooked them from their homes, and commissioned paintings to commemorate them'. Even English landscape artists frequently painted working rivers in their landscapes, typified by Constable's representations of the Stour as a navigable river with barges and associated economic activity, and by some of the work of members of the early nineteenth-century Norwich School of artists. In the later nineteenth century, the artist John Atkinson Grimshaw painted many scenes of industrial docks and rivers in both London and northern industrial towns, especially Liverpool and Leeds. His representation of the Aire at Leeds in 1880 captures the role of the river as a centre of economic activity particularly effectively.

Nineteenth- and twentieth-century writers also captured the economic activities associated with ports and rivers in their descriptions of urban life. Thus authors such Charles Dickens, Arnold Bennett, D. H. Lawrence and Alan Sillitoe all painted evocative pictures of urban industrial landscapes in which rivers and canals played an essential part. Thus in *Hard Times*, the only novel by Dickens set in the industrial north, he describes *Coketown* (loosely based on Preston) thus:

> It was a town of machinery and tall chimneys, out of which interminable serpents of smoke trailed themselves for ever and ever, and never got uncoiled. It had a black canal in it, and a river that ran purple with ill-smelling dye, and vast piles of building full of windows where there was a rattling and a trembling all day long, and where the piston of the steam engine worked monotonously up and down, like the head of an elephant in a state of melancholy madness. (Charles Dickens, *Hard Times*, 1854, chapter 5)

Unlike Dickens, who made only short excursions to industrial northern England, Arnold Bennett grew up in the Potteries and wrote from personal experience. While his books represent the dereliction and grime of an industrial landscape he could also see beauty in the products of industrialisation, drawing attention to the artificial rivers of molten slag produced by an ironworks (Drabble 1979, 221):

> To the south of them, a mile and a half off, in the wreathing mist of the Cauldron Bar Ironworks, there was a yellow gleam that even the capricious sunlight could not kill, and then two rivers of fire sprang from the gleam and ran in a thousand delicate and lovely hues down the side of a mountain of refuse. (Arnold Bennett, *Clayhanger*, 1910, chapter 1)

Although the role of rivers as centres of economic activity has declined greatly in recent decades, the bustle of productivity associated with river life can still attract artists and writers. For instance Alice Oswald won the 2003

J. Constable, *Scene on a Navigable River* (Flatford Mill), 1817

© TATE, LONDON 2003

J. Thirtle, *A View of Thorpe, with Steam Barge working up – Evening* (1815)

COURTESY OF NORWICH CASTLE MUSEUM AND ART GALLERY

T. S. Eliot prize with her 40-page poem *Dart*. In this work of verse and prose she captures the multiplicity of life on and around the River Dart in Devon. Characters in her poem include boat builders, sewage workers, water abstractors, salmon fishers, swimmers, water bailiffs and poachers. She spent some two years researching the poem and talking to people who lived and worked with the river and, in total, it provides an evocative picture of the wide range of activities which take place on a modern rural river, encapsulating 'the river's mutterings, a songline from the source to the sea' (Alice Oswald, introduction to *Dart*, 2002).

Rivers, landscapes and townscapes

Implicit in these examples is the link between British creative art and landscape, and how central rivers are within this context. Howard (1991) attempts to categorise the changing role of rivers in British landscape painting. He argues that in what he terms the 'Picturesque period' (1790–1830) rivers were a predominant element in landscape painting, especially upland rivers in North Wales, the English Lake District and the Scottish Highlands. The most popular rivers were of moderate size with rocky beds, clearly defined valleys, and special features such as waterfalls. Most such landscapes included a bridge

Leeds Bridge, 1880 (Oil on canvas) by John Atkinson Grimshaw (1836–93). LEEDS MUSEUMS AND ART GALLERIES (CITY ART GALLERY) U.K./BRIDGEMAN ART LIBRARY

to add to the picturesque effect. By mid-century, in the 'Romantic period' (1830–1870), Howard argues that representations of medium-sized upland rivers were especially popular, usually with waterfalls viewed looking upstream so that the fall of the water could be represented. The late nineteenth century is termed the 'Heroic period' (1870–1910), when it is suggested that, rather than simply viewing water as a prospect, rivers were viewed as a hazard to be overcome. Thus rivers were often torrents in full spate representing the savageness of nature. In the 'Vernacular period' (1910–50) Howard argues that rivers largely disappeared as the central feature of landscape paintings, appearing largely in the background, but that there was an upsurge of interest in representing ports and docks, a theme that continued into the 'Formal period' (1950–80). Although Howard's categorisation can be debated, many of the elements he describes appear in the examples of representations of rivers cited above.

One common theme is the way in which artists have used rivers to evoke particular moods in their creative work. This occurs in both urban and rural contexts, and has been used by composers, painters, novelists and poets alike. A few examples will suffice. Much of the work of Charles Dickens uses the Thames to create an appropriate atmosphere for the action and characters he portrays. The opening of Bleak House is particularly effective:

Fog everywhere. Fog up the river, where it flows among green aits and meadows; fog down the river, where it rolls defiled among the tiers of shipping, and the waterside pollutions of a great (and dirty) city. Fog on the Essex Marshes, fog on the Kentish heights. Fog creeping into the cabooses of collier-brigs; fog lying out on the yards, and hovering in the rigging of great ships; fog dropping on the gunwales of barges and small boats. (Charles Dickens, *Bleak House*, 1853, chapter 1).

Atkinson Grimshaw creates much the same effect in some of his paintings of dock scenes. Thus the series of pictures of the Thames by moonlight, painted in the 1880s and inspired by the grime of the city and the fog of the river, used subtle effects of lighting to convey the effect of the river at night. Robertson (1988, 75) describes *Nightfall Down the Thames* as 'a quintessentially London view, inviting the spectator to follow the path of light to St Paul's Cathedral, with a perfect balance between blocks of light and shadow'. Grimshaw was, of course, just one of very many artists who painted the Thames, including Canaletto, Turner, Monet, Sisley and Whistler. The significance of the Thames, and the iconic buildings along the river, for British artists such as Turner is emphasised by Daniels (1993, 130) who argues that, 'in English writing and painting the Thames and its scenery had long signified the nation's condition and power'. Some of the same qualities can also be encapsulated in music such as Vaughan William's *London Symphony*, in which the score represents many of the sights and sounds of London; and in Humphrey Searle's piece *Tamesis* (Op. 71), a musical history of the Thames.

The English rural landscape, and especially the pastoral idyll most usually associated with it, is widely represented in music, art, poetry and other literature. Composers such as Elgar, Vaughan Williams, Delius, Holst, Bax and Butterworth among others are inextricably linked to romantic images of the English countryside, even if in some instances their music may have been stimulated by other images (for instance the *Pastoral Symphony* by Vaughan Williams, in many sense quintessentially English, was probably inspired by the French countryside, and Delius' *By the River* is part of his Florida Suite for Orchestra). Such composers use a range of musical devices to link music and place. As Leyshon *et al.* (1998, 8) state: 'The imitation of natural sounds, the quotation of folk songs and dances, and references to localities and regions could rhetorically tie music to the rhythmical structures of land, landscape and language'. The sound of running water in rivers and streams often plays a role in such music.

English landscape painting which incorporates rivers is extensive, and cannot be covered comprehensively here. Much of this work is regionally based, with typical examples being the work of the Newlyn School in Cornwall and artists representing the English Lake District. In the early twentieth century the Lamorna valley, near Newlyn, was adopted by a group of Impressionist and Post-Impressionist landscape painters. They concentrated on coastal and rural scenes of the immediate locality, gaining most prominence in the 1930s. *Our Little Stream Lamorna* (1934) by John 'Lamorna' Birch is typical and represents the environment from which the artists gained their inspiration. Landscape painting also has a long tradition in the English Lake District, and is actively continued today by a range of contemporary Lakeland artists with a variety of artistic styles. Painters such as Jill Aldersley, Marion Bradley, Tiana Marie, James Ingham Riley, Jim Ridout, Peter Symonds and many others are widely exhibited in Lake District galleries and find a ready market for their work from tourists and collectors elsewhere. Although, inevitably, the hills and lakes of Cumbria form the basis of much of their work, upland streams and wooded river valleys are an essential part of contemporary representations of Lakeland. *Thunder of the Waters* by Tiana Marie provides a particularly evocative, impressionist, representation of the raw force of a Lakeland torrent.

The romantic representation of the English countryside and rivers has been constant over a long period of time. Thus William Wordsworth penned several poems to Lakeland streams, including thirty-four sonnets to *The River Duddon*, and a century and a half later the contemporary Lakeland poet, Norman Nicholson, wrote his own paean *To the River Duddon*. The Lakeland author A. Harry Griffin also captures the timeless quality of the Duddon,

RIVERS AND THE BRITISH LANDSCAPE

emphasising how little the valley has changed since Wordsworth was there in the early nineteenth century:

> All the fifteen miles from the Three Shires Stone to the sea, the Duddon dances down the dale through constantly varying scenery of crags and woodland – a twisting knobbly valley that, save for the afforestation on Harter Fell, has hardly changed since his [Wordsworth's] day. (A. Harry Griffin, *A Lakeland Mountain Diary*, 1990, 114).

Many other writers have tried to capture similar emotions in poems about English rivers and these are well represented in the collection *The River's Voice* (King and Clifford 2000). One example, not in that collection, which demonstrates the way in which concepts of the rural idyll can be applied even to rivers that may more usually be thought of as urban or industrial is Stevie Smith's poem *The River Humber* (1983):

> No wonder
> The river Humber
> Lies in a silken slumber
> For it is dawn
> And over the newly warm

Earth the mist turns,
Wrapping their gentle fringes
Upon the river where it hinges
Upon the perfected sleep of perfected images.
Quite in the thought of its felicity
A graven monument of sufficiency
Beautiful in every line the river sleeps complacently.
And hardly the dawn distinguishes
Where a miasma languishes
Upon the waters' farther reaches.
Lapped in the sleeping consciousness
Of its waves happiness
Upon the mudbanks of its approaches,
The river Humber
Turns again to slumber,
Deeper than deeps in joys without number.

While representation of the English landscape tend to focus on the romantic idyll, with more occasional references to the power of nature, artistic images of the Welsh landscape tend to place much more emphasis on the harshness of the environment and the struggle between humans and the elements. This comes through strongly in the work of R. S. Thomas who emphasises the hard side of the Welsh landscape, and the constant struggle to survive endured by the Welsh people. For instance, his poem *Welsh Landscape* begins:

To live in Wales is to be conscious
At dusk of the spilled blood
That went to the making of the wild sky,
Dyeing the immaculate rivers
In all their courses.

Although there are other representations of the Welsh landscape, for instance Dylan Thomas's penetrating and affectionate portrait of the fictional Llareggub, with its River Dewi, in *Under Milk Wood* (1954), it can be suggested that artistic representations of landscape in Wales do present a rather different picture from that produced by most English artists.

Rivers and spirituality

Spirituality and culture are closely intertwined, with many people defining their cultural norms through their spiritual beliefs. Many world religions identify specific holy places or have some affinity with the natural world, and for Hindus the river Ganges has particular significance. Most world religions are represented in Britain today, and many people with no religious belief may also find spiritual succour through contact with the natural environment. As such, rivers in the landscape can become a very personal source of support, rest and enlightenment for many people.

Pre-Christian Celtic religions in Britain were strongly associated with the natural world and rivers played a vital role in these belief systems. Stewart (1990, 15) argues that 'Celtic religion was primarily associated with the sanctity of the land and the power of certain key locations within the land. The entire landscape was alive ... The land was usually represented by a goddess, whose shape was clear to see in the rise of the hills and whose powers were apparent in the flow of the rivers, the rising of the springs and the growth of the plants.' Water worship was common, and the Celts had river goddesses and gods. For example, a large temple complex at Lydney on Severn was dedicated to the god Nodons, a god of both sea and water (Stewart 1990, 118). Many rivers developed particular associations with pagan rituals and belief systems, for instance the Derwent and Etherow in Derbyshire had reputations as evil rivers, and the bloodthirsty waters of the Spey in the Scottish Highlands were thought to require at least one victim every year (Clarke and Roberts 1996). Although such beliefs have largely been swept away by a combination of Christianity and scientific rationalism, there remains in Britain a small minority of people who follow Druidic, New Age or other belief systems which have their roots in early Celtic religions. It can also be argued that some aspects of modern environmentalism contain echoes of earlier Celtic traditions.

According to the 2001 census 71.6 per cent of the population of the United Kingdom consider themselves to be Christian, and rivers and the natural world play only a minor role in most of their belief systems. However, it can be suggested that many hymns and religious songs do make links between Christianity, national identity and the English landscape. This theme was developed in the 1930s and 1940s through the writings of H. J. Massingham. According to Palmer (2002) Massingham developed ideas of 'divine Englishness' defined primarily by his interpretation of the southern English countryside. Massingham was an acute observer of and commentator on contemporary rural life, and he linked his belief in 'natural' farming to his own Christian ideology. In his work he describes a 'rightful, divinely ordained universe, in which nature and human society are hierarchically related in a living, organic whole' (Palmer 2002, 35). Massingham's ideas both resonate with the notions of English rural identity outlined earlier, and have at least some roots in the Celtic religions which focused explicitly on the natural world.

J. Lamorna Birch,
*Our Little Stream
Lamorna* (1934), oil
on canvas.
ROYAL ACADEMY OF ARTS,
LONDON

Conclusions: British rivers and twenty-first-century culture

It is sometimes said that the twenty-first century is dominated by a culture of materialism, symbolised by patterns of high mass consumption and a throwaway society. Following from this, it can also be suggested that the role of the natural world in general, and of rivers in particular, is diminishing. Certainly, a review of what might broadly be termed popular culture suggests that the role of the landscape has changed. Even those television dramas and soap operas which are located in specific places usually use landscape only as a backdrop. Rarely does the natural world form a major part of the story line. Thus a television programme such as *EastEnders* opens with an aerial view of

London in which the characteristic shape of the Thames figures prominently. Yet, the storyline of the programme is based almost entirely on characters and relationships, and London as a place (including the Thames) rarely features prominently. Contrast this with the work of Charles Dickens, whose serialised stories were the nineteenth-century equivalent of the twenty-first-century TV soap. While Dickens was never short of good characters, relationships and plots, these were consciously set within an urban landscape which could be recognised by his readers. The Thames with its associated life was a key part of the narrative. Similar observations can be made about the long-running radio soap *The Archers*. Set in an English village the writers pride themselves on including topical references to rural affairs, and the village has a well-demarcated topography with key locations which are used repeatedly. However, few of these relate to the natural environment and the storyline focuses mainly on people, events and relationships. Although the fictional village is named Ambridge, giving a clear connection to the river which flows through the settlement, the river is rarely used in the storyline. In 2002 the Am flooded riverside property, giving a topical reference to the flooding

Tiana Marie, *Thunder of the Waters.*
TIANA MARIE
WWW.TIANAMARIE.CO.UK

which had occurred in much of Britain, and there are occasional references to poaching along the river. For the most part, however, the river that gives its name to the village remains as a silent backdrop to the drama.

In contrast, it can also be suggested that in other ways rivers have never been more important to British culture. Although rivers such as the Thames, Severn, Mersey, Tyne and Clyde are no longer the great centres of employment that they once were, rivers of all sizes and character have multiple significance for many aspects of British life. For instance, global climate change models predict that the British weather will become both stormier and wetter leading, in conjunction with possible sea level rise, to an increased risk of flooding from rivers and estuaries. In addition, the extension of urban development onto floodplains has exposed more homes to flood risk. Dealing with such risk is becoming an increasingly everyday aspect of British life, and some of the ways in which this is managed are explored in chapter 7. The use of rivers for leisure and pleasure is not new, but it can be argued that in what for most people is an increasingly busy and stressful world, rivers can provide a sense of timelessness and anti-material values which are often lost in modern society. Moreover, the importance given to riverside locations in contemporary urban redevelopment schemes highlights the significance attached to urban riverscapes. Some contemporary British creative artists have also turned towards nature to find inspiration for their work. For instance Stephen Turner works mainly with the natural world, and in 1998 produced an installation entitled *Tide & Change in the River Medway*. This was located in an abandoned nautical fort on a salt marsh island in the Medway estuary. Over the period of a month he recorded the movement of the tides on huge canvas tarpaulins stretched across the river bed, and used the deposits of alluvial silt to turn the tarpaulins into works of art which were then displayed on the ramparts of the fort. In an island nation, with many streams and rivers of all sizes, individual and group cultural identity is almost inevitably bound up to some degree with these fluid, entrancing and sometimes challenging elements in the environment. Although the role of rivers in British cultural identity is being constantly reworked, it is hard to escape their enduring presence.

CHAPTER 7 # The management of British rivers

Nigel Watson

Introduction

> The regulation of rivers has always been regarded as a matter of great public importance. Very few other forms of resource use and management have been subjected to such scrutiny and debate. The many attempts to reach a consensus, on the basis of an improved knowledge of the extent and nature of the resource itself and a reconciliation of the many conflicting interests, serve to draw attention to the long-standing nature of many of the problems being encountered in the planning of the environment at the present day. (Sheail 1988, p. 231)

The idea of river management is something of a misnomer. In isolated and unpopulated areas, rivers simply exist as 'neutral stuff' (Zimmerman 1951) and are free to flow and evolve as natural processes dictate. There is no need for intervention or 'management' of rivers in these circumstances since there are no human uses, values or constraints placed upon them. Interpreted in this way, 'river management' is really about management of human interactions with river spaces. Thus, we can think of river management as a collection of general and specific responsibilities and activities ranging from planning, development and regulation through to water abstraction, pollution control, navigation, fisheries, recreation and wildlife conservation. In some situations, emphasis is placed on the fullest possible development of the river in order to provide services such as water supply, navigation and waste disposal. However, if left un-checked, such activities can clearly harm the ecology of rivers, upon which we all ultimately depend. When this occurs, management must become more regulatory in character; human activities have to be controlled if valued rivers are to be protected and degraded rivers are to be restored. In reality the pressures for the development and protection of rivers exist at the same time. Those who have responsibility for the management of our rivers are therefore faced with a difficult task. The right balance between development and protection must be found and in so doing the demands of groups with opposing views and claims must be reconciled.

This chapter is concerned with how human interactions with rivers in Britain were dealt with in the past, how they are currently managed, and how the approach to river management is likely to change in the next few years. In broad terms, the history of river management in Britain has followed a pattern similar to the one outlined by the American geographer Gilbert F. White in the late 1960s (White 1969) (Figure 7.1). Initially river management is a relatively simple matter, with individuals and isolated communities using the resource freely with little if any adverse effect upon the river or other people. For example, scattered farms may use the river for the watering of cattle or for domestic water supply. However, with economic development

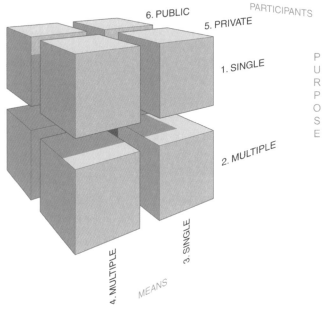

Figure 7.1.
The development of water management strategies.
(AFTER MITCHELL, 1986)

Strategy Combination	General Strategy Type	Example
1-3-5	Single purpose, single means, private sector	Farm pond for water supply
1-3-6	Single purpose, single means, public sector	Navigation canal
2-3-6	Multiple purpose, single means, public managers	Multiple purpose dam
1-4-6	Single purpose, multiple means, public managers	National flood damage reduction program
2-4-5-6	Multiple purpose, multiple means, public and private sector	

and the expansion of settlements, competition for available water and space next to the river starts to increase, giving rise to the need for some type of public body or authority to allocate water rights fairly in the interests of the whole community and to regulate against pollution and other harmful practices. At this time, river management is still limited to single structures (often dams) which are designed for single purposes, such as water supply.

With the passage of time, the demands of river-dependent communities become more diverse and a more sophisticated management approach is needed. At this point, a transition from 'single-purpose and single-means' to 'multiple-purpose and single-means' river management occurs. A good example of this phase in river management would be a dam (single means), paid for with public money and constructed for a range of purposes such as flood control, water supply, electricity generation and recreation.

The next phase in river management is characterised by the development of a much wider range of 'means' to satisfy the demands placed on the river. Rather than relying on a single means such as a dam, both structural and non-structural approaches are employed but often to satisfy a single need, such as flood control. Examples of structural or 'engineering' approaches include the use of levees and dams, water transfer schemes and waste-water treatment plants. In contrast, non-structural or 'behavioural' approaches include the use of licences and permits, farming practices designed to reduce the risk of river pollution, public education and awareness campaigns and charging schemes for angling and other recreational pursuits on rivers. Despite greater diversity in approach, during this phase river management is still carried out by public authorities under the direction of government officials and ministers.

According to White's model, the final and most desirable phase of river management is symbolised by a 'multiple-purpose, multiple-means and multiple-participant' approach. As such, the river is managed by both public and private organisations in a variety of different ways (structural and non-structural) in order to satisfy a range of uses and needs. Government agencies, private companies, environmental organisations, community associations, individual users and amenity groups are all considered to be legitimate players who can make important contributions to the effective management and sustainable development of rivers. Most commentators, including Gilbert F. White himself, agree that there are very few examples in the world where this final phase of river management has been put into practice fully. Significant challenges lie ahead in finding ways to involve a much wider array of non-governmental interests in river management.

Gilbert F. White's model provides a useful framework to examine how and why the management of British rivers has changed over time. This chapter traces the evolution of river management in Britain, from the impacts of the early hunters through to modern attempts to integrate the use of land and water management within entire river catchments. The chapter concludes by discussing some pressing issues which currently affect river management in Britain and by considering how those issues might be addressed.

The rise of river management in Britain

There is a long history within Britain of human interventions altering the flow and form of rivers. The first significant human impacts on the environment were the result of Mesolithic hunters and fishermen between 8000 and 3500 BC. However, it was the extensive removal of native woodland to create open land for farming, which pollen and other fossil evidence suggest began on a wide scale between 3000 and 2000 BC, that resulted in vast quantities of sediment being released into rivers (Eaton 1989). Not only were river run-off patterns extensively modified, but also aquatic vegetation started to develop because of the loss of bank-side shading; water quality was altered and floodplains were more frequently inundated. Despite the extensive nature of human impacts upon rivers during this early period there was little if any need for organised management, since people were few in number and capable of adapting to changes in the natural environment.

The arrival of the Romans in the late first century AD marked the introduction of direct forms of river management in Britain, particularly on the Somerset Levels and the East Anglian Fens. Many of the Roman water management schemes were for sea-defence purposes, but some were designed to drain the land into rivers, while other schemes enabled rivers to be navigated. Darby (1983) cites the example of Car Dyke in the East Anglian Fens, which linked the River Cam at Waterbeach to the River Witham near Lincoln via a chain of natural channels and artificial cuts. The Dyke served a land drainage function, but most importantly enabled grain and other goods to be transported from East Anglia to the north.

While the efforts of the Romans were confined to a few watercourses, by the fourteenth century many lowland rivers in Britain had been extensively changed by pre-industrial uses such as water milling and transportation. The construction of weirs, ponds and pound locks greatly altered the natural flow of many rivers throughout Britain. By the time of the Domesday Book in 1086, it is thought that the number of water mills on British rivers may have reached 6,000 (Darby 1977). In addition, wetland drainage schemes and the creation of water meadows to supply water and fertile silt to pastures from the fourteenth century onwards also caused lasting changes to the flow and ecological character of rivers.

At this point it is useful to reflect on the extent to which the early history of river management in Britain corresponds to the pattern suggested by Gilbert F. White. Before the arrival of the Romans in Britain, rivers were essentially used in a piecemeal fashion with little apparent attempt at formal control or management. From the first to the fourteenth century, water management in Britain was characterised by single purpose and single means schemes such as water mills and drainage networks operated for commercial profit rather than as public schemes for the benefit of whole river-dependent communities. As such, the initial phase in White's model does appear to describe the early development of river management in Britain remarkably well, even though it was based on much later experiences in North America.

There is some evidence to suggest that the need for formal administrative structures to control and manage rivers in Britain started to emerge in the fifteenth and sixteenth centuries, at a time when many private water schemes were operated and consequently the rights of the individual were pitched against the common good. For example, the Commissioners of Sewers established in 1427 and the General Sewers Act of 1531 both point towards the increasingly important role of statutory law, common law and central government generally in river management.

However, it would be wrong to claim that river management had become an entirely 'public' activity by this time. Throughout the seventeenth century, private capital was ventured by leading landowners in East Anglia, Lincolnshire and Cambridgeshire on schemes designed to speed the flow of water from low-lying areas to the sea, therefore improving the productivity of farmlands. For example, the Dutch engineer Cornelius Vermuyden was employed in the 1620s to complete a land drainage scheme for the Axholme district of Lincolnshire (Figure 7.2). Water from the River Idle was diverted into the Bykersdyke at Idle Stop and from there was able to follow a much shorter route to the River Trent at Stockwith. In addition, the eastern branch of the River Don was diverted at Thorne into the River Aire and eventually into the Yorkshire Ouse at Goole via an artificial channel called the Dutch River. The River Torne was also confined to a completely artificial channel designed to speed the flow of water across low-lying land to the River Trent at Althorpe.

Many of the drainage schemes constructed in the seventeenth century produced mixed results. Some could not cope with the highly variable volumes of flow and were washed away by heavy run-off in the winter or became blocked with sediment during the summer. Land was over-drained and in some cases actually became less productive. Because river run-off had to be directed somewhere, drainage schemes often resulted in disputes between landowners in different areas. The benefits gained from land drainage by some were often matched by flooding and increased losses for others.

River management schemes had become much more commonplace by the middle of the eighteenth century, but Britain was still essentially an

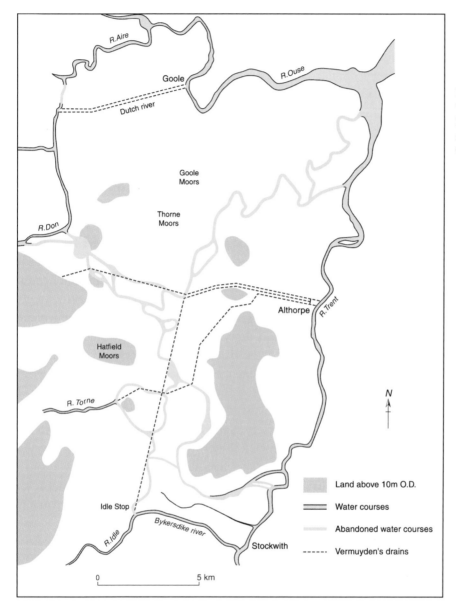

Figure 7.2.
The Isle of Axholme
land-drainage
scheme.
(AFTER SHEAIL, 1988)

agricultural country with a dispersed population of less than seven million (Petts 1988). While many rivers had been substantially altered by this time, their exploitation for human benefit and their ecological functioning essentially remained in balance.

The situation changed rapidly with the onset of the industrial revolution in the late eighteenth century, particularly in the river valleys of the Midlands and the North where large volumes of water could readily be supplied for powering machinery, for generating steam, for processing wool and cotton and for producing iron and steel. There is no question that industrialisation brought about enormous environmental change in Britain. Rivers were deepened and straightened and canals were dug to create extensive transport networks for the movement of raw materials and finished products. The Trent, Thames, Severn and Great Ouse were all navigable for more than 100 km inland from the sea as a result of engineering works. Although the development of railways and road transportation reduced the need for inland navigation, rivers continued to suffer other consequences as a result of industrialisation, including chronic pollution. For instance, Redford (1940) estimated that more than 33,000 tonnes of cinders and ashes were discarded annually into the Irwell in Manchester, the bed of which rose between 5 cm and 8 cm each year during the 1860s. In the case of the River Thames, parts became so polluted that 1858 became known as the 'Year of the Great Stink'.

The problems created by the industrial revolution prompted both innovative river engineering and change in the organisational structure of river management. One of the major effects of industrialisation was the growth of the urban population as workers were drawn to the towns and cities by the prospects of jobs in mills, factories and ironworks. For example, the population of Leeds was just 17,121 in 1775 but had grown to 53,000 by 1801; it had reached 123,000 by 1831, and 428,000 by 1901. This pattern was repeated in numerous other industrial towns and cities. The population of London grew

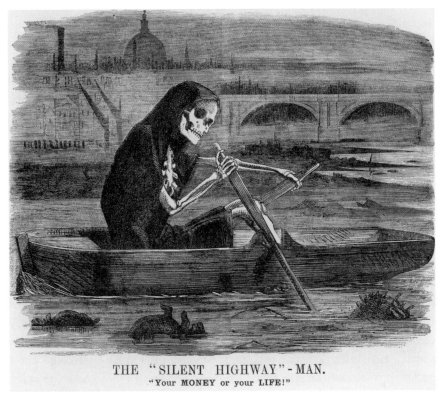

The Silent Highwayman, which appeared in *Punch* Magazine in 1858, is one of the most evocative and widely recognised images of water and air pollution. Between 1831 and 1867, more than 128,000 people died as a result of cholera epidemics in England alone.

THE "SILENT HIGHWAY" - MAN.
"Your MONEY or your LIFE!"

from 960,000 in 1801 to 1,776,566 in 1831 and that of Liverpool from 34,407 in 1773 to 202,000 in 1831 (Lawton 1990).

The rise of the industrial towns and cities led to both an increased demand for water and also greater discharges of domestic sewage and commercial waste. The River Aire in Yorkshire at the time has been described in the following terms:

> It was full of refuse from water closets, cesspools, privies, common drains, dung-hill drainings, infirmary refuse, wastes from slaughter houses, chemical soap, gas, dye-houses, and manufactures, coloured by blue and back dye, pig manure, old urine wash; there were dead animals, vegetable substances and occasionally a decomposed human body. (Wohl 1984, p. 285)

Since most water supplies were drawn locally, and waste was often returned to those same sources without any form of treatment, water-related diseases transmitted via the faecal–oral route, such as cholera and typhoid, became major concerns. In 1773, 50 per cent of Manchester's children died before the age of five (Lawton and Pooley 1992). Cholera first struck in England in 1831–32, killing 32,000 people. Further epidemics between 1848 and 1867 resulted in the deaths of a further 96,000 people (Wohl 1984).

A significant breakthrough came in 1855 when John Snow was able to establish a causal relationship between river pollution and the spread of disease. Snow demonstrated a higher incidence of cholera among Londoners who consumed polluted waters in Southwark and Vauxhall. Disease rates among similar social classes were much lower in Lambeth where the water supply came from a less polluted source (McDonald and Kay 1988). The evidence provided by Snow was seized upon by prominent public health reformers, most notably Edwin Chadwick, who argued for a total urban-environmental circular scheme for London involving a constant supply of piped water, water-carried sewage and disposal of human waste on to agricultural land for 'enrichment'.

As history has often demonstrated, it can take a considerable length of time before a scientific breakthrough is accepted by a professional community, and even longer before politicians are persuaded to use that breakthrough for public good. This was certainly the case with respect to water pollution and public health in Britain. At the time, lines between commercial interests and government responsibility were blurred and the notion of public accountability was barely recognised. Nineteenth-century reformers such as Chadwick, William Far, Edward Frankland and John Simon frequently complained that political power and money enabled water suppliers to procure 'scientific experts' willing to challenge evidence linking water pollution to disease (Luckin 1986).

Once the link between the contamination of domestic water supply and poor health was accepted, the initial response of most town councils was to establish an Improvement Commission. In a perverse way, the towns and cities were now reliant upon the polluting industries for a solution to the water supply and sewerage problem. Industry generated wealth and jobs, both of which were needed to provide capital for improvement works through taxes and rates.

Small towns in the southern Pennines of Lancashire and Yorkshire had begun to develop pure water supplies from reservoirs in the surrounding hills in the late eighteenth century. This practice was expanded throughout the nineteenth century under the Health Acts of 1875 and 1978, with the result that almost 200 water supply reservoirs were located in the Pennines by the early 1900s. While there had been only 11 municipal water supply undertakings in the 1830s, there were 78 in 1878 and more than 700 by 1914. The underlying principle in all such schemes was that the river upstream of the town was used as a 'zone of concentration' whereby pure water from the surrounding catchment could be gathered and piped to settlements and individual houses. Figure 7.3 provides an illustration of this approach, with a hypothetical city located midway in a river catchment. Upstream of the city, water is gathered from the surrounding rural landscape in order to provide an adequate supply for urban dwellers. One implication of this was that human activity, including the grazing of sheep and cattle, had to be kept to a minimum to prevent organic pollution of the water supply. To this day, it is not uncommon to find such upland catchments densely covered with conifer forest for this purpose, although the wisdom of this practice is now hotly debated among hydrologists. The area below the city was used as a 'zone of dispersal', for the disposal of sewage and industrial effluents (Figure 7.3). One

Figure 7.3. Zones of concentration and dispersal within a catchment.
(FROM McDONALD AND KAY 1988, P.36, PEARSON EDUCATION LTD)

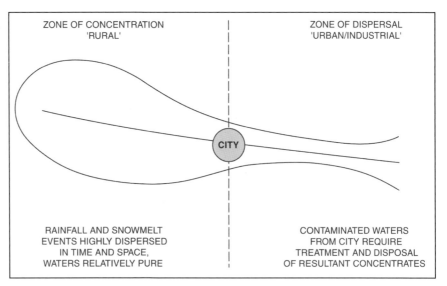

consequence of this approach was that lowland rivers in Britain tended to be forgotten and neglected at this time, since the priority of councils and river engineers was the acquisition and protection of upland water-gathering grounds. Although many towns did benefit from this rudimentary form of catchment-based river management, the majority of rural areas were not so fortunate. Low population densities meant that the cost per head of piped water was prohibitive for local parishes. Nearly all towns had piped supplies from reservoirs or other pure sources by the early 1900s but only one-third of rural parishes were in a similar position (Parker and Penning-Rowsell 1980).

With continued urban expansion in the mid- to late nineteenth century, it became increasingly difficult for local river management schemes to satisfy the requirements of the large conurbations. Cities such as Manchester, Liverpool and Birmingham had already exploited local rivers to the full, and therefore had to seek water from more distant places. As Stamp and Beaver (1963, p. 98–9) observed:

> Obviously the most suitable collecting grounds for water supply for a large city are the open moorlands or hilly areas which have heavy rainfall, but where there is not a large animal or human population living on the hills which would naturally pollute the water supply. Thus it is not too much to say that there has been a scramble amongst the more powerful city corporations to secure rights for this purpose over the more thinly inhabited parts of Wales, the Pennines, the Lake District and elsewhere.

In the 1850s, Liverpool was the first to adopt this approach, buying land and

William Ibbitt, *West View of Sheffield*, 1855.
Reservoirs in the hills to the west of Sheffield provided opportunities for local people to promenade as well as clean drinking water for some at least of the town's citizens.
SHEFFIELD GALLERIES AND MUSEUMS TRUST

RIVERS AND THE BRITISH LANDSCAPE

associated water rights in upland catchments in the Pennines and constructing a 40 kilometre aqueduct to the city. Liverpool completed a second scheme in 1880 involving the transfer of water over a distance of more than 100 kilometres from the Vyrnwy valley in Wales. At more than 40 metres in height, the Vyrnwy dam impounded nearly 60 million cubic metres of water to create the largest reservoir in Europe at that time. A similar scheme was completed for Birmingham in 1892 in which water was taken from the Wye valley in Wales and another scheme transferring water from Cumbria to Manchester was completed shortly after. In comparison to the rivers in close proximity to these large urban centres, schemes of this type could yield large volumes of high-quality water suitable for domestic use. Additional barriers against bacteriological contamination of the water supply, such as extended reservoir storage, sand filtration and eventually chlorination were added at later stages to produce very high standards of water quality (Eaton 1989).

Despite the benefits afforded to thousands of urban dwellers, the use of upland water supply systems created a number of problems. In addition to the obvious loss of scenic landscapes following the damming of river valleys, an inefficient and unfair pattern of water supply emerged as each town scrambled to acquire land and the water rights associated with it. Upland water sources were often bought by wealthy towns but subsequently wasted or not used to their full capacity while other communities could not obtain any form of water fit for human consumption. It was becoming increasingly clear that Britain needed a more co-ordinated approach to river management which gave consideration to other important aspects beyond mere water supply.

By the end of the nineteenth century, river management in Britain had clearly evolved from a situation where private capital and interests predominated to one in which public health, and therefore public water supply, dominated the agenda. The dams, reservoirs and transfer schemes first built by small towns in the eighteenth century and later commissioned on a much larger scale by the rapidly growing cities of the nineteenth century clearly reflect the single-purpose, single-means, public-funded and controlled approach identified by Gilbert F. White as the second phase of river management. The sixteenth and seventeenth centuries really represented a period of transition in which practical river management was largely carried out privately but with increasing efforts to create a system of public control and regulation.

The management of river basins in Britain

At the start of the twentieth century, some appreciation of the need to manage rivers in a more co-ordinated fashion had begun to emerge. Up to this time, management activities such as water supply and sewerage, land drainage and navigation had been carried out in a highly fragmented fashion by separate local authorities and other organisations which often had little to do with each other. For example, in England and Wales, public water supply was the responsibility of more than 2,000 separate organisations, ranging from council departments to licensed private companies. Sewerage and sewage treatment remained a separate local authority function. Similar situations existed in Scotland, where there were still 210 separate water undertakings as late as 1944, although private water companies did disappear in 1946. Central government responded by passing the 1945 Water Act and the Water (Scotland) Act of 1946, which empowered the Minister of Health and Secretary of State for Scotland to order amalgamations of local water supply undertakings so that economies of scale could be generated and conflicts between rival authorities could be resolved. In practice, central government relied on persuasion rather than legal force, with the result that very few water supply amalgamations actually occurred.

Before the 1930s, other important aspects of river management such as fisheries, the control of industrial pollution, conservation and recreation had been largely ignored by central government. Previous experience with the management of upland catchments had clearly shown that water quality and

Sheffield from Lady's Bridge (1875), by an unknown artist. Despite the pollution of the river Don, exacerbated by over-extraction of water upstream, a brewery is in full production on the riverbank.

water quantity were inextricably linked. Over-abstraction of water from a river could leave insufficient for the dilution of waste, a problem referred to as 'negative pollution' by the Yorkshire engineer Malcolm McCulloch Paterson when giving evidence to a parliamentary committee in 1896 on the state of the River Don at Sheffield.

Partly as a result of the lack of success in creating larger and more efficient arrangements for water supply, attention was turned to other aspects of the hydrologic cycle in an attempt to develop administrative arrangements which would allow rivers to be managed in a co-ordinated fashion from source to mouth. Such thinking coincided with advances in the science of hydrology, which provided new insights into the functioning of river catchments, such as the impacts of agriculture and forestry on water quantity and quality and the relationship between upland drainage and lowland flooding. The goal was to place entire river catchments under the control of a single authority that in theory would be more efficient and would enable different uses and claims on available water to be balanced more effectively.

It is perhaps surprising that initial attempts at whole catchment management in Britain were focused on land drainage. However, as Newson (1992) explained, drainage has been of paramount importance in the settlement and optimum use of land. To this day, approximately half of lowland Britain would be waterlogged and unfit for habitation without the maintenance of drainage and flood defence works. A total of 47 separate Catchment Boards were first established in England and Wales under the 1930 Land Drainage Act. Under the direction of the Ministry of Agriculture, each Board drew together the various public and private interests to plan and allocate investment for land drainage across the entire catchment. Each catchment area was sub-divided among several Internal Drainage Boards (IDBs), which were granted powers to levy rates for the construction and maintenance of arterial drains. The IDBs still exist and have been accused by some of being slow to adopt conservation practices in the planning and construction of drainage works, and also of being overly protective of landed interests.

Throughout the 1920s and 1930s, the Ministry of Agriculture also introduced a system of catchment-wide Fisheries Boards in England and Wales. Fishing rights were economically important and riparian landowners were keen to protect their interests against the growing pressures of water abstraction and waste disposal. These emergent drainage and fisheries management organisations provided a platform from which more sophisticated arrangements for catchment management would subsequently be developed. Commenting on their significance, Kinnersley (1988, pp. 71–2) stated:

These new (or in some cases reshaped) boards were bringing together various local interests or lobbies such as elected councillors, landowners, anglers and others directly engaged in river basin activities, in a close relationship with central government also, but in each case for a river-related territory. The significance of the systematic revision of legislation and administration in this way was that, while local influence was being kept very strong, the central government (in the shape of the Ministry of Agriculture and Fisheries) was becoming more committed in the 1920s and 1930s to a coherent pattern covering these specialist water functions across England and Wales.

The arrangements for catchment management in England and Wales were advanced once again by the 1948 River Boards Act. Replacing the Catchment and Fisheries Boards with 32 new River Boards was a major step towards multi-purpose river basin management. Each River Board was responsible for land drainage, fisheries and navigation in a jurisdiction defined by hydro-logical rather than political boundaries. Under the 1951 Rivers Pollution Prevention Act, River Boards were given additional powers to license new, but not existing, waste discharges. Furthermore, local councils were usually heavily represented on the River Boards and hence there was little attempt to improve discharges from municipal sewerage systems. The absence of water supply planning and operation from this arrangement was, without doubt, another major deficiency. The towns, cities and other owners of land adjacent to rivers fiercely resisted the suggestion that responsibility for water supply should be given to the River Boards.

The 1963 Water Resources Act finally removed riparian water supply rights in England and Wales and introduced a system of licensing for all water taken from rivers and underground sources. Although local authorities could no longer claim automatic rights to water, they remained in control of sewage disposal, and the water supply function was placed in the hands of statutory water undertakings either in the form of local authority agencies or private water companies.

The main advance achieved through the 1963 Act was a change in emphasis from single-purpose river management to a more multi-purpose approach in which agricultural drainage, flood alleviation, pollution prevention, fisheries and navigation were all carried out by 29 River Authorities organised along similar hydrologic boundaries as the 34 River Boards which they replaced. While the River Authorities were not responsible for the operational aspects of water supply, they did have additional powers related to water resource development, conservation, abstraction and forward planning. The division of responsibility for national water policy within central government placed further constraints on the ability to deliver multi-purpose catchment management. Under the 1963 Act, the Ministry of Agriculture, Fisheries and Food retained overall control of land drainage, flood alleviation and fisheries while the Ministry of Housing and Local Government oversaw all the remaining functions of the River Authorities. This fragmented approach within central government proved to be particularly problematic in later years when agricultural practices were pinpointed as some of the most significant causes of organic pollution in British rivers.

The 1963 Water Resources Act was ambitious for its time, but still failed to live up to the ideal of fully co-ordinated river basin management. Parker and Sewell (1988, p. 762) captured the essence of the problem:

> The 1963 Water Resources Act did not go far enough in consolidating water management units. The major flaw – the continued separate management of the 'dirty' [sewage disposal] and 'clean' [water supply] sides of the water cycle – quickly surfaced in the late 1960s as a major continuing coordination problem. The issue was exacerbated by the increased reliance upon 'dirty' lowland river sources as new 'clean' upland sites for water storage became increasingly difficult to find, owing in part to the increased public concern about adverse environmental and social impacts of reservoir developments.

The inability of the River Authorities to tackle the sewage disposal problem effectively had enormous implications because of post-war population growth and economic expansion. Improved sewage treatment and pollution control could have allowed more water to be taken from lowland rivers for water supply purposes. The closure of this option meant that even more emphasis was placed on expensive long-distance transfer schemes, culminating in the release of a national water plan in the early 1970s which envisaged a national water grid.

Only a decade after the River Authorities had been established, they were swept away by what has been described as a 'revolution' in water management in England and Wales. The 1973 Water Act combined most of the water supply agencies, all of the sewage treatment units and all of the functions of the River Authorities to create 10 Regional Water Authorities (RWAs). Approximately thirty private water companies were retained as agents to the new RWAs to provide 22 per cent of the public water supply. Each RWA operated within river basin boundaries and was responsible for water development and conservation, water treatment and distribution, sewerage and sewage treatment, water quality regulation, pollution control, flood alleviation, land drainage, recreation, fisheries and navigation. For the first time, parts of Britain could legitimately claim to be practising a true form of multi-purpose river basin management, but the move was not without risks. Perhaps most problematic of all was the combination of regulatory and operational functions within the same organisations (Kinnersley 1988). In effect, the RWAs were expected to police themselves to ensure that effluent from sewage treatment works was within consented limits. This situation has been referred to as the 'poacher and gamekeeper problem'. This was not helped by the continued division of responsibility for water within central government between the Ministry of Agriculture, Fisheries and Food and what had become by that time the Department of the Environment.

From the beginning, the RWAs were faced with an almost impossible task. The RWAs inherited massive debts, and they could not obtain local support grants from central government because the 1973 Act had removed water management from local authority control. Charges to water users were increased, but this was not enough to generate sufficient revenue for the RWAs to fulfil all their duties competently. The 1974 Control of Pollution Act (COPA) also proved to be problematic for the RWAs. Increased expenditure by industry and the RWAs was viewed as an inflationary pressure at a time when anti-inflationary policy was a government priority. Thus, it became necessary for the RWAs to relax discharge consents at some of their own sewage treatment works in order to comply with the law while also avoiding additional expenditure. Not surprisingly, water quality in the lowland sections of many rivers in England and Wales was extremely poor in the late 1970s and early 1980s.

Attempts were also made in Scotland to move towards multi-purpose river management from the 1960s onwards. At around this time there were no fewer than 210 water supply authorities and 234 local drainage authorities in Scotland. In 1968 responsibility for water supply was transferred to thirteen Regional Water Boards and a Central Scotland Water Development Board. The Rivers (Prevention of Pollution) Act of 1951 created seven catchment-based River Purification Boards to maintain river quality and to conserve water resources through a system of discharge consents.

Following a re-organisation of local government in 1975, the duties of the Regional Water Boards plus responsibilities for land drainage and flood prevention were transferred to nine Regional Councils. The Central Scotland Water Development Board was retained and the powers of the River Purification Boards were extended to include all inland and coastal waters. According to Hammerton (1989), the independence of the River Purification Boards is ensured by their membership, one-third being appointed by Regional Councils, one-third by District Councils and one-third by the Secretary of State for Scotland to represent agricultural, industrial and environmental interests. Different arrangements were created for the Western Isles, Orkney and Shetland, where all-purpose authorities were given dual responsibility for water pollution control and water services. Thus, with some exceptions, the relationship between the operational and regulatory aspects of river management was much clearer and less prone to conflicts of interest in Scotland than it was in England and Wales at this time.

The account of river management in Britain between the early 1900s and late 1970s shows some resemblance to the multiple-purpose, single-means, public management strategy described by White. Rivers were increasingly viewed as multi-functional resources which should be managed at the catchment scale. The integration of different river management functions into progressively larger administrative units was the primary means by which river managers worked towards the multi-purpose approach. However, as experiences in England and Wales demonstrated, this approach was not always successful because of conflicts between the regulatory and operational duties of the water authorities.

From the 1980s onwards, the pattern of river management in Britain became more complex and the chronology described by White was less closely observed. In practice, the multi-purpose and single-means approach continued to predominate but at the same time examples of single-purpose and multiple-means river management started to emerge. The management of river floods is probably the clearest example of the single-purpose, multiple-means approach in Britain.

The natural function of rivers is to drain land. It is inevitable that, after rainfall of high intensity or long duration, rivers will occasionally overflow their banks. Over-confidence in our ability to control the flow of rivers has produced a situation in which floodplains are judged to be completely safe for human habitation. Many of the areas affected by the widespread floods of 1947 are now heavily urbanised and it has been estimated that as many as 250,000 people in England and Wales are at risk from river floods which can be expected to occur on average once every 100 years (Penning-Rowsell and Handmer 1988).

In Britain the traditional approach to the control of river flooding has been predominantly 'structural' or 'engineered' in character. Typically, the threat of flooding has been tackled by deepening and straightening river channels to accommodate more water and by removing rough bed material to reduce resistance to flow. In addition, flood walls or levees have been constructed to contain the flow of water that does overspill the riverbanks. Investment in such flood alleviation schemes was often based on a simple cost-benefit analysis in which the costs of construction and maintenance were compared to the damages to be avoided. Unfortunately, calculations based on purely economic criteria failed to take account of other factors such as environmental damage caused by river engineering or the consequences of flood alleviation works for settlements further downstream.

The enormous financial and environmental costs associated with flood alleviation have led to calls for a more diverse 'multiple-means' approach to flood hazard management in Britain in which structures are used more sensitively alongside non-structural responses such as catchment control, land-use planning, flood warnings, flood proofing and flood insurance. As such, the more modern approach is to try to prevent river flooding in an economically and environmentally sustainable way while at the same time preparing for those larger floods which cannot be prevented. Catchment control involves the modification of land cover in order to manipulate the flow of water. For example, the establishment of forest cover in upland areas can reduce water yields by up to 40 per cent. However, one of the drawbacks of this approach is that a dense network of drainage ditches is required for early tree growth and this can have the effect of increasing the short-term risk of flooding.

A combination of land-use planning, flood warnings and flood insurance can be used to reduce our vulnerability to river flooding. In the last few years, the Environment Agency has formally objected to many housing development proposals in parts of England and Wales that are prone to flooding. Unfortunately, the Environment Agency does not have the legal authority to prevent such developments and planning approval is often granted because of the high demand for new housing. Positively, more emphasis has been placed on automated flood warning schemes and the flood-proofing of buildings. For example, the Environment Agency issues flood warnings via the telephone and radio broadcasts to the City of York on the River Ouse. Furthermore, many buildings along the banks of the River Ouse are designed to minimize the impacts of flooding. The photograph below shows a hotel

Flooding of the River Ouse at York is common during the winter months. Businesses adjacent to the river, such as this hotel, have installed their own flood defences such as movable barriers in doorways. In addition, the lower floors of buildings are often used for car parking which can be quickly evacuated when a flood warning is received.
S. OWEN

RIVERS AND THE BRITISH LANDSCAPE

entrance fitted with a movable flood barrier. The lower floor of the hotel, which is used as a car park, can be cleared quickly when a flood warning is received. Despite the move away from total reliance on flood control structures in recent years, there have been some worrying developments regarding flood insurance. An increasing number of insurance companies no longer include flood risks as part of standard home insurance policies and residents in particularly high-risk areas are finding it increasingly difficult to obtain any form of flood insurance. In the long term the practice adopted by the insurance industry may have the desirable effect of discouraging building in flood-prone areas. However, at present many people living in low-lying areas of Britain are in an extremely vulnerable position.

Towards integrated management of river basins in Britain

Much of the history of river management in Britain has been dominated by attempts to satisfy increasing human requirements for clean water and for cost-effective waste disposal. As a result, most rivers in Britain have been altered from their natural state in some way, and many have become degraded. In the last decade a new management philosophy has emerged which seeks to restore rivers to a healthy state and to ensure that their future use is set within a stronger framework of environmental protection. This most recent development reflects in part the idea of multiple-purpose, multiple-means and multiple participant river management first advocated by Gilbert F. White. From this perspective, rivers are seen as valuable resources that fulfil many different economic, social, cultural and environmental needs. In order to balance those needs, a wider range of management tools and techniques must be used, ranging from legislation and regulation through to voluntary action and community campaigns. Advocates of this approach argue that truly integrated river basin management cannot be achieved by legislation and other conventional means alone. Furthermore, river manage-ment is no longer regarded as the exclusive domain of government and public agencies. A partnership approach, in which government, industry, commerce and community groups work cooperatively, is now regarded as an essential prerequisite for balanced and integrated river management.

The Mersey Basin Campaign provides an interesting example of how different groups are working together to restore Britain's most heavily used and polluted rivers. The Mersey is the largest river in North West England and is formed at the confluence of the Rivers Goyt and Tame in the town of Stockport. The total length of the river from source to mouth is only 60 km, but the basin itself covers 4,680 square kilometres, includes more than 2,000 km of watercourse and is home to more than 5 million people. Until the late eighteenth century, the Mersey was a clean river with a sizeable fishing industry. Salmon could be caught up to 40 km upstream from the sea. The Manchester Ship Canal is a significant feature of the Mersey Basin. Built in 1894 to enable sea-going vessels to travel inland to Manchester, the canal is now largely disused upstream of the tidal limit.

During the industrial revolution, water for the rapidly expanding population in the Mersey Basin was transferred from the un-polluted uplands of Wales, the Pennines and Cumbria. However, the Mersey was heavily used for the disposal of industrial waste and sewage and by the middle of the nineteenth century it was among the most polluted rivers in the country.

Gradual progress towards the restoration of the Mersey was made between the 1950s and 1970s when new legislation established limits on pollution and required all discharges to be authorised. A significant step was taken in 1980 when the government and what was then the North West Regional Water Authority launched a £170 million scheme to clean up the estuary. This was followed in 1985 by the launch of the Mersey Basin Campaign (MBC), a twenty-five year initiative to clean up the main river and all its tributaries at an estimated cost of £4 billion.

Jones (1999, p. 133) summed up the managerial philosophy and approach of the MBC in the following terms:

River Mersey, Manchester
CHRIS E. MAKEPEACE

RIVERS AND THE BRITISH LANDSCAPE

The Manchester Ship
Canal in the 1920s.

In order to be successful the Campaign had to establish constructive partnerships between a whole range of organisations. It was recognized that big, bureaucratic approaches did not work (indeed money for this method was not available) and that local communities had to be involved in the design, implementation and management of schemes. These concerns moved environmental action away from confrontational approaches adopted in the 1960s and 1970s. It is the ability of the Mersey Basin Campaign to capitalise on its partners' strengths and abilities that underlies its success.

Three broad objectives for the MBC were defined at the outset:

- To improve water quality so that by 2010 all rivers, streams and canals are clean enough to support fish.

- To stimulate the development of attractive waterside environments for businesses, housing, tourism, heritage, recreation and wildlife.

THE MANAGEMENT OF RIVERS

- To encourage people living and working in the Mersey Basin to value and cherish their watercourses and waterfront environments.

The MBC has an unusual but interesting mode of operation. Essentially federal in character, the MBC works by generating what is often termed a 'collaborative advantage'. Since no single organisation has the resources, expertise or authority to tackle the problems of the River Mersey, effective action is dependent on a partnership approach in which additional gains are achieved by two or more organisation working together rather than working alone and possibly at cross-purposes.

There are two key organisations within the MBC, each of which has responsibility for developing and maintaining relationships with a different sector. The MBC Administration Limited is responsible for liaison with the public sector (such as local authorities, the Environment Agency and the North West Development Agency) and for the overall management and promotion of the Campaign. The Mersey Basin Business Foundation helps businesses to improve their environmental performance and encourages their involvement in the Campaign. These two key organisations have equal status and are headed by executive directors. The Secretary of State for the Environment appoints a new chairperson for the whole of the MBC every three years and an MBC Council meets on a quarterly basis. In addition, a major conference is held every three years at which all of the organisations involved in the Campaign review progress and plan new collaborative initiatives.

Initially formed as part of the MBC, the Mersey Basin Trust now works independently with approximately 600 wildlife, angling, recreational, heritage, canal and civic groups. The Trust operates a Stream Care initiative which encourages communities to adopt and clean up local watercourses, a 'Water Detectives' initiative which encourages schools to use local watercourses for study, and a Grant Scheme for projects such as new fishing facilities, habitat creation and footpath improvements.

In less than twenty years, the actions of the MBC and its partner organisations have had a marked impact on the river and the surrounding area. The percentage of river length capable of supporting fish life has risen from just 56 per cent to more than 70 per cent and thirty-five different species can now be found in the Mersey estuary. More than £700 million has been spent on improved waste-water treatment facilities and the input of heavy metals has declined from approximately 60 tonnes per year to one tonne per year. More than £500 million has been spent on infrastructure renewal and economic generation in the Campaign area and public access has been either improved or opened along more than 60 km of waterside (Jones 1999). One of the major innovations attempted by the MBC concerned the River Valleys Initiatives (RVIs). Launched in 1993, the RVIs were designed to achieve the objectives of the MBC by concentrating efforts locally on individual tributaries within the Basin. As Kidd and Shaw (2000, p. 198) observed:

> Through the RVIs it was envisaged that the partnership approach of the MBC, which had been brought to bear so successfully at the strategic Mersey Basin level, could be developed to encourage local stewardship of individual watercourses. The fundamental principle behind the RVIs was that there was a need to harness the MBC's message at the local level by giving communities and individuals the opportunity to identify with its vision and objectives and be stimulated to take action themselves.

Six different RVIs were established between 1993 and 1996 (the Rivers Alt, Bollin, Darwen, Weaver, plus the Sankey Brook and Canal and also the Wirral peninsula catchments). The main benefit derived from the RVIs has been an ability to fine-tune larger publicly and privately funded river management projects (such as waste-water treatment facilities) to fit local needs and conditions. While some of the RVIs have been criticised for failing to mobilise local community action, it should also be pointed out that effective partnership arrangements take time to develop and perhaps it is too early to judge the overall success of the RVI initiative.

The River Tweed provides a further example of an innovative and collaborative approach to the management of rivers. With a catchment area of 5,000 km², the Tweed is Scotland's second largest river and provides 15 per cent of all the spawning waters available in Scotland for Atlantic salmon. The Tweed covers a distance of 160 km from the source in the Lowther Hills to the breakwater at Berwick upon Tweed and is among the UK's least polluted rivers. Tributaries of the Tweed include the River Teviot, the River Till, Megget Water and Whiteadder Water, many of which include reservoirs. Average rainfall decreases from west to east, with 2000 mm typically falling in the western upper reaches and approximately 650 mm falling in the eastern reaches near Berwick. Although the primary purpose of the reservoirs is to collect and store water for public supply, they also enable the flow of the river to be enhanced during the dry summer months by the return of 'compensation water' in order to satisfy requirements for conservation and recreation. While the Scottish Environmental Protection Agency (SEPA) has a statutory responsibility for the protection and regulation of water flows in the Tweed, increasing emphasis has been placed on a voluntary and co-operative approach to the management of this important river during the last decade.

The Tweed Forum was created in 1991 as an informal collection of public and private organisations dedicated to the wise and sustainable use of the Tweed catchment through holistic and integrated management and planning. In 1998 the Tweed Forum was formally established as a not-for-profit company with five directors and a management group of fifteen people drawn from the wider membership of twenty-nine different organisations. In effect, the Tweed Forum is an intermediary organisation which addresses issues that fall outside the remit of government agencies and seeks to facilitate decision-making by consensus rather than by coercion. In many respects, the Tweed Forum symbolises current thinking about sustainable river management. For instance, the importance of managing the land and water components of the catchment in a co-ordinated fashion was recognised at the outset. Great importance was also attached to the fundamental role of the Tweed in the economy and the landscape of the Borders region. The Tweed Forum also reflects a managerial philosophy which favours information exchange, collaboration and negotiation rather than the heavy hand of government regulation as a way of developing and implementing river management policy and, as such, may offer some important lessons for the future.

Prospects for the future

Although the Mersey Basin Campaign and the Tweed Forum provide useful examples of how the efforts and interests of multiple participants can be combined in a collaborative approach to river management, it would be wrong to suggest that this is the norm in Britain. In reality, river management is still in general considered to be the domain of public authorities, albeit with some form of public consultation and private sector involvement in areas such as public water supply and sewerage. Water supply and sewerage services in England and Wales were privatised in 1989. The multi-functional Regional Water Authorities were disbanded and a new National Rivers Authority (NRA) with responsibilities for pollution control and river management was created. The NRA itself was merged with Her Majesty's Inspectorate of Pollution and the local waste regulation authorities in 1996 to form the Environment Agency for England and Wales. In addition to its powers for the control of water, land and air pollution, the Environment Agency also has duties related to the management of river catchments and the promotion of river conservation. Similar institutional changes occurred during 1996 in Scotland, where the Scottish Environmental Protection Agency (SEPA) assumed the previous responsibilities of the River Purification Boards.

River management is generally regarded as a matter for government and its agencies rather than something that is of direct interest or concern to local communities. There are, however, signs that this may change in the near future. Public officials are paying increasing attention to the partnership approach demonstrated by the Mersey Basin Campaign and other similar initiatives such as the Tweed Forum in Scotland. European environmental legislation has been instrumental in bringing about this change in professional attitudes to river management. The European Water Framework Directive (WFD) requires all member states to develop comprehensive strategies to restore water quality and to achieve good ecological status in all rivers. What is more, the WFD requires a consistent approach to river management, including the development of river basin management plans, full assessments of the impacts of human activities upon rivers plus economic studies of the value of rivers and the costs associated with their use. A dominant theme running through the WFD is the importance of public participation during all phases of river management, from initial planning through to final implementation. As such, each member state of the EU must be able to demonstrate that each river within its jurisdiction is managed in a balanced and sustainable way and that the full range of interests are involved in the decision-making process.

It seems, therefore, that Britain may, finally, move towards a situation in which rivers are managed in a balanced fashion, taking into account the full range of economic, social, cultural and environmental purposes, using a wide variety of tools and techniques and engaging public and private interests at many different levels. Whether Gilbert F. White's vision of integrated river management becomes a reality in Britain will depend on many things, not least the extent to which public agencies are prepared to relinquish a degree of control and the willingness of private companies, community groups and voluntary organisations to step forward and contribute their time, energy and resources to a common cause.

This account has attempted to show that river management in Britain is not just a technical activity but is inherently political and institutional in character. River management involves choices regarding which needs and interests will be fulfilled (and equally which will not), what means will be used to control the flow and quality of the watercourse, and where managerial power and responsibility will reside within society. Such choices are never simple and often require some sort of compromise between human and environmental requirements. The historical account shows that we have tended to place great emphasis on the satisfaction of immediate human needs and have overlooked the environmental consequences and the resulting longer-term problems for ourselves. It will be interesting to see over the next few years whether the current fascination with collaborative river management in Britain is successful in redressing the balance fully.

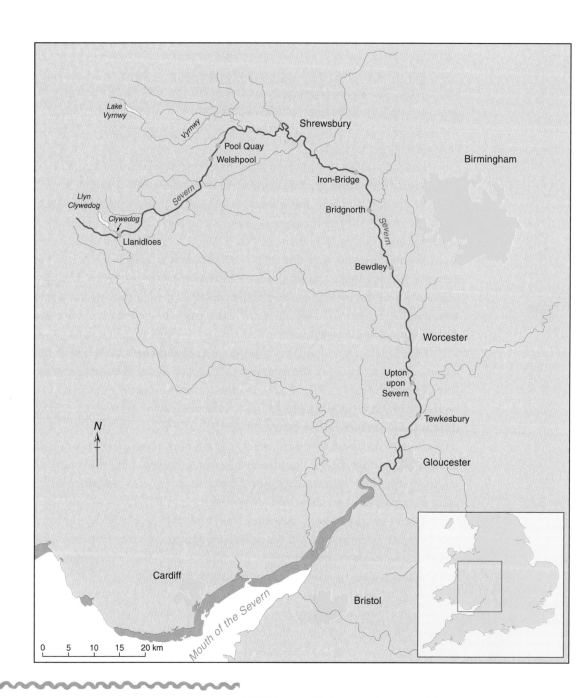

CHAPTER 8

A journey down the river Severn

Sue Owen

Introduction

I undertook a journey along the course of the River Severn in the summer of 2003. The Severn, as an exemplar of British rivers and the issues raised in this book, seemed an obvious choice as not only is it a significant feature of the landscape, it also flows through a variety of scenery and historically significant towns. A journey along the river would therefore offer an opportunity to explore the development of the river together with the historical and cultural landscape of the Welsh and English towns and countryside it passes through.

At 354 km the Severn is the longest river in Britain and has the largest single river basin in England and Wales. Yet in comparison to other European rivers the Severn's basin, or catchment, is small, for example its mean discharge is less than one-fiftieth of the flow of the Danube (Wood 1987). The particular combination of geology, distinctive landscape, climate and human interventions, particularly related to economic activities through time, has produced a unique river, one which illustrates well many of the issues explored elsewhere in this book.

It is not often that one makes a journey from a river's source to the sea, to be able to absorb the changing nature of a river, the diversity of its landscape and its response to a variety of natural conditions and human interventions. This journey takes Gunn's (1991: 42) advice that, 'going from the mouth to the source may well seem to be reversing the natural order, to be going from the death of the sea, where individuality is lost, back to the source of the stream, where individuality is born'.

Figure 8.1.
The course of the river Severn, together with some places mentioned in the text.
DEPARTMENT OF GEOGRAPHY, LANCASTER UNIVERSITY

Along the journey particular examples of the physical, economic, management and cultural features of the river and its landscape are taken from three distinct areas (as designated by the Environment Agency 1997, 1998, 1999): the Severn Uplands, the Middle Severn and the Severn Vale. The Severn Uplands include the Welsh mountain area and the southern Shropshire plain west of Shrewsbury; the Middle Severn contains Shrewsbury, the Ironbridge Gorge, and the broad river valley with its alluvial terraces from Bridgnorth down to Worcester; and the Severn Vale runs from north of Tewkesbury to the river's outflow into the Bristol Channel. The examples that I give within the chapter are not exhaustive and represent only my impression of the river during a hot August visit. For the sake of clarity and to avoid repetition, I have highlighted specific places to represent one particular issue.

The river

The River Severn, or Hafren in Welsh, rises at 613 m, only 4 km from the source of the River Wye, on the flanks of Plynlimon (741 m) in the Cambrian Mountains (Fig 8.1). It subsequently flows from Wales into England through the local authorities of Powys, Shropshire, Worcestershire, Gloucestershire, South Gloucestershire and Bristol. Travelling through its upper, middle and lower reaches it is joined by a number of streams and tributaries including the rivers Clywedog, Vyrnwy, Avon and Wye, which significantly add to its volume.

Unsurprisingly certain reaches, landscapes and settlements appealed to me more than others. In terms of the 'natural' aesthetic appearance of the river these reaches tended to be in the Welsh and Shropshire upland region, where the stream gathers pace after its boggy source and passes through narrow, green and fertile valleys. Not only can the river be seen in these reaches, but it also can be heard as the sound of its passage along the channel competes only with the noise of the woodland and forest. Here, also, the settlements on its banks appear to have an obvious attachment to the river. This contrasts with the lower reaches where the river, now travelling through a wider valley, seems physically removed from the settlements on its banks. This in part is due to the flood defences protecting the larger towns and cities from the most extreme effects of floodwaters. Yet many of these settlements, like the upland villages and towns, also owe their origins to the presence of the river. Also in these middle and lower reaches the river appears to have lost its 'liveliness' and 'freshness', evolving from its earlier dynamic form into a wide snake of brown water, hardly appearing to move, its noise now muted, lost among the increasing background noise.

My own subjective attraction to the wilder, narrower, noisier reaches of the river is indicative of the instinctive human preference for the more natural phenomena of water, forests, mountains and valleys (Tuan 1974b, Appleton 1975). Interestingly Brown and Daniel (1991) point out that even the flow rate of a river affects the viewer's estimation of its scenic quality. The optimum flow rate, between 31 and 42 m^3 s^{-1}, is quite a lively flow which corresponds closely to that of the Severn's upland reaches (see Table 8.1 p. 201).

In August the river appeared benign and at times sluggish; however, a visit in the winter and spring would offer a river of completely different character not only in its appearance and flow rate but also in its effect on the adjacent landscape. Where appropriate, therefore, issues such as flooding are incorporated in this account. The information within the chapter has been gathered from personal observation and sources gathered along the way, for example in published literature, local history museums such as those at Llanidloes and Welshpool, and information centres. Other sources included a great deal of published literature on the River Severn ranging from academic articles (the Severn catchment being one of the most studied catchments in Britain), to walking guides including one on the newly instigated long distance footpath, the Severn Way (The Severn Way Partnership 1999), and information available on the internet.

The popularity of the river as a cultural resource and a venue for recreation was also reflected in the many local walking guides and pamphlets available in local Tourist Information Centres, and pamphlets and books written with a particular interest in mind, which reflect more personal attachments to the river (Witts 1998, 1998a, Bibby 2002). For example Witts (1998) in *A Century of Bridges* provides an illustrated account of all the bridges crossing the river. Such concerns with bridges recalls Hardy's recognition within *The Mayor of Casterbridge* of the many purposes and appearances of bridges:

> These bridges had speaking countenances. Every projection in each was worn down to obtuseness partly by the weather, more by friction from generations of loungers, whose toes and heels had from year to year made restless movements against these parapets, as they stood there meditating on the aspects of affairs.

Indeed, many of the photographs of the river taken for this chapter included, or were taken from, bridges. Standing on a bridge gives a good view of the river and the adjacent settlement and landscape and in many cases offers our only opportunity of getting close to a river. There were a number of occasions where access to the river's banks proved difficult due to private ownership and dense vegetation, and even the negotiated Severn Way footpath occasionally has to follow canal towpaths and roads because of restricted access to the riverside. Yet important components of a relationship with a river include the ease of access to its banks and the ability to become immersed in both a natural habitat and the wildlife within it (Green and Tunstall 1992, Tapsell *et al.* 2001). This apparent need to be close to moving water is also reflected in the many pastimes undertaken on the river or its bank. Fishing, boating, including canal boats, commercial crafts and privately owned leisure cruisers, and canoeing were well represented, all offering opportunities to come closer to the river, to experience peacefulness and relaxation (Tapsell *et al.* 2001) and to gain a different perspective of the river and its landscape.

The historical landscape of the Severn looked very different from how it appears today. The pre-glacial landscape of the Severn was one of contrasts between the west and the east, between the Ordovician and Silurian grits, slates and shales of central Wales and the higher Welsh borderland and the younger sedimentary rocks of the Devonian, Carboniferous, Triassic and Jurassic period in the lower Welsh borderland and Severn valley, which can be seen for example in the outcrops of Old Red Sandstone around Welshpool. The Devensian glaciation, which reached its greatest extent between 25,000 and 18,000 BP (before present), also had a geographical division, with much of the western uplands covered with glacial sands and tills and some 42 per cent of the present Severn valleys glaciated (Lewin 1987).

In contrast, the eastern valley was free from glaciation but was subject to periglacial/freeze–thaw processes which caused extensive erosion and later fluvial activity, when substantial amounts of sediment and debris were washed down in the torrential streams and rivers and deposited on the eastern plain (Mitchell and Gerrard 1987). During this period the path taken by the

right Gravel bed channel, Hafren Forest.
S. OWEN

far right Bedrock channel, Hafren Forest.
S. OWEN

The source of the River Severn, Plynlimon.
S. OWEN

RIVERS AND THE BRITISH LANDSCAPE

upper Severn was distinctly different from today, draining to the north into the estuary of the Dee rather than the south (Hamblin 1986). It was the subsequent blockage of the river flow by ice sheets and the breaching of the divide between the Upper and Lower Severn during the Devensian glaciation, which connected the two systems and re-channelled the river's flow southwards, thus producing a single Severn. The present Severn, is therefore as Lewin (1987) notes a surprisingly 'modern' river system.

Severn-Break-its-Neck-Falls.
s. OWEN

The Severn Uplands

The source of the river Severn is a boggy pool on the slopes of Plynlimon, from where it moves through moorland and forest, and through deeply incised valleys and rounded hills, before entering the Shropshire Plain and the extensive floodplain below the Breidden Hills at the confluence of the Severn and Vyrnwy. This is an attractive rural landscape, with a variety of natural habitats and a mixture of land uses including sheep, arable and dairy farming and forestry plantations.

In its mountain reach the stream is narrow, lively and shallow, passing over gravel beds and exposed bedrock. Depressions in the bedrock become sediment traps, retaining gravel and small stones which swirl around the depression, further excavating the channel. There are also a number of waterfalls in this reach including the 'Severn-Break-its-Neck-Falls' where the bedrock has proved more resistant than the neighbouring rocks to the erosive power of the flowing water. Near

Montgomery, the river leaves its mountain landscape and begins to flow across a floodplain, the interaction of flow, sediment load and channel altering the river's character so that it becomes deeper and wider and the flow swifter than that of the narrower upland stream.

Much academic work has been undertaken relating to the upland catchment of the Severn, including the channel form and the historical development of the channel and floodplain (Lewin 1983, Gregory 1987), and the headwater characteristics and dynamics. Information for the latter has been gathered from the dense network of monitors in the Hafren forest high up in the catchment. High rainfall levels in the west of the catchment, compared to the relatively low precipitation in the east (see Table 8.1 for a comparison of annual rainfall at the Plynlimon Flume station in the west (3207 mm), and at the Saxon Lode station in the east (969 mm)) combined with the gradient of the slope, and the reduced ability of the soil to absorb intense rainfall caused by changes within farming practice and afforestation (Higgs 1987), has produced a catchment with a flashy (i.e. quick) response to rainfall, the pattern of which can be determined by these monitors.

A daily record of river levels, including rainfall and flow rate is available from a number of gauging stations situated along the whole length of the river (Table 8.1). Certain gauging stations also collect river quality data including the chemical load of the water. Data is then relayed via telemetry to Environment Agency offices. Haw Bridge, the lowermost full-range gauging station on the river, incorporates the discharge values from all the upstream flows. It therefore monitors some 9,895 km² of the 11,422 km² of the Severn

Hafren monitors.
S. OWEN

Table 8.1: Data from eight gauging stations situated on the Severn, 1994

Gauging station	Catchment area (sq km)	Rainfall (mm)	Run-off (mm)	Mean flow ($m^3 s^{-1}$)	Peak flow ($m^3 s^{-1}$)	Minimum daily flow ($m^3 s^{-1}$)
Hafren Flume	3.6	3257	2577	0.29	6.3	0.03
Plynlimon Flume	8.7	3207	2521	0.70	14.6	0.08
Abermule	580	1567	1093	20.10	252.1	1.44
Montford	2025	1363	827	53.07	341.1	5.94
Buildwas	3717	1080	632	74.47	386.6	10.70
Bewdley	4325	1036	539	73.9	383.1	9.24
Saxons Lode	6850	969	479	104.04	394.7	13.06
Haw Bridge	9895	885	414	129.89	470.2	16.27

Source: Institute of Hydrology and British Geological Survey (2003)

catchment. However, this station is situated some distance upstream of the river's discharge into the Bristol Channel and is also heavily affected by tides. As such the figures at Haw Bridge refer only to the 'gauged' catchment area and 'gauged' length, as opposed to actual area and length; also the figures here are subject to tidal influences (Wood 1987).

To return to the upland catchment, this area is particularly important in terms of the strategic provision of high quality water, particularly for people living further down stream (Environment Agency 2003). Thus the flow of the Severn quickly becomes 'useful'. Even from just downstream of the Plynlimon flume the flow is substantially modified by public water supply exports, effluent returns, releases from the Clywedog and Vyrnwy reservoirs and the Shropshire Groundwater Scheme, and exports for power generation at the Ironbridge Power Station. Despite these human manipulations of flow, the table above serves to show that as the river moves from west to east rainfall and run-off decline, while the catchment size and flow rate increases primarily due to the number of tributaries joining the main river. However, the flow regime of the Severn, although typical of many large rivers in temperate climates (Wood 1987), can be subject in certain reaches to periods of low flow levels, primarily due to impermeable strata and poor groundwater supply.

The minimum daily flow figures in Table 8.1 indicate how releases into the river from reservoirs and the Shropshire Groundwater Scheme, particularly in the summer, are necessary not only to maintain a viable river in terms of its fisheries, conservation and recreation, but also to maintain its ability to meet abstraction demands for public and industrial water supply and irrigation (Environment Agency 2002a). For example, as of 1998 there were six abstraction licences (of greater than 1ml/d – mega-litres per day) granted for the Severn uplands, one for public water supply on the Afon Clywedog, one for industrial usage at Newtown and the remaining four for spray irrigation near Shrewsbury (Environment Agency 1998). Abstractions occur throughout the course of the river, apart from downstream of Gloucester where the salinity of the water makes it unsuitable, although these are reassessed at times of particularly low flow.

The monitoring of flow rate and decision-making about the release of reservoir water into the Severn and strategies for flooding are undertaken by the Environment Agency. Wood (1987: 80) notes that it is this integrated management of the whole basin by one authority which 'has allowed the development of a consistent hydrometric policy and eased the problems of network management'. In terms of its management and 'naturalness', and because industrial abstraction and discharge are small throughout much of the basin, many people feel that the Severn is a 'natural' river. However, the river is very carefully managed in terms of regulation for water-supply purposes (Ledger 1972) and to preserve its 'natural' appearance (Wood 1987), albeit that little of its course remains unaffected by human intervention (Brookes 1982, Gregory 1987).

Llyn Clywedog, an artificial reservoir constructed on the river Clywedog, a tributary of the Severn, capitalises on the heavy rainfall in the western part of the catchment and is jointly managed by the Environment Agency and Severn Trent Water Ltd. Built between 1964 and 1967 it supports the provision of water to 6 million people (Environment Agency 1998). The dam is one of Britain's tallest buttress dams and the reservoir covers an area of 250 hectares, with a length of 9.5 km and capacity of 50,000 mega-litres of water. Contrary to popular belief, the reservoir has a negligible effect on alleviating flooding by the Severn, its key function being the topping up the river flow. At times of high demand and low flow the rainfall captured and stored in the dam is released into the river thus, together with releases from the Vyrnwy reservoir, maintaining sufficient water flow downstream to the estuary. The reservoir is also a recreational venue for sailing, canoeing and angling and provides an important wildlife habitat.

Following the river downstream

Llyn Clywedog.
S. OWEN

from the Hafren Forest one comes to Llanidloes, the first settlement on the river, which is reached by passing over the 'Short Bridge'. Llanidloes originally developed from the site of a ford where old tracks met at the confluence of the rivers Severn and Clywedog. It is an attractive medieval town with a half-timbered market hall and terraced houses and fine stone buildings, which betray its wealthy past. Llanidloes has a long history of woollen production (Morris 1993) and a heavy reliance on the Severn. The *Laws of Howel Dda*, written around 950, frequently mention woollen cloths and plaids, 'which appear to have been converted from webs by "weaving women"' (Hamer 1872: 33). Originally carding, spinning and weaving took place in local farms and terraced houses and eventually mills such as the Bridgend Factory. By 1833 there were forty carding machines, eight fulling mills and nearly 35,000 spindles in operation in the town and neighbourhood. Production reached approximately 300 pieces of flannel, averaging 150 yards each in length, which were sent to Welshpool market every fortnight. By 1838 this had risen to 8,310 pieces per fortnight. Later power looms and other machinery, powered by the Severn, allowed full machine production of the flannel. Such was Llanidloes' importance in the nineteenth century that it was able to support nine principal factories on the Severn and Clywedog and many others of lesser importance (Hamer 1872).

One such flannel mill, The Bridgend Factory (1834), now providing high quality apartments, used the power of the river to drive its machinery and shared the same weir and watercourse as the town's cornmill. The carding engine was housed on the ground floor, the spinning machines on the first floor and the looms above. However, low flows on the river affected the availability of the water to drive the mill machines and at such times mill workers resorted to the traditional manual means of carding, spinning and weaving wool. The finished flannel from The Bridgend Factory was stored in the adjacent Britannia yard (Morris 1993) before being transferred to the market at Welshpool.

The borough and market of Welshpool were founded between 1241 and 1245. Laid out on a typical medieval plan, the town contains many fine examples of late eighteenth- and nineteenth-century houses, dating from the time when the town reached its peak as a centre of manufacturing, commerce and trade. A flannel market was held every other Thursday in the Town Hall and, as well as manufacturing cloth itself, Welshpool also acted as a trading and export centre for flannel and woollen products made in Llanidloes and Newtown, the latter being known as the 'busy Leeds of Wales' (Bibby 2002: 32). By the late nineteenth century Welshpool was a large and populous town with 70 working tailors and over 20 grocers (Trant and Griffin 1998).

Goods were transported to and from the town via the river at Pool Quay, effectively the quay of Pool or Welshpool, four miles north of Welshpool. This was the highest navigable point on the Severn, albeit only at times of high flow, when the water was sufficiently deep to cover the many sequences of pools and rock bars upstream of Gloucester. Measures were taken to improve the passage and as far back as the seventeenth century navigation works helped the movement of goods by boat.

Many trows – the 'workhorses of the Severn' – were built in the boatyards of Bridgnorth, downstream of Shrewsbury (Gwilt, n.d.), and up until the 1820s brought cargoes from Bristol, including wine, tobacco, oil, salt, brassware and soap, together with goods such as ironware, textiles, earthenware, cider and coal collected from wharves along the river. With shallow drafts and no fixed keels, trows were ideally suited to negotiate the shallow waters of the Severn; they relied on spring tides to move them upstream and floodwater to move them downstream, using sails whenever the wind was in the right direction. Of the two types of trow, the larger ones (60 feet in length and weighing between 40 and 80 tons, with main, top and occasionally mizzen masts that could be lowered to pass under bridges) worked between Bristol and Gloucester where the channel was deeper and wider, while the smaller trows (up to 60 foot in length and between 40 and 60 tons in weight) worked upstream of Gloucester where the depth was shallower (Witts 2003).

In 1796 the building of the Montgomery Canal, part of the Shropshire Union Canal (Roberts 1999), to Newtown, allowed Pool Quay and Welshpool to uphold their position as trading centres and overcome the difficulties of navigation on the river. The canal brought much prosperity to Welshpool and allowed the town and its inhabitants to participate in the new industrial age.

The canal soon became lined with wharves, warehouses, cottages and workshops (The Welshpool Partnership n.d.) and the canal transported a variety of goods for import and export including grain, dairy produce and luxury goods.

One canalside building is now home of the Powysland Museum, which contains information on the development of the town and its prehistory. Archaeological evidence demonstrates that the forests of the Severn basin were converted into farmland in the late sixth millennium BP, so that by the time of the Roman conquest there was already a long history of farming in the area (Limbrey 1987). The landscape betrays evidence of early settlement and land-use; for example, neolithic tombs have been found in the foothills of the Black Mountains, as well as on the adjacent lowlands and Cotswold scarp, while aerial photographs of crop marks have revealed a henge and cursus on low terraces of the Severn just south of Welshpool. The occurrence of polished stone axes also suggest that the Severn basin was crossed by important communication routes including the route between Craig Llywd, North Wales and the Preseli Mountains in the west (Limbrey 1987).

Indeed, the upper valley near Welshpool and Montgomery, a small prosperous agricultural town just on the Welsh side of the border, was probably one of the most militarised areas of Britain for hundreds of years, with castles along the border signifying the political conflict and tensions not only between the English and Welsh but also between the north and south Welsh and local rivalries. Within five miles of Montgomery there are the remains of

Powysland Museum, Welshpool.
S. OWEN

several Iron Age hillforts, a large Roman fort, Offa's Dyke and one Welsh and two Norman castles (The Welshpool Partnership n.d.). Further downstream early land boundaries on the gravels of the Severn–Vyrnwy confluence are thought to be neolithic, while excavations have confirmed neolithic settlements at Sharpstones Hill, near Shrewsbury, on The Breiddin, overlooking the Severn where it emerges from the Welsh hills (Musson 1976) and on the nearby Long Mountain (Britnell 1982).

As the Severn moves through the valley from Welshpool, and below the Breidden Hills, it is joined by the river Vyrnwy (catchment size 878 km^2 (Lewin 1987)). The valley here is one of a number of major floodplains within the whole catchment (Environment Agency 1998) and is thus subject to intense and regular flooding in the winter. Settlements are isolated, with roads often covered with water at times of flood, and residents live under the threat of regular winter flooding. During one flood a farmer, looking down from his land on Long Mountain, described the valley as '… like a sea with islands floating in it'. In February 2002 Tony and Liz Dawson in Llandrinio (north-north-west of Shrewsbury) celebrated that the newly built flood defence banks on their land had held back the worst of the water, yet farmer Roger Davies at Maesbrook was still having to herd his dairy cows through knee-high water to the milking parlour (Witts 2003).

Attempts have been made to mitigate the major effects of the flood-waters, including the early recognition and warning of flood risks provided to the

The Severn's confluence with the Vyrnwy (right).
S. OWEN

Environment Agency by the gauging stations along the route of the Severn. Along this section of the river flood embankments, specifically low earth embankments (known locally as argaes), which were mostly constructed in the late eighteenth century, also serve a dual purpose; providing a limited form of protection for the land behind, and at times of high flow when the bank is overtopped, substantially reducing major flows passing down the system by enhancing the storage of water on the natural floodplain (Environment Agency 1998). Yet, despite the threat of flooding, the floodplain both here and upstream is subject to intense pressure for development, particularly in view of the hilly topography, and one of the tasks of the Environment Agency is to monitor any such developments, mindful of the consequences of flooding.

Increasingly this upland area of the Severn is also being promoted as a venue for recreation. The Countryside Agency is keen for local authorities to open up new footpaths particularly alongside rivers including the Severn. From the Forestry Commission visitor centre, which lies within the dense Hafren forest, a series of white-topped posts leads the visitor on a three-mile route through the forest and up on to the moorland to reach the source of the river Severn. The lower section of the walk is accessible to the disabled, with the construction of a raised wooden platform running parallel with the stream allowing access for wheelchair users.

Wooden walkway, Hafren Forest.
S. OWEN

The river also offers high quality angling, with designated salmonid fisheries in the upper reaches, coarse fishing further downstream, and designated

cipronid fisheries within the Montgomery branch of the Shropshire Union Canal. The river and its banks also offer much for those interested in wildlife because of the variety of flora and fauna including floating water plantain, otter and crayfish (Environment Agency 1998). Although certain sections of the Montgomery Canal are now dry or inaccessible, a programme of restoration is underway (British Waterways 2003) with the aim of opening up the whole of its length and reconnecting it to the Shropshire Union Canal. This will provide an additional recreational resource, requiring careful management of the environment and water quality.

The Middle Severn

The river in the Middle Severn passes through two distinct landscapes, divided by the Ironbridge Gorge. The flatter landscape of the Shropshire Plain lies to the north. Here the river snakes through a wide floodplain, with sequences of meanders such as the one near Buildwas. To the south of the gorge the river flows through an undulating, steep-sided wooded valley before finally reaching a floodplain once again at Worcester (Environment Agency 1997). In this section of the river there are numerous villages and historic towns such as Ironbridge, Bridgnorth and Bewdley, with their Georgian features and buildings of brick and local sandstone (White et al. 2000).

The Severn immediately up and downstream of Shrewsbury flows through a series of meanders and well-defined sequences of pools and riffles (Figure

Meander, Buildwas.
S. OWEN

Sandstone cliff,
Bridgnorth.
S. OWEN

8.1) (Dury 1987). The meander pattern upstream of Shrewsbury is particularly distorted. With the use of aerial photographs, Dury (1987) has shown the existence of relict meanders much wider and larger those of today, indicating that the river was originally much larger, deeper and more erosive than it is now.

The landscape of the Middle Severn is underlain by a complex geology, visible in the outcrops of red sandstone at Bridgnorth. The river was also significant in the establishment of commerce and industry, as seen by the major Roman city of Wroxeter nearby the Severn, and the medieval settlements of Shrewsbury and Worcester (Environment Agency 1997). A clear example of the ways in which geology and the river have combined to make the area significant is at the Ironbridge Gorge, now a World Heritage Site.

Ironbridge

Ironbridge developed as a major centre of the industrial revolution, due in large part to the commercial use of abundant local supplies of coal, clays, iron and limestone deposits, all accessible at different points along the Severn valley. The river played a significant role by providing an effective means of access to these deposits along the valley, as well as for the transport of goods both up and down stream.

It is difficult today visiting the village of Ironbridge, with its multiple museums, 'theme park' appearance and premises manufacturing and selling cuddly toys, to appreciate how this valley must have looked from the sixteenth to nineteenth centuries. Then it was

A winding glen ... hemmed in by lofty hills and hanging woods ... [its] considerable iron works ... the forges, mills and steam engines with all their vast machinery – the flaming furnaces, and smoking chimneys. (from Samuel Bagshaw's *History, Gazetteer, and Directory of Shropshire 1851* in Cossons 1977: 28).

Other than the museum, which aims to recreate the industrial heritage of the gorge, there is little which truly suggests the levels of activity, noise and pollution that used to exist in the valley and how this would have impacted on the river and its immediate landscape. For centuries river water powered industrial machinery, including the bellows for the blast furnaces; now, the only industrial use of the river is as a source of cooling water for the coal-fired

above left Ironbridge.
S. OWEN

above Ironbridge Power Station.
S. OWEN

The Iron Bridge.
S. OWEN

Ironbridge power station, its four cooling towers coloured in order to blend in with the surrounding red sandstone landscape (Cossons 1977).

An iconic focal point on the Severn is provided by Abraham Darby III's iron bridge of 1781, symbolising in its design and location – connecting the industries on both banks of the gorge – the important role played both by the river and by local manufacturing industries during the early phase of the industrial revolution. Cossons (1977) traces the significance of the valley, and the river, back to the early seventeenth century when the small coal mines in the gorge relied on the navigable river for transport to external markets. While Coalbrookdale provided the initial focus of industrial activity within the gorge, soon the valley sides became scenes of industrial and commercial activity when

> … upwards of 100,000 tons of coals are annually shipped from collieries about Broseley and Madeley to the towns situate on its [the Severn's] banks, and from thence into the adjacent counties; also great quantities of grain, pig and bar iron, iron manufactures and earthenwares; as well as wool, hops, cyder and provisions, are constantly exported to Bristol and other places from whence merchants' goods are brought in return. (Perry 1758 in Cossons 1977: 16)

The wharfage stands as a testament to the historical quayside activity, running by the river from the old Coalbrookdale Company's gothic warehouse on Loadcroft wharf to the iron bridge itself. Loadcroft was one of the busiest and most important places in the gorge, the point at which raw materials and goods were delivered, and where iron products from the

Loadcroft Wharf,
Ironbridge.
S. OWEN

Coalbrookdale Company, delivered via waggonways, were transferred on to barges for passage to Stourport and Bristol (Cossons 1977).

Goods from Loadcroft and other wharfs were taken downstream by barges and trows, the former able to carry 20 to 49 tons, the latter 40 to 80. In 1756 a total of 376 barges and trows were in use on the river between Welshpool and Gloucester, of which 139 were owned in the Gorge (Cossons 1977). Gangs of men known as 'bow-haulers' towed the trows upriver, although the opening of a towpath in 1800 enabled horses to draw the trows. At times of high water Witts (2003) notes that as many as 80 trows left Ironbridge Gorge, and in 1874 as much as 4,000 tons were taken by barge from the Gorge. What is particularly surprising about the industrial development of the valley and its vital reliance on the river for transport, were the limitations that the river imposed because of its low flow. Navigation here, as in the upland reaches, was confined to only a short period in the year, usually eight weeks in autumn, when river conditions were suitable (Environment Agency 1997). When the river was impassable, goods were often stored in the warehouses at Ironbridge.

Ironbridge continued to prosper in the nineteenth century and it was only with the opening of the Severn Valley Railway that trade on the river began to decline so that by the early 1900s the wharves and warehouses fell into disrepair. The more recent revival of the area, and its designation as a World Heritage Site, has 'sanitised' the valley's appearance and the river, and particularly its riverbanks, are now only used for boating, canoeing and an annual coracle regatta. The coracle, a bowl shaped ash timber construction with an outer skin of waterproofed calico or canvas, was a traditional river craft for fishing and transporting passengers on Shropshire rivers. The craft was particularly appropriate to this stretch of the Severn, its modest draft suiting the shallow water. Within the Ironbridge gorge there was a variation in style, its design owing much 'to the needs of poaching and rabbit-catching ... [and] some stability has been sacrificed to speed and manoeuvrability' (Cossons 1977: 116). Eustace Rodgers, the builder of the Ironbridge variant, had such skill in its use and a familiarity with the river that 'the underwater geography of the Severn [was] as clear to him as if there were no water' (Cossons 1977: 116).

Fishing

One key leisure use of the Middle Severn (and indeed the Lower Severn) is fishing. The middle reaches of the Severn in particular have a long history of the commercial exploitation of fish including the trapping of salmon and eels in fish weirs and traps; today angling remains a popular pastime on the river-banks. The river provides good quality coarse fishing, with barbel, chub and roach being found in the moderate gradient, moderate flow and alternating

Rivers are at the very heart of many towns and villages. This is Bewdley.
S. OWEN

rapids and quieter waters found upstream of Bewdley, while bream are to be found in the deeper and slower flowing water of the Severn downstream of Worcester.

Salmon fishing is also popular, especially below weirs as the salmon migrate to their upstream spawning areas (Environment Agency 1997). The Environment Agency in its River Severn Salmon Action Plan (Environment Agency 2003a) has devised means of improving and protecting habitat, and of increasing spawning areas together with the protection of young salmon. Fishing for salmon also takes place within the Severn estuary with rods and nets, some of which are peculiar to the area, for example the use of draft nets, lave nets and putchers. The river downstream of Gloucester is also popular for elvering. In 1553 Henry VIII prohibited the removal of elvers from the river, an order which was made permanent by Elizabeth I in 1558, and later overturned by George II (Witts 2003). However, illegal coarse fish and salmon removals by rod and line are cause for concern to the Environment Agency, as is the impact on the indigenous fish stocks of predatory species such as pike and zander (Environment Agency 1997).

Flooding

The Environment Agency and the Department for Environment, Food and Rural Affairs' (Defra) joint strategy 'The River Severn Strategies' (Environment Agency 2003b) covers flooding issues on two sections of the river. The Fluvial Severn Strategy covers the river from its source to Gloucester and takes account of flooding caused by high river flows, while The Tidal Severn

Strategy covers the river downstream from Gloucester to Avonmouth in the Bristol Channel, where flooding is predominantly caused by high tides. These documents take a holistic approach to the problem of flooding of the whole of the Severn rather than adopting the traditional approach which focused on individual towns and reaches of the river.

As in the floodplain east of Shrewsbury, the Middle Severn – including the towns of Shrewsbury, Ironbridge, Bewdley and Upton upon Severn – are subject to flooding. Some settlements such as Shrewsbury, Worcester and Gloucester have a variety of flood defences, but unprotected parts of the river such as at Upton upon Severn, and Tewkesbury, particularly around the river Swilgate and the Severn's confluence with the Avon, flood more frequently (Environment Agency 1999).

Shrewsbury, a well-preserved medieval town which sits high up on a sandstone cliff above the tight meanders of the Severn (White *et al.* 2000), owes its development to the river, yet is subject to regular floods dating back to at least 1338. Two bridges, the English Bridge (1774) to the east and the Welsh Bridge (1795) to the west allow access to the centre of the town, and help indicate the severity of historic floods: the highest recorded level of the river, at 5.7 metres above the river bed at the Welsh Bridge, was in 1795, nearly half a metre deeper than the floods of 2000, which peaked at a level of 5.25 metres.

The severe floods of 2000, the worst for over fifty years, affected the whole length of the river, causing the flooding of agricultural land and extensive damage to homes and businesses. Shrewsbury was badly hit, with many properties severely flooded three times in a period of six weeks (Environment Agency 2003c). The problems of flooding were exacerbated in many places because the natural floodplain, which might have served to dissipate the energy of the flood-waters, was artificially constricted due to building developments, including the flood defence structures themselves. According to the Environment Agency (1997) there are approximately 400 residential and commercial properties, as well as major transport links, subject to flood risk throughout the town. Steps taken to minimise risk include the Environment Agency's continuing regular maintenance of the river channel by dredging, tree and debris removal, weed cutting and initiation of the Flood Warning Scheme at times of risk, allowing owners to take steps to minimise damage (Environment Agency 1997). Also, the construction of earth embankments, walls and demountable defences in Frankwell, as part of the Shrewsbury Flood Alleviation Scheme, will offer some protection to local people.

As of 1999 there were a total of 28 km of flood defence embankments from Worcester to Tewkesbury and a further 34 km from Tewkesbury to Gloucester, but flooding further downstream from Shrewsbury prompted the Environment Agency to begin installing more innovative 'demountable' defences. These are walls which are only erected at times of flood. For example, demountable flood barriers were erected on New Year's Day 2003 at Bewdley as a precautionary measure, the first time they had been deployed in a real emergency situation (Environment Agency 2003d). Such initiatives form part of the Severn Catchment Flood Management Plan (CFMP). Catchment Flood Management Plans are a new strategy introduced by Defra and the Environment Agency (Environment Agency 2003b) following the 2000 floods and are currently being piloted in five catchments, of which the Severn is one. The aim of the plan is to undertake an assessment of flood risks and flood management policies for the whole of the catchment, and to take account of their long-term sustainability and economic, environmental, social and technical implications.

The next stage, the Fluvial Severn Strategy (FSS), involves implementing the policies derived from the CFMP related to specific sub-catchments on the river. The Environment Agency has been keen to involve and consult local stakeholders regarding the options for flood management. Information displays at libraries and on the internet summarise where and why flooding occurs along the river and the available options, including alteration of land management practices, for example encouraging afforestation and amending agricultural practices, and building defences or storage. These options will subsequently be modelled in order to identify their potential effects on the whole of the catchment.

The Severn as a cultural resource

Chapter 6 related how rivers can act as a cultural focus for groups or individuals and can provide meaning and attachment to the local landscape. One material example of the myth of the Severn can be found in the Worcester City Art Gallery and Museum, where a bronze statue of 'The Legend of Sabrina' (1880) by William Calder Marshall, depicts the myth of Habren, illegitimate daughter of the ancient British king Lorcine and the Hunnish princess Estildis. Habren is known as Hafren in Welsh, and Sabern in Latin, the probable etymology of the word Severn (Ashe 1990).

Leaving his wife Gwendoline, daughter of the ruler of Cornwall, King Lorcine established Estildis in his court. An angry Gwendoline amassed a Cornish army to fight Lorcine, who was killed in the subsequent battle and Gwendoline as the new ruler ordered that Habren and her mother be thrown into the river and drowned. She also ordered that the river be named Habren as a reminder of the sins of Lorcine and, according to Rogers (2003), as a tribute to the innocent Habren.

Just as the river provided an actual geographical boundary between England and Wales, and as such became the scene of many skirmishes including the battle between the Romans and the British leader Caractacus at Caersws, just south of Llanidloes, and the Saxons and retreating Britons near Arlingham (Rogers 2003), it also became associated with boundaries and frontiers in other myths and legends, particularly those associated with liminality and links with the Underworld. For example the symbolism of the water implies both death and a rebirth, a regeneration and enabler of life. Thus Palmer (1992) notes the belief that the hermits of Blackstone Rock near Bewdley renamed all infants they rescued from the river with the surname Severn, as if they were reborn. Rogers (2003) also identifies this notion of rebirth in Milton's masque *Comus*, where he captures this rebirth of Sabrina as a spiritual goddess of the river:

> She, guiltless damsel, flying the mad pursuit
> Of her enraged stepdame Guendolen,
> Commended her fair innocence to the flood
> That stayed her flight with his cross-flowing course …
> The water-nymphs, that in the bottom played,
> Held up their pearled wrists, and took her in,
> Bearing her straight to aged Nereus' hall;
> Who, piteous of her woes, reared her lank head,
> And gave her to his daughters to imbathe
> In nectared layers strewed with asphodel,
> And through the porch and inlet of every sense
> Dropped in ambrosial oils, till she revived,
> And underwent a quick immortal change,
> Made Goddess of the river.

The river and its surrounding landscape also became an inspiration for the music of Edward Elgar, his statue near the cathedral in Worcester suggesting the close connection between the composer and the local landscape. The Elgars also named their London home Severn House. The sounds of the river in particular inspired his music. On one composition written by the Severn he wrote, 'I made this on the banks and it's rather like' (Anderson 1993: 192), and according to Kennedy (1982: 334):

> Always, through his life and music there runs his motif of the river – 'I am at heart the child on the Severn side' … [writing in his music] 'what the reeds were saying' … [and urging the orchestra to play] 'like something you hear down by the river'. By some alchemy he put this into his music, a fresh wistful quality, whenever his thoughts went back to his youth, to the land of lost content, alone by the river.

Elgar also made direct references to the river as in the title of the *Severn Suite* (1930) a composition for brass band, and in *Caractacus* (1898), a choral and orchestral work where he uses the history of the landscape to inform his music. In particular Scene III is set in a forest near the Severn and Scene V, the fatal battle scene between Caractacus and the British, somewhere along the river Severn. How Elgar wrote about the river signifies what it meant to him, and in his music what the English landscape means to others. For Hall (1997: 3), 'meaning is what gives us a sense of our own identity, of who we are and with whom [and what] we belong'.

The Worcester City Art Gallery and Museum holds many landscape paintings portraying the rural idyll by Worcester-born Benjamin Williams Leader (1831–1932). His works include 'On the Severn', 'On the Severn below Worcester' and 'The Smooth Severn Stream' (1886), the latter depicting the Severn, a trow and quayside from the Bishop's Palace, Worcester. According to Dean (n.d.) the countryside of Worcestershire with its little villages or 'the long, glassy sweep of the River Severn were particular favourites … [of Leader's and] we are left with a timeless image of Worcestershire untouched by progress and technological advance'.

Upton upon Severn

Before leaving the middle reaches of the Severn it is worth mentioning Upton upon Severn, a particularly attractive town to the south of Worcester. Like many other villages, it benefited from its position on the river. It was a crossing point and went on to use the river for industrial, trade and commercial purposes. The architecture of Upton upon Severn's buildings demonstrate the town's earlier economic success. Buildings include mansion-size houses, the one remaining warehouse and the Pepperpot, the tower of a now demolished medieval church, which, as the town's heritage centre, contains much information on the significance of the river to the town's history.

Historically, Upton upon Severn served as an important European trading location and acted as the port of Hereford, Monmouth and the rich agricultural land in the surrounding area. Such was its importance that Henry VII freed its users from the taxes charged on most waterways. Trade transported by trows carrying up to 200 tons included cargoes of salt from Droitwich, pottery from nearby Hanley Castle, coal, bricks, corn and cider. The thriving town offered opportunities not only for merchants but also for innkeepers catering to the needs of travellers, fishermen and boat builders. The decline in trade familiar to other ports on the river caused Upton to fall back once more on fishing and farming, and more recently it has marketed itself as a leisure venue, holding annual jazz and water festivals, many of which take place in the Fish Meadow.

The bridge across the river here is noteworthy. A timber bridge mentioned in accounts of the town in 1480 replaced the original ford or ferryman. This in turn was replaced in 1605 by a sandstone bridge, which despite being damaged in the Civil War, lasted until 1854. This bridge not only allowed

W. Leader. *The Smooth Severn Stream* (1886). WORCESTER CITY MUSEUM AND ART GALLERY

access across the river but also acted as a mooring for boats and a compound to house pigs. The bridge fell into such disrepair that a new bridge was needed and an iron bridge with a drawbridge replaced it. The present steel bridge was built early in the Second World War, only the fourth bridge on the site in five hundred years.

Upton upon Severn.
S. OWEN

The Severn Vale

The Severn Vale extends from north of Tewkesbury through a wide flood-plain down to the Bristol Channel. Unlike the upland and middle reaches, this is mainly an open landscape, with little woodland, and, as the now wider and deeper river nears the sea it becomes a more dominant feature of the land-scape, snaking its way through the wide floodplain (White *et al.* 2000), being joined on its passage by five major river outlets, including the Wye.

The landscape of the Severn Vale is also home to greater population numbers than in the upland reaches, so the river acts as a major source of water in this area, supplying domestic and industrial users to urban settle-ments such as Worcester, Tewkesbury and Gloucester and other users as far away as Bristol and Coventry (Environment Agency 1999). Public water supplies account for approximately 67 per cent of water abstracted from the Severn, the majority of which is taken from three sites; Upton on Severn, Mythe near Tewkesbury and at Gloucester. Indeed, the abstractions from Mythe supply most of Gloucestershire.

Tewkesbury and Gloucester

Tewkesbury and Gloucester both offer clear examples of the economic, polit-ical and strategic importance of this part of the river. Tewkesbury has a fine example of a medieval mill. The original Abbey Mill, a grade-2 listed building situated on the banks of the Mill Avon, a leat supplying water to the mill which had been 'improved' by widening as far back as the fifteenth century, was built in *c*.1190 for the Priory of Tewkesbury and was operated by the Benedictine monks who received their supplies from local farmers. The mill

Mythe Treatment Works, near Tewkesbury.
S. OWEN

was later rebuilt in 1793 with four waterwheels powering the mill stones. Later flood-gates were also added to the Abbey Mill's weir in 1935 in order to assist in flood control, and these have since been replaced by a new 'belly' sluice, with an integral elver pass. However in 1865 the construction of Healing's Flour Mill at the northern end of the Ham (see below), led to the Abbey Mill's eventual demise in 1920. This area between the Healing's Mill and Abbey Mill is also a good example of the regeneration of the riverside which has taken place in a number of towns and cities along the Severn. New housing is in keeping with the city's traditional style and care has been taken to maintain easy access to the Ham, a Site of Special Scientific Interest and one of the last remaining traditionally managed 'ham' meadows in the Severn Vale. Ham is the traditional lower Severn valley name applied to alluvial meadows adjoining the river. The ham meadows designated as SSSIs are all lammas land in that hay rights and pasturage had separate tenures. The land was usually divided into strips and most commonly regulated by manorial courts. Many, but not all, hams are botanically very rich.

The Battle of Tewkesbury in 1471 in the Bloody Meadow just outside the city illustrates the town's strategic importance as well as the significance of the

Abbey Mill, Tewkesbury.
S. OWEN

RIVERS AND THE BRITISH LANDSCAPE

river as a barrier between England and Wales. The Lancastrian Army, trying to wrest the crown from Edward IV for their own leader Henry IV, were being led northwards in 1471 by Queen Margaret, Henry's wife, in order to meet up with her ally Jasper Tudor, Earl of Pembroke. Learning of their plan, Edward IV mustered his army to prevent the Lancastrians crossing the Severn into Wales. Margaret's first attempt to cross the river was at Gloucester which, until the construction of the first Severn Bridge, was the lowest point at which it was possible to ford or bridge the river. Edward's supporters, however, barred the Westgate Bridge and prevented Margaret's passage across the river. Thwarted, she moved north to try and ford the river at Tewkesbury; once again she was prevented from crossing the river and was instead forced to fight in the fields just south of Tewkesbury. The battle had devastating consequences with the Lancastrian army routed and some 2,000 killed.

Gloucester, too, owed much of its importance to its location on the river (Heighway 1985). The Romans, who had established a fort overlooking the river crossing, used the site for incursions into Wales. Later in the second century a stone wall was built to surround the town, including the Roman riverside suburb and its wooden quay along the easternmost of the three channels of the river Severn. The Saxon town of Gloucester extended towards the westernmost of the three channels to the medieval bridge known as the 'Foreign Bridge', which denoted its significance as marker of the town boundary.

The river at Gloucester has been an important arterial route for commerce for many hundreds of years, with military and other supplies such as timber and coal being regularly shipped to and from the city. The city went on to develop as an important centre for the production of iron nails, horseshoes and tools, together with cloth, agricultural produce and the 'Severn Fisheries'. This company received fish from local fish weirs and villages from riverside parishes downstream of Gloucester, which it distributed to other markets. It also supplied lampreys to the royal houses. Water bailiffs were appointed by the city to supply salmon and shad to the royal house and to settle disputes over fishing rights, many of which arose between villagers and landowners including Gloucester Abbey, particularly over the latter's rights to various stretches of river.

The disused Cadbury's chocolate plant, Frampton on Severn.
S. OWEN

Lockkeeper's cottage, Frampton on Severn.
S. OWEN

The quays at Gloucester were busy, with local products including cloth, apples, pears, honey and corn being traded, and produce such as jugs and cooking pots from Bristol and Worcester and other ports on the river. Foreign imports such as wine, salt, fish and Baltic timber, and later luxury goods such as oranges, oils and raisins were also transported upstream from Bristol on crafts with shallow drafts, seagoing vessels being unable to negotiate the treacherous waters just south of the city.

Gloucester also benefited from cross-river trade. Wales became a source of cattle for the city's meat and leather industries, and iron arrived on pack-horses from the Forest of Dean. Thus the thriving quayside trade contributed to the city's formal designation as a port in 1580, and as a result of its new customs role the city's revenues increased dramatically. Such developments brought about fierce competition between Gloucester and the upstream settlements, and a number of disputes arose relating to trading rights and river tolls (Heighway 1985). Even Bristol, despite retaining the majority of trade, protested at Gloucester's new-found economic position (Heighway 1985).

The Herbert, Kimberly and Phillpott Warehouses, Gloucester Dock
S. OWEN

By 1619 Gloucester had three trading ships, yet this was fewer than other ports upstream: Bewdley had five ships, Tewkesbury eight and Worcester ten. The key inhibitor of Gloucester's expanding trade was the difficult river passage below the city, the river being navigable here for only a few days a month on the spring tides. The solution was to build the sixteen-mile Gloucester and Sharpness Ship Canal, which, when completed in 1827, bypassed the difficult river sections and linked Gloucester to the Severn downstream. The docks built at Sharpness were able to receive large ships from Bristol whose cargo was then loaded onto barges and taken upstream to Gloucester.

The canal side as well as the Sharpness Docks housed warehouses and processing plants, including a Cadbury's chocolate works. The factory, which was opened in 1916 near the Fretherne Bridge, Frampton on Severn, produced chocolate crumb (a baked mixture of ground cocoa beans, sugar and milk from local farms), which was later transported by boat to Cadbury's main works at Bournville for final processing. The factory closed in 1983 and the site is now used by a number of other businesses. Near the factory can also be seen an example of a lock-keeper's cottage, designed by Robert Mylne in the neo-classical style.

The fully completed docks at Gloucester, which connected north to the Severn by a lock, had three dock basins, two dry docks and fifteen warehouses, including the Herbert, Kimberley and Phillpott's warehouses (Roberts 1999). Trade flourished and soon railway links were established which allowed for more effective transportation of goods inland. Increased dock activity stimulated other industries in the area, including those connected with the principal imports of timber and corn, such as oil and flour mills. The Moreland Match Factory and the Gloucester Railway Carriage and Wagon Company, were both established on or near the docks.

Trade continued to flourish all along the Severn until the development of the railway, and the steady silting up of the river gradually pushed the economic centres on the river downstream towards Bristol. With its separate canal link to the Severn estuary, Gloucester managed to hang on to trade longer than most (White et al. 2000), so that the total tonnage of imported and exported goods passing through Gloucester docks increased from 107,000 tons in 1827 to a total of 694,000 tons in 1892. Eventually, however, Gloucester lost out to Bristol and Avonmouth docks, and suffered a complete decline in canal and export trade.

Following a long period of disuse the warehouses and associated dock buildings, including the old custom house, are now being renovated, part of an ongoing programme of redevelopment which includes the conversion of warehouses into tourist, residential, commercial and retail premises. The Lock Warehouse built in 1834 is now used as an antiques centre, while Llanthony Warehouse on Llanthony Quay, which was built for the Gloucester and Dean Forest Railway in 1852, has since 1987 been the home of the National Waterways Museum. The area is a popular tourist attraction with shops and cafes, and the dock basin now provides berths for canal and leisure craft.

The Severn estuary

Downstream of Gloucester the river, now meandering through a wide floodplain, becomes prone to the effects of tidal surges. The Severn estuary experiences the third highest tides in the world, with its tidal range (the difference between the lowest and highest tide in any one day) as much as 14.5 metres (Environment Agency 1999). The effect becomes particularly pronounced when a spring tide coincides with an active depression producing on-shore south-westerly winds into the Bristol Channel. At such times surges in excess of 1 metre above predicted tide levels can occur (Ward 1987).

One of the most notable physical phenomena of this reach of the river is the Severn Bore, a naturally occurring tidal wave which affects the river below Gloucester. The funnel shape of the Severn estuary contributes to the development of a bore, which is created when the rising tide flows into a converging channel with a rising funnel-shaped riverbed (Environment Agency 2003e). The bore has been known to reach almost two metres in height and can average speeds of 16 km an hour particularly during periods when there is a following wind (Environment Agency 2003e). The bore can be seen at various locations along the river and such events, which are timetabled in a yearly calendar, are a popular visitor attraction (see page 59).

The landscape of the Severn south of Gloucester is significantly different to that of the upland reaches of the river. The area is wide and flat and, because of the risk of flooding, mostly used for grazing land. A key feature of the Severn Vale landscape, however, is the large and important area of wetland habitat. The Slimbridge Wildfowl and Wetlands Trust with its famed white-fronted geese, Bewick swans and many duck species occupies a 2,000-acre riverside location, capitalising on the abundant feeding and breeding grounds. Estuaries hold extremely rich food resources for birds. At low tide vast expanses of sand and mud banks are exposed which, together with saltmarsh and reed banks, provide both a year-round and overwintering feeding site and habitat for birds. Large flocks of birds including resident and migrant wild-fowl and waders such as dunlin, curlew and wildfowl can be seen on the exposed saltwater marshes and flats.

The Llyn Clywedog, some 340 km away in the Upland Severn also plays its part in the maintenance of this habitat. The release of water from the reservoir during periods of low flow not only ensures a healthy river and wildlife habitat in the upland and middle reaches, but has particular importance in the

The First Severn
Crossing.
S. OWEN

The Second Severn
Crossing.
S. OWEN

estuary and its wetlands. The estuary's wide variety of insects, birds and animals would be adversely affected by low flows and saline intrusions from the sea. Yet despite the apparent healthiness of the landscape the construction of embankments to dissipate the major effects of flooding, together with agricultural improvement such as land reclamation and drainage, has affected the hydrology and ecology of the floodplain wetlands (Environment Agency 1999), and consultations are currently under way to reconsider the drainage of the area. A further threat to the wildlife habitats is the proposed tidal barrage across the estuary (Hoare 2002, Professional Engineering 2003). The alteration of flow by the barrage would eliminate certain intertidal areas and result in loss of habitat for birds, particularly shelduck, curlew and redshank (Clark and Prys-Jones 1994).

The landscape of the estuary offers a sharp contrast in colour and land-use to the upland Severn with its topography of hills, trees and fields. The site is dominated by the two Severn bridges, the Second Severn Crossing completed in 1996 being, at over 5 km, Britain's longest river crossing. Here, there is a greyness and unattractiveness about the scenery. This feels like an industrial

Hampton Loade.
S. OWEN

landscape: the area around Avonmouth is home to a variety of industries ranging from pharmaceuticals to zinc smelting, while opposite stand the oil refineries of Newport. Oldbury power station on the east bank is also clearly visible. The river in the estuary therefore offers a different resource to its middle and upland reaches, providing sea transport for the export of goods and fuel including the historical movement of coal from the Forest of Dean. The nuclear power station also relies on the river for cooling water hence the presence of a large offshore tidal reservoir, which provides the approximately 70 million litres of water an hour required for cooling (The Severn Way Partnership 1999). This is therefore an area of complex management issues and there is a need for a coherent management plan which meets the social and economic needs of the local population and industry, while sustaining the estuarine and coastal ecosystem and its wildlife (Hoare 2002).

In the past the Severn could be crossed on foot at several points, particularly in its upland reaches, while further downriver crossings could be made by ford or ferry, for example the ferry at Aust in the Severn estuary and the ford at Hampton Loade. The 'loade' (an old English name for ford or river crossing) dates back at least to 1594, while a ferry carrying passengers and goods was established in the 1880s, a service which continues today. However, as transportation of goods became increasingly important from the eighteenth century bridges were constructed in order to make the passage of goods and travellers across the river easier. For example Mythe Bridge, constructed in 1826 and adjacent to the Mythe water treatment works, is one of the many bridges on the Severn designed by Thomas Telford. Two toll houses, one at either end of the bridge collected the tolls, the right bank collecting from people passing over the bridge, the left bank collecting from river users (Witts 2003). Witts (1998) notes that as of 1994 a total of 102 bridges and one tunnel now cross the river from source to sea, including aqueducts, road, railway and foot bridges.

Conclusion

For Marsh and Meech (1999: 2), 'a walk along the length of the Severn is a geography lesson brought vividly to life'. So it proved with this journey through the ever-changing landscape of the river, from the sluggish bog of Plynlimon, through fast-flowing upland reaches in narrow valleys, and quickly out on to wider floodplains, joined by streams and rivers and eventually discharging into the windswept estuary and Bristol Channel. Since the Ice Age, when the river's course changed drastically to follow the path we know today, small-scale changes to the channel and the erosive power of the water flow have cut new paths through rock and alluvium and have also produced classic fluvial features such as meanders and mid-channel bars. Despite its natural appearance, however, this is a river which has served a wide variety of purposes, has been manipulated by human activity over many centuries, and has been moulded to meet the requirements of an increasingly industrialised age.

The river Severn can be thought of as a microcosm of all rivers in the British Isles, displaying the physical, ecological, economic, social and cultural features associated with rivers, from the north of Scotland to Cornwall and from west Wales to East Anglia. While some themes are peculiar to the Severn, a journey along its course stimulates interest in, and amply illustrates the use and development of, other rivers that anyone may encounter in the course of a day.

Appendices compiled by Sue Owen

Appendix 1. Facts and figures for primary rivers[1]

River name	Catchment size[2] sq km	Mean flow 1996–2000[3] Cubic m per sec	EA Area and LEAP no.[4] and SEPA area	Designated rivers[5] (SSSI) (SAC)
Annan	925	29.55	SEPA - WEST	
Arun	379 (disc)	4	SOUTHERN – 82	
Avon (Warwickshire or Upper)	2674*	16.71	MIDLANDS – 32	
Avon (Hampshire)	1706	19.87	SOUTH WEST – 110	SSSI
Avon (Avon)	1595 (disc)	20.47	SOUTH WEST – 104	
Brue	135.2	1.92	SOUTH WEST – 107	
Clyde	1903.1	49.17	SEPA – WEST	
Dee (Aberdeenshire)	1844	46.93	SEPA – NORTH	SAC
Dee (Afon Dyfrdwy)	1816.8 (disc)	29.71	WALES – 47	SSSI
Derwent (Humberside)	1634.3 (disc)	16.46	NORTH EAST – 20	SSSI
Deveron	954.9	16.56	SEPA – NORTH	
Dochart	239	16.08	SEPA – EAST	
Don (Aberdeenshire)	1273	20.41	SEPA – NORTH	
Eden	2286.5	52.22	NORTH WEST – 7	SSSI
Exe	600.9	16.27	SOUTH WEST – 91	
Findhorn	781.9	19.22	SEPA – NORTH	
Forth	1036	47.84	SEPA – EAST	
Frome	414.4	6.43	SOUTH WEST – 111	SSSI
Great Ouse	3430	11.77	ANGLIAN – 70, 72, 73, 74, 75	
Great Stour	345	3.24	SOUTHERN – 88	
Kennet	1033.4	9.8	THAMES – 126	SSSI
Lea or Lee	1364	5.55	THAMES – 115, 117	SSSI
Little Stour	0	0	SOUTHERN – 88	
Lugg	885.8	11.15	WALES – 46	SSSI
Lune	994.6 (disc)	33.71	NORTH WEST – 3	SSSI
Medway	1256.1	11.2	SOUTHERN – 85	
Mersey	2030	37.22	NORTH WEST – 10, 11	
Moors River	143.3	1.73	SOUTH WEST – 112	
Nene	1634.3 (disc)	9.3	ANGLIAN – 62	
New Bedford River or Hundred Foot Drain	0	0	ANGLIAN – 73	
Nith	799	27.47	SEPA – WEST	
North Tyne	1043.8 (disc)	17.23	NORTH EAST – 17	SSSI
Old Bedford River	0	0	ANGLIAN – 70	
Ouse	3315	50.1	NORTH EAST – 21	
Ouse	395.7	3.86	SOUTHERN – 81	
Parrett	74.8	1.21	SOUTH WEST – 106	
Ribble	1145	33.15	NORTH WEST – 5	SSSI
Rother	424 (disc)	5.16	SOUTHERN – 86	
Severn	9895	107.12	MIDLANDS – 28, 30, 33	SSSI
South Tyne	751.1	18.48	NORTH EAST – 17	SSSI

River name	Catchment size[2] sq km	Mean flow 1996–2000[3] Cubic m per sec	EA Area and LEAP no.[4] and SEPA area	Designated rivers[5] (SSSI) (SAC)
Sow	591	6.17	MIDLANDS – 34	
Spey	2861.2	64.99	SEPA- NORTH	SSSI / SAC
Stour	844.3 (disc)	3.1	ANGLIAN – 67	
Stour	1073	13.91	SOUTH WEST – 112	SSSI
Swale	1363	20.09	NORTH EAST – 21	
Tamar	916.9	22.61	SOUTH WEST – 99, 100	
Taw	826.2	18.18	SOUTH WEST – 90	
Tay	4587.1	168.11	SEPA – EAST	† SAC
Tees	1264	18.84	NORTH EAST – 19	
Teifi	893.6	28.93	WALES – 52	SSSI
Teme	1480	17.52	MIDLANDS – 31	SSSI
Thames or Isis	9948	66.23	THAMES – 119, 122, 127, 129–31	
Tone	202	3.15	SOUTH WEST – 105	
Torridge	663	15.9	SOUTH WEST – 89	
Trent	8547 (disc)	90.71	MIDLANDS – 34, 40	
Tweed	4390	78.87	SEPA – EAST	SSSI / SAC
Tyne	2175.6	45.24	NORTH EAST – 17	SSSI
Tywi	1090.4	39.41	WALES – 53	SSSI
Ure	914.6	21.2	NORTH EAST – 21	SSSI
Usk	911.7	28.22	WALES – 42, 44	SSSI
Waveney	670 (disc)	0.59	ANGLIAN – 68	
Wear	1008.3	14.69	NORTH EAST – 18	SSSI
Weaver	1370	16.55	NORTH WEST – 15	
Welland	717.4	3.96	ANGLIAN – 60	
Wey	1008	6.98	THAMES – 124	
Witham	297.9	1.83	ANGLIAN – 59, 64	
Wye (Afon Gwy)	4010	74.3	WALES – 46	SSSI

Notes

[1] *Primary river*: The extent of a naturally flowing watercourse above the normal tidal limit which at its widest point is greater than 8 metres wide.
Secondary river: The extent of a naturally flowing watercourse course above the normal tidal limit which at its widest point is equal to or greater than 4 metres and less than 8 metres in width.
Source: Written correspondence from Ordnance Survey, 22.11.01

Data relating to primary rivers

[2] Catchment size refers to the measurement at the lowest gauging station on the river, ie not from source to sea. Some gauging stations may be discontinued (disc). For gauging station data Ward (in Lewin 1981: 6) also notes that the final station may not always be near the river's outlet to the sea so that the total discharge/flow rate and other data for the river may not be accurate ie it will not include data post-gauging station. Also in lowland Britain some 17km at least of most major rivers are ungauged (Ward 1981).
* Avon flows into the Severn. Source: Concise Register of Gauging Stations. EA Website. 23.10.03. www.nwl.ac.uk/ih/nrfa/station_summaries/crg.html

[3] Source: As above
For discontinued stations, mean flow is derived from last record of mean flow at the discontinued station closest to the estuary 0 = no gauging station

[4] **EA** – Environment Agency; **LEAP** – Local Environment Agency Plan; **SEPA** – Scottish Environment Protection Agency

[5] **SSSI**, Site of Special Scientific Interest – Can refer to a particular reach, multiple reaches in one river, or from source to sea. Can relate to biological and geological features. Geological features include waterfalls, meanders and shingle.
SAC denotes Special Area of Conservation – can refer to a particular reach, or from source to sea
† denotes awaiting designation.

NB: Not a complete list as rivers other than primary and secondary have also been designated

Source: English Nature Website – 22.10.03 www.english-nature.org.uk
Scottish National Heritage (E-mail 22.11.01)
Countryside Council for Wales (Tel. 26.11.01)

Appendix 2. Longest rivers in Britain

	Name of watercourse	Length km (miles)*	Mouth
1	**Severn**	354 (220)	Bristol Channel
2	**Thames** (for 178 km) – **Isis** (69 km) – **Churn**	346 (215)	North Sea
3	**Trent** (for 236 km) – **Humber** (61 km)	297 (185)	North Sea (as Humber)
4	**Aire** (for 126 km) **Yorkshire Ouse** (72 km) and **Humber** (61 km)	259 (161)	North Sea (as Humber)
5	**Ouse** (Great of Bedford)	230(143)	The Wash
6	**Wye**	215 (135)	Into Severn S of Chepstow, Gwent
7	**Tay** (for 150 km) – **Tummel**	188 (117)	North Sea
8	**Nene**	161(100)	The Wash
9	**Clyde** (incl. **Daer Water**)	158 (98.5)	Firth of Clyde (measured to Port Glasgow)
10	**Spey**	157.5 (98.0)	North Sea
11	**Tweed**	155.3 (96.5)	North Sea
12	**Dee** (Aberdeenshire)	137.1(85.2)	North Sea
13	**Avon** (Warwickshire or Upper)	136.7 (85)	Into Severn at Tewksbury
14	**Don** (Aberdeenshire)	129.5 (80.5)	North Sea
15	**Tees**	127 (79)	North Sea
16	**Tyne** (for 55 km) – **North Tyne** (63 km)	118.5 (73)	North Sea
17	**Dee** (Cheshire)	112.5 (70)	Irish Sea
18	**Eden** (Cumbria)	111 (69)	Solway Firth, Irish Sea
19	**Usk**	104.5 (65)	Bristol Channel
20	**Wear**	104.5 (65)	North Sea
21	**Wharfe**	104.5 (65)	Into York Ouse, nr Cawood, North Yorks
22	**Forth**	103.5 (64.5)	Firth of Forth, North Sea

* These measurements are strictly for the course of a river bearing the one name; thus, for example, where the principal headstream has a different name its additional length is ignored unless otherwise indicated.

Source: *The Guinness Book of Answers* (9th edn) (1993: 711) Enfield: Guinness Publishing Ltd

Appendix 3. Largest catchments

	River name	Catchment size (sq km)
1	**Severn**	9895
2	**Thames** or **Isis**	9948
3	**Trent**	8547 (disc)
4	**Tay**	4587.1
5	**Tweed**	4390
6	**Wye (Afon Gwy)**	4010
7	**Great Ouse**	3430
8	**Ouse**	3315
9	**Spey**	2861.2
10	**Eden**	2286.5

Appendix 4. Highest mean flows

	River name	Mean flow ($m^3\,s^{-1}$)
1	**Tay**	168.11
2	**Severn**	107.12
3	**Trent**	90.71
4	**Tweed**	78.87
5	**Wye (Afon Gwy)**	74.3
6	**Thames** or **Isis**	66.23
7	**Spey**	64.99
8	**Eden**	52.22
9	**Ouse**	50.1
10	**Clyde**	49.17

Source: Concise Register of Gauging Stations. EA Website. 23.10.03 www.nwl.ac.uk/ih/nrfa/station_summaries/crg.html

Appendix 5. Major freshwater lochs and lakes

Name	Area km² (sq mi)		Maximum length km (mi)		Maximum breadth km (mi)		Maximum depth m (ft)	
Scotland								
Loch Lomond	712	(27.5)	36.4	(22.64)	8	(5)	189	(623)
Loch Ness	56.6	(21.87)	36.6	(22.75)	3.2	(2)	228	(751)
Loch Awe	38.7	(14.95)	41	(25.5)	3.2	(2)	93	(307)
Loch Maree	28.4	(11)	21.7	(13.5)	3.2	(2)	111	(367)
Loch Morar	26.6	(10.3)	18.5	(11.5)	2.4	(1.5)	309	(1017)
Loch Tay	26.3	(10.19)	23.4	(14.55)	1.7	(1.07)	154	(508)
Loch Shin	22.5	(8.70)	27.7	(17.35)	1.6	(1.0)	49	(162)
Loch Shiel	19.5	(7.56)	28.1	(17.5)	1.4	(0.9)	128	(420)
England								
Windermere	14.7	(5.69)	16.8	(10.50)	1.47	(0.9)	66	(219)
Ullswater	8.9	(3.44)	11.8	(7.35)	1.0	(0.6)	62	(205)
Bassenthwaite Water	5.3	(2.06)	6.1	(3.83)	1.18	(0.7)	21	(70)
Derwentwater	5.3	(2.06)	4.6	(2.87)	1.94	(1.2)	21	(72)
Wales								
Lake Vyrnwy (dammed)	8.2	(3.18)	7.5	(4.7)	0.6	(0.6)	36	(120)
Bala Lake (**Lake Tegid**)	4.3	(1.69)	6.1	(3.8)	0.53	(0.5)	38	(125)

Source: *The Guinness Book of Answers* (9th edn) (1993: 712) Enfield: Guinness Publishing Ltd.

Appendix 6. Major reservoirs

Reservoir/location	Area km²	Area sq mi	Capacity megalitres
England			
Rutland Water	12.6	4.86	124,000
Kielder Water	11	4.25	199,175
Pitsford Water	7.39	2.85	17,500
Grafham Water	7.38	2.85	56,000
Chew Valley	4.86	1.88	20,457
Derwent	4.05	1.56	9,478
Wales			
Trawsfynydd	4.78	1.84	32,550
Llyn Brenig	3.72	1.44	60,008
Alaw	3.14	1.21	7,456
Scotland			
Carron Valley	3.9	1.51	19,400
Megget	2.59	1	61,400
Loch Bradan	2.09	0.81	20,700

Source: *The Guinness Book of Answers* (9th edn) (1993: 712) Enfield: Guinness Publishing Ltd.

Appendix 7. Highest British waterfalls

	Waterfall	height m	(ft)
1	**Eas A'Chual Aluinn**, Scotland	200	(658)
2	**Falls of Glomach**, Scotland	112	(370)
3	**Pistyll-y-Llyn**, Wales	73*	(230)*
4	**Pistyll Rhaiadr**, Wales	73	(240)
5	**Foyers**, Scotland	62	(205)
6	**Falls of Clyde**, Scotland	62	(204)
7	**Falls of Bruar**, Scotland	60	(200)
8	**Cauldron Snout**, England	60	(200)

* cascades

Source: *The Guinness Book of Answers* (9th edn) (1993: 712) Enfield: Guinness Publishing Ltd.

Appendix 8. The busiest rivers and inland waterways in the UK

Goods moved[1] in billion tonne-kilometres[2] on rivers and inland waterways, 1989 and 2000

River/ waterway	A – Internal traffic			B – Seagoing traffic			Busiest[4]
	1989[3]	2000	% change	1989[3]	2000	% change	
River Thames	0.15	0.13	−13	0.92	0.51	−45	.32/1
River Medway	N	N		0.06	0.03	−50	.015/9
River Severn (incl. **Gloucester and Sharpness Canal**)	N	N		0.02	0.01	−50	.005/11
River Mersey	N	N		0.11	0.13	15	.065/4
Manchester Ship Canal	0.01	0.01	0	0.10	0.11	−10	.06/5
River Clyde	N	N		0.07	0.04	−42	.02/8
River Forth	N	N		0.18	0.23	22	.115/3
River Humber	0.04	0.01	−75	0.37	0.26	−30	.135/2
River Ouse	0.01	0.01	0	0.04	0.04	0	.002/12
Aire and Calder Navigation	0.03	0.03	0	N	N	0	.015/9
River Trent	0.03	0.02	−33	0.05	0.03	−40	.025/6
River Orwell	N	N		0.09	0.05	−44	.025/6
Total of all above waterways	0.26	0.2	−23	2.01	1.45	−28	
All waterways (UK) total	0.31	0.21	−32	2.09	1.47	−30	

Notes
[1] Goods moved = weight of load multiplied by the distance it is carried.
[2] One billion tonne–kilometres = one supertanker travelling across the Atlantic.
[3] 1989 was chosen in order to show the decline in movements after 1989.
[4] Mean of A + B and ranked in terms of busiest, based on 2000 figures
  (N = nil or negligible.)

Sources:
2000 data: Department of Transport (2003) *Transport Statistics Great Britain: 2002 edition*. London: The Stationery
  Office
1989/1990 data: Department of Transport (1994) *Transport Statistics Great Britain*. London: The Stationery Office

Appendix 9. Freight[1] moved by mode of transport, 1990 and 2000

Country	Road		Rail		Inland waterway[2]		Total[3]	% road	% rail	% inland waterway
	1990	2000	1990	2000	1990	2000				
Great Britain	130.6	150.5	6.3	18.3	0.3	0.2	169	89	10.8	0.1
France	193.9	266.5	50.7	55.4	7.6	9.6	331.5	80	17	3
Germany	182.8	347.2	81	75.8	54.8	66.5	489.5	71	15	14
Netherlands	31.8	45.7	3.1	3.8	35.7	41.3	90.8	50	4	46
USA	1,073	1,499[4]	1,510	2,010[4]	516	521[4]	4030	37	50	13

Notes
[1] In billion-tonne kilometres.
[2] Excluding coastal and one port traffic.
[3] Based on 2000 data.
[4] 1998 data as 2000 data not available.

Sources:
2000 data: Department of Transport (2003) *Transport Statistics Great Britain: 2002 Edition*. London: The Stationery Office
1989/ 1990 data: Department of Transport (1994) *Transport Statistics Great Britain*. London: The Stationery Office

Appendix 10. General Quality Assessment (GQA) for rivers in England and Wales: aesthetic quality

Region	Aesthetic quality 2000 (percentage of sites)			
	Good	Fair	Poor	Bad
Anglian	20.4	34.5	13.8	15.5
Midlands	30.8	33.3	31.6	19.3
North East	36.2	44.6	12.5	17.9
North West	15.8	40.7	5.1	10.2
Southern	25	34.1	22	14.6
South West	44.1	39.4	22.5	9.9
Thames	29.3	25.5	9.1	18.2
Wales	28.2	37	24.1	18.5
England and Wales	47.3	36.3	17.5	15.5

Notes
1. Information for the English regions is based on the Environment Agency's river catchment boundaries. We have used the national boundary for Wales.
2. These results are based on a snapshot survey of 452 sites on selected rivers and canals in late 2000. Sites in rural and urban areas were selected that people visit frequently

Source: Environment Agency website 30.11.01.

Bibliography

Acarlar, M. S. and Smith, C. R. (1987a) A study of hairpin vortices in a laminar boundary layer. Part 1. Hairpin vortices generated by hemisphere protuberances. *J. Fluid Mech.* 175: 1–41

(1987b) A study of hairpin vortices in a laminar boundary layer. Part 2. Hairpin vortices generated by fluid injection. *J. Fluid Mech.* 175: 43–83

Allan, J. D. (1995) *Stream Ecology: Structure and Function of Running Waters.* London: Chapman and Hall

Allen, P. A. (1997) *Earth Surface Processes.* Oxford: Blackwell

Anderson, R. (1993) *Elgar.* London: J. M. Dent

Angelier, E. (2003) *Ecology of Streams and Rivers.* Enfield: Science Publishers

Appleton, J. (1975) *The Experience of Landscape.* Chichester: John Wiley

Ashe, G. (1990) *Mythology of the British Isles.* London: Methuen

Babakaiff, C. S. and Hickin, E. J. (1996) Coherent flow structures in Squamish river estuary, British Columbia, Canada. In P. J. Ashworth, S. J. Bennett, J. L. Best and S. J. McLelland (eds) *Coherent Flow Structures in Open Channels.* Chichester: Wiley: 321–342

Bagnold, R. A. (1966) An approach to the sediment transport problem from general physics. *U.S. Geological Survey Professional Paper.* 422-I

(1988) *The Physics of Sediment Transport by Wind and Water: A Collection of Hallmark Papers.* New York: American Society of Civil Engineers

Bennett, A. (1910) *Clayhanger.* London: Methuen and Co.

Bennett, S. and Best, J. L. (1996) Mean flow and turbulence structure over fixed ripples and the ripple-dune transition. In P. Ashworth, S. Bennett and J. Best (eds) *Coherent Flow Structures in Open Channels.* London: Wiley: 281–304

Best, J. L. and Bristow, C. S. (1993) (eds) *Braided Rivers.* London: Geological Society

Bibby, B. (2002) *Dancing with Sabrina: A Walk from Source to Sea of the River Severn.* Bridgnorth: TravellersEye.

Biron, P. M., Richer, A., Kirkbride, A. D., Roy, A. G. and Han, S. (2002) Spatial patterns of water surface topography at a river confluence. *Earth Surface Processes and Landforms.* 27 (9): 913–928

Booij, R. and Tukker, J. (2001) Integral model of shallow mixing layers. *Journal of Hydraulic Research.* 39 (2): 169–179

Boston, L. (1959) *The River at Green Knowe.* London: Faber and Faber

Boughey, J. (1998) *Hadfield's British Canals: the Inland Waterways of Britain and Ireland.* 8th edn. Stroud: Budding Books

Bragg, M. (2001) *A Son of War.* London: Sceptre

British Waterways (2003) *Montgomery Canal News.* Spring: Issue 3. Llanymynech: British Waterways

Britnell, W. (1982) The excavation of two round barrows at Trelystan, Powys. *Proceedings of the Prehistoric Society*, 48: 133–201

Brookes, A. (1982) *River channelization in England and Wales: downstream consequences for the channel morphology and aquatic vegetation.* Unpublished Ph.D thesis, University of Southampton

Brown, T. C. and Daniel, T. C. (1991) Landscape aesthetics of riparian environments: relationship of flow quantity to scenic quality along a wild and scenic river. *Water Resour. Res.* 27 (8): 1787–1795

Caradog Jones, D. (1934) *The Social Survey of Merseyside.* Liverpool: University Press of Liverpool

Chadwick, A. and Morfett, J. (1998) *Hydraulics in Civil and Environmental Engineering.* 3rd edn. London: E.&F.N. Spon

Chanson, H. (1999) *The Hydraulics of Open Channel Flow: An Introduction.* London: Arnold

Clark, N. A. and Prys-Jones, R. P. (1994) Low tide distribution of wintering waders and shelduck on the Severn Estuary in relation to the proposed tidal barrage. *Biological Journal of the Linnean Society.* Vol. 51: 199–217

Clarke, D. and Roberts, A. (1996) *Twilight of the Celtic Gods: An Exploration of Britain's Hidden Pagan Traditions.* London: Blandford

Coleridge, S. (1816) *Kubla Khan.* London: Bulmer

Colley, L. (1992) Britishness and otherness: An argument. *Journal of British Studies*, 31: 309–329

Cosgrove, D. (1984) *Social Formation and Symbolic Landscape.* London: Croome Helm

Cosgrove, D., Roscoe, B. and Rycroft, S. (1996) Landscape and Identity at Ladybower Reservoir and Rutland Water. *Transactions, Institute of British Geographers* 21, 3: 534–48

Cossons, N. (1977) *Ironbridge: Landscape of History.* London: Cassell

Daniels, S. (1993) *Fields of Vision: Landscape Imagery and National Identity in England and the United States.* Cambridge: Polity Press

Dann, C. (1979) *The Animals of Farthing Wood.* London: Heinemann

Darby, H. C. (1977) *Domesday England.* Cambridge: Cambridge University Press

— (1983) *The Changing Fenland.* Cambridge: Cambridge University Press

Dean, D. (No date) *Benjamin Williams Leader: A Rural Vision.* Catalogue: City Museum and Art Gallery: Worcester

de Salis, H. R. (1969) *Bradshaw's Canals*

and Navigable Rivers of England and Wales. Reprint of 1904 edition. Newton Abbot: David and Charles

Dickens, C. (1836) Sketches by Boz. Illustrative of Every-Day Life and Every-Day People. London: James Macrone

— (1854) Hard Times. London: Bradbury and Evans

— (1853) Bleak House. London: Longman, Brown, Green and Longmans

Drabble, M. (1979) A Writer's Britain. London: Thames and Hudson

Dunston, G. (1909) The Rivers of Axholme with a History of the Navigable Rivers and Canals of the District. London: Brown

Dury, G. H. (1987) Osage-type underfitness on the River Severn near Shrewsbury, Shropshire, England. In K. J. Gregory (ed.) Background to Palaeohydrology: A Perspective. John Wiley and Sons: Chichester: 399–412

Dyer, K. R. (1997) Estuaries: A Physical Introduction. 2nd edn. Chichester: Wiley

Eaton, J. W. (1989) Ecological aspects of water management in Britain. Journal of Applied Ecology. Volume 26: 835–849

Eliot, G. (1860) The Mill on the Floss. Edinburgh and London: William Blackwood and Sons

— (1876) Daniel Deronda. Edinburgh and London: William Blackwood and Sons

Eliot, T. S. (1922) The Wasteland. New York: Boni and Liveright

Elliott, M. and Kingston, P. F. (1987) The sublittoral benthic fauna of the estuary and Firth of Forth, Scotland. Proceedings of the Royal Society of Edinburgh, 93B: 449–465

Elliott, M., O'Reilly, M. G. and Taylor, C. J. L. (1990) The Forth estuary: a nursery and overwintering area for the North Sea fishes. Hydrobiologia, 195: 89–103

English Nature (1998–2003) Natural Areas: 56 Severn and Avon Vales. www.english-nature.org.uk

Environment Agency (1997) Local Environment Agency Plan: Middle Severn Consultation Report. Shrewsbury: Environment Agency

— (1998) Local Environment Agency Plan: Severn Uplands Consultation Report. Almondsbury: Environment Agency

— (1999) Local Environment Agency Plan: Severn Vale Environmental Overview. Almondsbury: Environment Agency

— (2002a) Salmonid and Freshwater Fisheries Statistics for England and Wales, 2001. Bristol: Environment Agency

— (2002b) The Severn Corridor Catchment Abstraction Management Strategy. October. Consultation Document. Almondsbury: Environment Agency

— (2003) A Water Resources Strategy for the West Midlands. www.environment-agency.gov.
uk/regions/midlands/Corporatedocuments/112954/?version=1&lang=_e

— (2003a) River Severn Salmon Action Plan. www.environment-agency.gov.uk/regions/midlands/455652/455657/?lang=_e

— (2003b) Severn Catchment Flood Management Plan and Fluvial Severn Strategy update. June. Almondsbury: Environment Agency

— (2003c) Shrewsbury Flood Alleviation Scheme. www.environment-agency.gov.uk/regions/midlands/202790/?lang=_e

— (2003d) Demountable Defences installed at Bewdley – New Years Day 2003. environment-agency.gov.uk/regions/midlands/230279/432591/?lang=_e

— (2003e) The Severn Bore and Trent Aegir. Almondsbury: Environment Agency

Featherstone, R. E. and Nalluri, C. (1982) Civil Engineering Hydraulics: Essential Theory with Worked Examples. London: Granada

Ferrier, G. and Anderson, J. M. (1997) A multi-disciplinary study of frontal systems in the Tay Estuary, Scotland. Estuarine, Coastal and Shelf Science, Volume 45, Issue 3, September: 317–336

Forrester, H. (1974) Twopence to Cross the Mersey. London: Cape

Gauckler, P. G. (1867) Etudes Théoriques et Pratiques sur l'Ecoulement et le Mouvement des Eaux (Theoretical and Practical Studies of the Flow and Motion of Waters) (Comptes Rendues de l'Académie des Sciences: Paris, France) Tome 64: 818–822. (in French)

Gaudet, J. M. and Roy, A. G. (1995) Effect of bed morphology on flow mixing length at river confluences. Nature. 373 (6510): 138–139

Graf, W. H. and Altinakar, M. S. (1998) Fluvial Hydraulics: Flow and Transport Processes in Channels of Simple Geometry. Chichester: John Wiley and Sons

Graham, B., Ashworth, G. J. and Tunbridge, J. E. (2000) A Geography of Heritage: Power, Culture and Economy. London: Arnold

Grahame, K. (1908) The Wind in the Willows. London: Methuen and Co.

Green, C. H. and Tunstall, S. M. (1992) The amenity and environmental value of river corridors in Britain. In P. J. Boon, P. Calow and G. E. Petts (eds) River Conservation and Management. John Wiley: Chichester: 425–41

Greenwood, J. D. (1994) Realism, Identity and Emotion: Reclaiming Social Psychology. London: Sage

Gregory, K. J. (1987) Introduction. In K. J. Gregory, J. Lewin and J. B. Thornes (eds) Palaeohydrology in Practice: A River Basin Analysis. Chichester: John Wiley and Sons: 1–15

Gregory, K. J. (1997) Fluvial Geomorphology of Great Britain. London: Chapman and Hall

Gregory, K. J. and Walling, D. E. (1973) Drainage Basin Form and Process: A Geomorphological Approach. London: Edward Arnold

Griffin, A. H. (1990) A Lakeland Mountain Diary. Swindon: Crowood

Gunn, N. M. (1991) Highland River. Edinburgh: Canongate Classics

Gurnell, A. M. and Clark, M. J. (1987) Glacio-Fluvial Sediment Transfer. London: Wiley

Gwilt, C. F. (No date) The Port of Bridgnorth: Including the Chapel on the Bridge. Bridgnorth Publications: Bridgnorth

Hadfield, C. (1981) The Canal Age. Newton Abbot, David and Charles

Hall, S. (1995) New cultures for old. In D. Massey and P. Jess (eds) A Place in the World: Places, Cultures and Globalization. Oxford: Oxford University Press: 175–214

Hall, S. (ed.) (1997) Representation: Cultural Representations and Signifying Practices. London: Sage

Hamblin, R. J. O. (1986) The Pleistocene sequence of the Telford district. Proceedings of the Geologist's Association, 97: 365–77

Hamer, E. (1872) A Parochial Account of Llanidloes. In Montgomery Collections. Vol. V. Collections: Historical and Archaeological Relating to Montgomery. London: J. Russell Smith

Hamill, L. (1999) Bridge Hydraulics. London: E.&F.N. Spon

Hammerton, D. (1989) River basin management in Scotland. Water Science and Technology. Volume 21, 10–11: 1501–1508

Hanham, F. G. (1930) *Report of Enquiry into Casual Labour in the Merseyside Area.* Liverpool: Young

Hardy, T. (1878) *The Return of the Native.* London: Smith, Elder and Co.

Haslam, S. M. (1978) *River Plants: The Macrophytic vegetation of Watercourses.* Cambridge: Cambridge University Press

— (1982) *Vegetation in British Rivers.* London: Nature Conservancy Council

— (1997) *The River Scene: Ecology and Cultural Heritage.* Cambridge: Cambridge University Press

Hastings, A. (1997) *The Construction of Nationhood: Ethnicity, Religion and Nationalism.* Cambridge: Cambridge University Press

Heighway, C. (1985) *Gloucester: A History and Guide.* Gloucester: Alan Sutton

Herbert, N. M. (ed.) (1988) *Gloucester City. Vol. V of The Victoria History of Gloucestershire.* Gloucester: Gloucestershire Record Office

Hey, D. (1997, 2005) *A History of Sheffield.* Lancaster: Carnegie Publishing

Higgs, G. (1987) Environmental change and hydrological response: Flooding in the Upper Severn catchment. In K. J. Gregory, J. Lewin and J. B. Thornes (eds) *Palaeohydrology in Practice: A River Basin Analysis.* Chichester: John Wiley and Sons: 131–60

Hoare, A. G. (2002) Natural harmony but divided loyalties: the evolution of estuary management as exemplified by the Severn Estuary. *Applied Geography.* 22: 1–25

Hobsbawm, E. (1990) *Nations and Nationalism since 1780: Programme, Myth, Reality.* Cambridge: Cambridge University Press

Howard, P. (1991) *Landscapes: The Artists' Vision.* London: Routledge

Hughes, T. (1983) *River: Poems.* London: Faber

Institute of Hydrology and British Geological Survey (2003) *Hydrological Data UK: Hydrometric Register and Statistics 1996–2000.* Wallingford: Institute of Hydrology

Jackson, R. G. (1976) Sedimentological and fluid-dynamic implications of the turbulent bursting phenomena in geophysical flows. *J. Fluid Mech.* 77: 531–60

Jerome, J. K. (1889) *Three Men in a Boat.* Bristol: J. W. Arrowsmith

Jones, T. (1999) The Mersey Basin Campaign. *Water Science and Technology.* Volume 40, 10: 131–136

Kennedy, M. (1982) *Portrait of Elgar.* 2nd edn. London: Oxford University Press

Kidd, S. and Shaw, D. (2000) The Mersey basin and its river valley initiatives: An appropriate model for the management of rivers?' *Local Environment.* Volume 5.4: 191–209

King, A. and Clifford, S. (eds) (2000) *The River's Voice: An Anthology of Poetry.* Dartington: Green Books Ltd.

Kinnersley, D. (1988) *Troubled Waters: Rivers, Politics and Pollution.* London: Hilary Shipman

Kjerfve, B. (1988) *Hydrodynamics of Estuaries. Vol 1. Estuarine Physics. Vol 2. Estuarine Case Studies.* Boca Raton, Florida: CRC Press

Knighton, D. (1998) *Fluvial Forms and Processes: A New Perspective.* London: Arnold

Lamb, H. H. (1972) *The Changing Climate: Selected Papers by H. H. Lamb.* London: Methuen

Lane, S. N., Bradbrook, K. F., Richards, K. S., Biron, P. A. and Roy, A. G. (1999) The application of computational fluid dynamics to natural river channels: three-dimensional versus two-dimensional approaches *Geomorphology* 29 (1–2): 1–20

Lane, S. N., Hardy, R. J., Elliott, L. and Ingham, D. B. (2002) High-resolution numerical modelling of three-dimensional flows over complex river bed topography. *Hydrol Process* 16 (11): 2261–2272

Larkin, P. A. (1947) *A Girl in Winter.* London: Faber and Faber

Lascelles, E. C. P. and Bullock, S. S. (1924) *Dock Labour and Decasualisation.* London: King and Son Ltd.

Lawler, D. M. (1987). Spatial variability in the climate of the Severn basin: A palaeohydrological perspective. In K. J. Gregory, J. Lewin and J. B. Thornes (eds) *Palaeohydrology in Practice: A River Basin Analysis.* Chichester: John Wiley and Sons: 49–78

Lawrence, D. H. (1915) *The Rainbow.* London: Methuen and Co.

Lawton, R. (1990) Population and society: 1730–1914. In R. A. Dodgshon and R. A. Butlin (eds) *An Historical Geography of England and Wales.* Second Edition London: Academic Press Limited

Lawton, R. and Pooley, C. (1992) *Britain 1740–1950: An Historical Geography,* London: Edward Arnold

Ledger, D. C. (1972) The Warwickshire Avon: a case study of water demands and water availability in an intensely used river system. *Transactions Institute of British Geographers,* 55: 83–110

Leeder, M. J. (1983) On the interactions between turbulent flow, sediment transport and bed form mechanics in channelised flows. In J. D. Collinson and J. Lewin (eds) *International Association of Sedimentologists Special Publication,* 6: 5–18

Leopold, L. B. and Maddock, T. (1953) The hydraulic geometry of stream channels and some physiographic implications. *US. Geological Survey Professional Paper,* 252: 55

Leopold, L. B. and Wolman, M. G. (1957) River channel patterns: braided, meandering and straight. *US. Geological Survey Professional Paper,* 282: B

Lewin, J. (ed.) (1981) *British Rivers.* London: Allen and Unwin

— (1983) Changes of channel patterns and floodplains. In K. J. Gregory (ed.) *Background to Palaeohydrology.* Chichester: Wiley: 303–19

— (1987) Historical river channel changes. In K. J. Gregory, J. Lewin and J. B. Thornes (eds) *Palaeohydrology in Practice: A River Basin Analysis.* Chichester: John Wiley and Sons: 161–176

Lewin, J. and Weir, M. J. C. (1977) Morphology and recent history in the lower Spey. *Scottish Geographical Magazine.* 93: 45–51

Lewis, R. (1997) *Dispersion in Estuaries and Coastal Waters.* Chichester: Wiley

Leyshon, A., Matless, D. and Revill, G. (1998) Introduction: music, space and the production of place. In A. Leyshon, D. Matless and G. revill (eds) *The Place of Music.* New York: The Guildford Press: 1–30

Limbrey, S. (1987) Farmers and farmland: Aspects of pre-historic land use in the Severn Basin. In K. J. Gregory, J. Lewin and J. B. Thornes (eds) *Palaeohydrology in Practice: A River Basin Analysis.* Chichester: John Wiley and Sons: 251–268

Little, C. (2000) *The Biology of Soft Shores and Estuaries.* Oxford: Oxford University Press

Lovell, J. C. (1969) *Stevedores and Dockers: A Study of Trade Unionism in the Ports of*

London, 1870–1914. London: Macmillan

Lowenthal, D. (1991) British national identity and the English landscape. *Rural History*, 2: 205–30

Luckin, B. (1986) *Pollution and Control: A Social History of the Thames in the Nineteenth Century*. Bristol: IOP Publishing Limited

Marsh, T. and Meech, J. (1999) Introduction to the Severn Way. In the *Official Severn Way Walkers' Guide*. Worcester: Worcestershire County Council: 2–4

Mason, C. F. and Macdonald, S. M. (1986) *Otters: Ecology and Conservation*. Cambridge: Cambridge University Press

Matless, D. (1998) *Landscapes and Englishness*. London: Reaktion Books Ltd

Matthes, G. H. (1947) Macroturbulence in natural stream flow. *Trans AGU*. 28: 255–62

McDonald, A. T. and Kay, D. (1988) *Water Resources: Issues and Strategies*. Harlow: Longman

McDowell, D. M. and O'Conner, B. A. (eds) (1977) *Hydraulic Behaviour of Estuaries*. London: Macmillan

Milne, A. A. (1928) *The House at Pooh Corner*. London: Methuen

Mitchell, D. J. and Gerrard, A. J. (1987) Morphological responses and sediment patterns. In K. J. Gregory, J. Lewin and J. B. Thornes (eds) *Palaeohydrology in Practice: A River Basin Analysis*. Chichester: John Wiley and Sons: 177–200

Morisawa, M. (1985) *Rivers*. London: Longman

Morris, E. R. (1993) *Llanidloes: Town and Parish: An Illustrated Account*. Llanidloes: Great Oak Bookshop

Muller, A. and Gyr, A. (1996) Geometrical analysis of the feedback between flow, bedforms and sediment transport. In P. Ashworth, S. Bennett and J. Best (eds) *Coherent Flow Structures in Open Channels*. London: Wiley: 237–47

Musson, C. (1976) Excavations at The Breiddin 1969–1973. In D. W. Harding (ed.) *Hillforts: Later Prehistoric Earthworks in Britain and Ireland*. London: Academic Press

Newson, M. D. (1992) *Land, Water and Development: River Basin Systems and Their Sustainable Management*. London: Routledge

Nicholson, N. (1966) To the river Duddon in *Collected Poems*. London: Faber & Faber

Nikuradse, J. (1933) *Strömungsgesetze in rauhen Rohren* (Laws of Turbulent Pipe Flow in Rough Pipes) (VDI-Forschungsheft. No. 361) (in German) (Translated in NACA Tech. Memo. No. 1292, 1950)

Novak, P., Moffat, A. I. B., Nalluri, C. and Narayanan, R. (1996) *Hydraulic Structures*. 2nd edn London: E & F. N. Spon

Oswald, A. (2002) *Dart*. London: Faber and Faber

Palmer, C. (2002) Christianity, Englishness and the southern English countryside: a study of the work of H. J. Massingham. *Social and Cultural Geography*, 3.1: 25–38

Palmer, R. (1992) *The Folklore of Hereford and Worcester*. Almeley: Logaston

Park, C. C. (2001) *The Environment: Principles and Applications*. London: Routledge

Parker, D. J. and Penning-Rowsell, E. C. (1980) *Water Planning in Britain*. London: George Allen and Unwin

Parker, D. J. and Sewell, W. R. D. (1988) Evolving water institutions in England and Wales: An assessment of two decades of experience. *Natural Resources Journal*. Volume 28: 751–785

Pearce, P. (1958) *Tom's Midnight Garden*. Oxford: Oxford University Press

Penning-Rowsell, E. C. and Handmer, J. W. (1988) Flood hazard management in Britain: A changing scene. *Geographical Journal*. 154: 2: 209–220

Petts, G. E. (1988) Regulated rivers in the United Kingdom. *Regulated Rivers: Research and Management*. Volume 2: 201–220

Petts, G. E. and Foster, I. (1985) *Rivers and Landscapes*. London: Edward Arnold

Philo, C. (1991) Introduction, acknowledgements and brief thoughts on older words and older worlds. In *New Words, New Worlds: Reconceptualising Social and Cultural Geography*. Conference Proceedings. Aberystwyth: Cambrian Printers: 1–13

Prater, A. J. (1981) *Estuary Birds of Britain and Ireland*. Calton: T. and A. D. Poyser

Price, M. (1996) *Introducing Groundwater*. 2nd edn. London: Chapman Hall

Professional Engineering (2003) Report: Severn barrage plan refloats. *Professional Engineering*. Vol 16, Issue 2: 16

Pye, K. (ed.) (1994) *Sediment Transport and Depositional Processes*. Oxford: Blackwell Scientific

Redford, A. (1940) *The History of Local Government in Manchester. Volume II: Borough and City*. London: Longman

Richards, K. S. (1982a) *Rivers: Form and Process in Alluvial Channels*. London: Methuen (ed.)

— (1982b) River Channels: Environment and Process. Oxford: Blackwell

Roberts, B. (1999) *Britain's Waterways: a Unique Insight*. Reading: GEOprojects

Robertson, A. (1988) *Atkinson Grimshaw*. Oxford: Phaidon

Robinson, S. K. (1991) Coherent motions in the turbulent boundary layer. *Ann. Rev. Fluid Mech.* 23: 601–39

Rodaway, P. (1991) Self, geography, postmodernism. In *New Words, New Worlds: Reconceptualising Social and Cultural Geography*. Conference Proceedings. Aberystwyth: Cambrian Printers: 196–203

Rogers, L. (2003) *Sabrina and the River Severn*. Originally published by Beltane (1999) now available on www.whitedragon.org.uk/articles/ Sabrina.htm

Rolt, L. T. C. (1950) *The Inland Waterways of England*. London: George Allen and Unwin

Rose, G. (1995) Place and identity: a sense of place. In D. Massey and P. Jess (eds) *A Place in the World: Places, Cultures and Globalization*. Oxford: Oxford University Press: 87–132

Royal Society for the Protection of Birds (1994) *The New Rivers and Wildlife Handbook*. Sandy: RSPB

Sack, R. D. (1986) *Human Territoriality: Its Theory and History*. Cambridge: Cambridge University Press

Saugeres, L. (2002) The cultural representation of the farming landscape: masculinity, power and nature. *Journal of Rural Studies*, 18.4: 373–84

Schumm, S. (1977) *The Fluvial System*. London: Wiley

Scott, W. (1814) *Waverley*. Edinburgh

Sheail, J. (1988) River regulation in the United Kingdom: An historical perspective', *Regulated Rivers: Research and Management*. Volume 2: 221–232

Smith, C. R. (1996) Coherent flow structures in smooth-wall turbulent boundary layers: Facts, Mechanisms and speculation. In P. J. Ashworth,

S. J. Bennett, J. L. Best and S. J. Mc-Lelland (eds) *Coherent Flow Structures in Open Channels*. Chichester: Wiley: 1–40

Smith, I. and Lyle, A. (1979) *Distribution of freshwaters in Great Britain*. Edinburgh: Institute of Terrestrial Ecology

Smith, S. (1983) The River Humber. In *Stevie Smith: A Selection*. H. Lee (ed.) London: Faber and Faber

Smith, S. J. (1994) Soundscapes. *Area*, 26.3: 232–40

Smithson, P., Addison, K. and Atkinson, K. (2002) *Fundamentals of the Physical Environment*. London: Routledge

Stamp, L. D. and Beaver, S. H. (1963) *The British Isles: A Geographic and Economic Survey*. London: Longman

Stewart, R. J. (1990) *Celtic Gods, Celtic Goddesses*. London: Blandford

Storey, D. (2001) *Territory: The Claiming of Space*. Harlow: Prentice Hall

Strickler, A. (1923) *Beiträge zur Frage der Geschwindigheitsformel und der Rauhligkeitszahlen für Ströme, Kanäle und Geschlossene Leitungen* (Contributions to the Question of a Velocity Formula and Roughness Data for Streams, Channels and Closed Pipelines) Vol. 16. (Mitt. des Eidgenössischen Amtes für Wasserwirtschaft, Bern, Switzerland) (In German) (Translation T–10, W. M. Keck, Laboratory of Hydraulics and Water resources, California Institute of Technology, USA, 1981)

Swift, G. (1983) *Waterland*. London: Heinemann

Swinburne, A. (1904) 'Garden of Proserpine' in *Poems and Ballads*. London: Chatto

Tapsell, S., Tunstall, S., House, M., Whomsley, J. and Macnaghten, P. (2001) Growing up with rivers? Rivers in London children's worlds. *Area*, 33.2: 177–89

Tennyson, A. (1833) 'The Lady of Shallott' in *Poems by Alfred Tennyson*. London: Edward Moxon

The Severn Way Partnership (1999) *Official Severn Way Walkers' Guide*. Worcester: Worcestershire County Council

The Welshpool Partnership (No date) *Welshpool Visitor Guide: Activities and Attractions*. Welshpool: WPG Limited

Thomas, D. (1954) *Under Milk Wood*. London: J. M. Dent and Sons

Thomas, R. S. (1955) Invasion on the Farm. In *Song at the Year's Turning. Poems 1942–1954*. London: Rupert Hart-Davis

—(1955) Welsh Landscape. In *Song at the Year's Turning. Poems 1942–1954*. London: Rupert Hart-Davis

Townsend, C. R. (1986) *The Ecology of Streams and Rivers*. The Institute of Biology's Studies in Biology no. 122. London: Edward Arnold

Trant, I. and Griffin, M. W. (1998) *The Changing Face of Welshpool*. 2nd edn. The Powysland Club: Welshpool

Tuan, Y. F. (1974a) Space and place: humanistic perspective. In C. Board, R. J. Chorley, P. Haggett and D. R. Stoddart (eds) *Progress in Geography*. 6: 213–52. Edward Arnold: London

—(1974b) *Topophilia: a study of environmental perception, attitudes and values*. Englewood Cliffs. N. J.: Prentice Hall

Turrell W. R., Brown J. and Simpson J. H. (1996) Salt intrusion and secondary flow in a shallow, well-mixed estuary. *Estuarine, Coastal and Shelf Science*. 42.2: 153–169

University of Liverpool, Social Science Department (1954) *The Dock Worker: An Analysis of Conditions of Employment in the Port of Manchester*. Liverpool: Liverpool University Press

Varley, M. E. (1967) *British Freshwater Fishes*. London: Fishing New Books

Walsh, R. (1990) Fluvial landforms. In N. Stephens (ed.) *Natural Landscapes of Britain from the Air*. Cambridge. Cambridge University: 147–90

Walton, I. (1653) *The Compleat Angler*. 1983 edition. Oxford: Clarendon Press

Ward, R. C. (1981) River systems and river regimes. In J. Lewin (ed.) *British Rivers*. London: George Allen and Unwin, 1–33

Warwick, R. M. and Uncles, R. J. (1980) Distribution of benthic microfaunal associations in the Bristol Channel in relation to tidal stress. *Marine Ecology Progress Series*, 3: 97–103

Waters, B. (1947) *Severn Tide*. London: J. M. Dent and Sons

Werrity, A. and Ferguson, R. I. (1981) Pattern changes in a Scottish braided river over 1, 30, and 200 years. In

R. A. Cullingford, D. A. Davidson and J. Lewin (eds) *Timescales in Geomorphology*. Chichester: Wiley: 53–68

White, G. F. (1969) *Strategies of American Water Management*. Ann Arbor: University of Michigan Press

White, N., Zeff, L., Phillpott, S. and Daniel, P. (eds) (2000) *The English Landscape*. London: Profile Books

Witts, C. (1998) *A Century of Bridges*. Gloucester: River Severn Publications

—(1998a) *Tales of the River Severn*. Gloucester: River Severn Publications

—(1998b) *Along the Severn from Source to Sea*. Leckhampton: Reardon

Wohl, A. S. (1984) *Endangered Lives: Public Health in Victorian Britain*. London: Methuen

Wood, T. R. (1987) The present-day hydrology of the River Severn. In K. J. Gregory, J. Lewin and J. B. Thornes (eds) *Palaeohydrology in Practice: A River Basin Analysis*. Chichester: John Wiley and Sons: 79–99

Wordsworth, W. (1820) *The river Duddon, a series of sonnets*. London: Longman

—(1850) *The Prelude*. London: Edward Moxon

Zimmerman, E. W. (1951) *World Resources and Industries*. New York: Harper and Brothers

Websites

British Waterways website: www.britishwaterways.co.uk

The Canal website – www.canaljunction.com

Department of Transport (annual). *Port Statistics* www.transtat.dft.gov.uk

Port profiles at
  (i) www.britishports.org.uk (the British Ports Association)
  (ii) www.abports.co.uk (Associate0d British Ports)
  (iii) www.portofliverpool.co.uk (Mersey Docks and Harbour Company)
  (iv) www.portoflondon.co.uk (Port of London Authority)

Severn Stories (2003) www.secretshropshire.co.uk/content/Learn/Severn/index.aspx

Witts, C. (2003) *Severn Tales* www.severntales.co.uk/

Index